Advance Praise for *Horseshoe Crab: Biography of a Survivor*

ANTHONY FREDERICKS, IN A FOLKSY, STORY-WITHIN-A-STORY approach, has created an accurate and very readable introduction to *Limulus polyphemus*, the American horseshoe crab, and to some of the people associated with it. It is an informative and well-written book; I highly recommend it. —*Carl N. Shuster, Jr., adjunct professor of marine science at the College of William & Mary and co-author of* The American Horseshoe Crab

IN *HORSESHOE CRAB: BIOGRAPHY OF A SURVIVOR*, ANTHONY FREDERICKS takes us on a fascinating tour of horseshoe crabs and the people who study them. Through interviews and vivid descriptions of his experiences, Fredericks shares his journey to understand the complexities of horseshoe crab biology and the history of their exploitation. Along the way we learn a lot about earth history and the ancient origins of horseshoe crabs; about systematics and how animals acquire their names; about the visual system and the similarities between very different species; and about ecology and the relationships among organisms. We get to see how scientific knowledge is acquired, which is sometimes quite by accident. We discover that horseshoe crabs are important to medicine and to the survival of other species. We look in on how the species is managed, and how educators and scientists collaborate to teach the public about the value of this important species. Horseshoe crabs are a model for how committed citizens and scientists worldwide can work together to make a difference. —*H. Jane Brockmann, professor of biology, University of Florida and co-author of* The American Horseshoe Crab

WITH A HARD, HOOF-SHAPED JOINTED SHELL TRAILING A DANGEROUS-looking spike tail, they bear no resemblance to any creatures you know, looking for all the world like something you would expect to find on the planet Zarkon. They move slowly over the sand like two-foot-long armored tanks, their means of locomotion hidden from view. They were here during the Triassic Period, when the earliest dinosaurs first appeared, and they're still here. We know these "living fossils" as horseshoe crabs (technically *Limulus polyphemus*), although they're not crabs at all, but more closely related to scorpions and ticks. And if their uniqueness and astonishing longevity doesn't impress you, consider this: the light-blue blood of *Limulus* contains sensitive chemicals that can be used by researchers to discover harmful endotoxins in human blood. Do you need another reason to read this fascinating, relevant, revealing, and endlessly enjoyable book by Anthony Fredericks? —*Richard Ellis, research associate at the American Museum of Natural History in New York City and the author of* The Great Sperm Whale *and twenty-four other books*

CONSIDER AN ESCAPE FROM THE CACOPHONY OF THE 24-HOUR NEWS cycle and spend some time instead with one of Earth's oldest creatures. In *Horseshoe Crab*, Anthony Fredericks takes readers on a quest to understand an important animal easy to overlook. His *Biography of a Survivor* is a reminder that a skillful storyteller can find a good tale anywhere, and it is a warning that we ignore the perils humankind creates for other animals at our own selfish risk. —*Peter Laufer, author of* The Dangerous World of Butterflies

IN THE OPENING CHAPTER OF *HORSESHOE CRAB: BIOGRAPHY OF A Survivor*, author Anthony Fredericks likens his philosophy for exploring the natural world to that of a four-year-old child—buzzing with questions, brimming with curiosity, and teeming with passion. Such qualities shine forth in Tony's travelogue-esque accounting of the wonders of the horseshoe crab, one of Earth's oldest and most unique, interesting, and beneficial animals. His journey to discover and distill all he can about this amazing animal takes Tony up and down the Atlantic coast, from the broad expanses of Delaware Bay beaches, where horseshoe crabs congregate each spring in incredible masses, to more remote stretches of west coast Florida. Along the way (in his telling, Tony manages to make you feel like you are indeed along for the ride), you'll not only learn a lot of cool stuff about horseshoe crabs, but you'll also meet an equally engaging cast of human characters who have devoted their life, talents, and remarkable passion to the study, interpretation, and conservation of this ancient mariner.

As an environmental educator who has spent the better part of two decades in the school of horseshoe crab learning, I have had the good fortune of meeting many of the people in this book, and what impresses me most is how well Tony captures what makes them, as well as the horseshoe crab, special and worth knowing. So pack up your travel sack, roll up your pant legs, and bring on your best prepared-to-be-awed spirit of discovery. Meet the grand survivor through Tony's eyes—I expect you'll find the journey an enjoyable and enlightening one. —*Gary Kreamer, co-founder and partner in the Green Eggs & Sand (Horseshoe Crab/Shorebird Education) project*

EVERY TEN YEARS OR SO THE AMAZING STORY OF HOW HORSESHOE crab blood saves millions of human lives changes, and has to be told all over again. This book takes readers on a whirlwind ride up and down the East Coast visiting the many people who are now working to protect this species that is so crucial to human health and the ecology of the East Coast of America. —*William Sargent, director of the Coastlines Project in Ipswich, Massachusetts, and author of* Crab Wars: A Tale of Horseshoe Crabs, Bioterrorism and Human Health

AN ENTERTAINING GUIDE TO A CREATURE THAT IS 445 MILLION years old and still having sex on the beach. —*Richard Conniff, author of* Spineless Wonders: Strange Tales from the Invertebrate World

AS ONE WHO HAS DOCUMENTED THE HORSESHOE CRAB/SHOREBIRD phenomenon and the associated resource management challenges since 1986, I feel this book is an enjoyable, informative, and well-balanced profile of the horseshoe crab resource, and the passionate characters who interact with it. For those who know little about this creature and its vital connections to migratory shorebirds and to human health, this is an accessible, playful introduction to an ancient animal that continues to amaze us. —*Michael Oates, video documentarian and producer of* Dollars on the Beach

HORSESHOE CRAB: BIOGRAPHY OF A SURVIVOR IS ONE OF THOSE RARE natural history books that makes clear the deep interdependence and relationship of humans to the natural world in ways they would little dream of without reading the book. What does a a horseshoe crab have to do with your daily life? A whole lot! Read the book and you'll find that you have relations you had never met before. —*Anne Rudloe, Gulf Specimen Marine Laboratory*

FREDERICKS TAKES THE READER ON HIS JOURNEY OF DISCOVERY OF this fascinating, unassuming creature. Fredericks is both student, as he learns about *Limulus*, and teacher, as he adds the historical, ecological, and scientific perspectives. You will be entertained and not even realize you are learning something. You will meet just a few of the horseshoe crab enthusiasts and learn how this ancient animal helps humanity. Compared to the 445 million years the horseshoe crab has survived, its interaction with humans has been a small blip, but that interaction has perhaps affected the crabs more than other events in time. After reading Fredericks' book, you too will become a fan of the horseshoe crab. With our help, the horseshoe crab story can be "never-ending." —*Maribeth Donovan Janke, Ph.D., Lonza Walkersville Inc.*

Horseshoe Crab

Horseshoe Crab

Biography of a Survivor

Anthony D. Fredericks

Ruka Press®
Washington, DC

First edition published 2012 by Ruka Press,® PO Box 1409, Washington, DC 20013. www.rukapress.com

See page 250 for photography credits.

Library of Congress Control Number: 2012930107

ISBN 978-0-9830111-8-7

10 9 8 7 6 5 4 3 2 1

Printed in the United States of America

Design by Sensical Design & Communication

For Nancy Weikert,

who first introduced me to
these ancient wonders of the sea

Table of Contents

FOREWORD   ix
By Glenn Gauvry

INTRODUCTION: Ten Thousand Friends   3
(And Some Human Party Crashers)

CHAPTER 1: Mr. Roger N. Parker of Golden, Colorado,
   Lives Another Day   11
How Horseshoe Crabs Saved His Life (and Yours, Too)

CHAPTER 2: Long Before the Dinosaurs   24
Yes, They've Been Around a While

CHAPTER 3: Lord De La Warr's Bay   40
A Short Course in Geology and History

CHAPTER 4: From Fertilizer to Bait   56
Taking Advantage of an Ancient Creature

CHAPTER 5: Horseshoe Crab-ology 101   74
All That Anatomy and Physiology Stuff

CHAPTER 6: Can You See What Eye See? 91
The Creature with Ten Eyes

CHAPTER 7: Ménage a Trois, Ménage a Quatre, Ménage a...Whatever 104
Reproduction Among the Arthropods

CHAPTER 8: Free Food! All You Can Eat! Come and Get It! 117
The Birds and the Eggs

CHAPTER 9: Hatching Out and Moving On 133
Growing Up is Hard to Do

CHAPTER 10: Where the Boys Are 146
Spring Break in Florida

CHAPTER 11: "To Protect This Remarkable Mariner" 167
How an Intrepid Band of Citizens is Defending Horseshoe Crabs

CHAPTER 12: A Friend in Need is a Friend Indeed 182
One Man and His Lifelong Passion for Limulus

CHAPTER 13: Back to School 197
Green Eggs & Sand

CHAPTER 14: "'Cause they're ugly!" 216
Are Horseshoe Crabs Worth It?

POSTSCRIPT: Orgy on Gandy's Beach 225

AUTHOR'S NOTE: How Horseshoe Crabs Saved My Life 229

ACKNOWLEDGMENTS 231

APPENDIX: Timeline 234

BIBLIOGRAPHY 239

INDEX 251

Foreword

By Glenn Gauvry

MANY YEARS AGO, IN THE SPRING OF 1996, I STOPPED FOR lunch at the local convenience store in the small Delaware Bay coastal town of Broadkill Beach, where I lived at the time. The nonprofit organization I had founded to promote awareness and advocate for the conservation of the world's four horseshoe crab species was in its infancy, struggling to make a difference. As I approached the counter to pay for my lunch, Lois, the store's owner, told me that a man had stopped by the other day looking for me and had bought a few of the horseshoe crab T-shirts we had designed. "He left his business card, along with this small pewter horseshoe crab pin," she said, and handed me the items. As I fiddled with the pin, I looked at the card, curious as to who had left this gift and had taken such interest in our work. I was astonished to read the name Carl N. Shuster, Jr., Ph.D.—the world's authority on horseshoe crabs.

It would be days before I would find the courage to call this remarkable man. Although I considered myself well informed about this animal, at least within the scope of the programs our organization was promoting, I was equally aware of my limitations. After much procrastination, I made the call; to my relief, I was greeted by a warm and inviting voice, a man secure with himself. We talked for quite some time about horseshoe crabs, and our call concluded with Dr. Shuster inviting me on a road trip to introduce me to others whom he felt could be helpful to our organization's conservation efforts.

We began our four-day journey at his modest home in Arlington, Virginia, which was filled with memorabilia, specimens, and scientific literature reflective of a lifetime of inquiry about a species he knew more about than anyone. As we drove, we talked mostly about horseshoe crabs and how our lives had led us to the paths we found ourselves following. The miles and days passed all too quickly, and Dr. Shuster's relaxed and unpretentious manner of sharing information was like lounging in a comfortable chair with a good book. We have been friends ever since.

I share this story because, over the years, I have learned that the right message, told in a casual manner, can deepen one's understanding, nurture compassion, and turn what may have been a disinterested observer into a committed advocate. To that end, Anthony has done a remarkable job with the book you are about to read. Through humor and a casual, inviting, layman style of writing, he has taken the tedium out of scientific information without removing the science. I believe that as you read this book, you will become drawn into an incredible journey of survival spanning hundreds of millions of years, and along the way you will meet extraordinary individuals whose knowledge and commitment to the understanding and conservation of this often misunderstood creature is truly inspiring, leaving you with a profound depth of knowledge of a most remarkable survivor. I have no doubt that you will also be left with much to think about, for it will be very difficult to ever look at a horseshoe crab again in quite the same way.

We all carry within us, consciously or not, an imaginary line of concern. We take interest in that which rises above this line and ignore that which doesn't. Many in the animal realm in need of an advocate have the good fortune to capture our interest, perhaps through their appearance, sound, or mannerisms; whatever the reason, their life is made easier as a result of our attention. What chance does a bottom-dwelling marine creature that most people find unappealing have? Yet through the dedication and compassion of a small but growing global community of individuals, this ancient mariner, who long ago discovered how to harmonize with the environment it depends on for survival, has reached the threshold of our concern. The journey has not been easy, and its outcome is still uncertain. However, if one were to ask me just a few years ago whether a book like this one were possible, I would have thought not. Many thanks to Anthony and his courage to give life to this important story.

Glenn Gauvry is founder of Ecological Research & Development Group, the leading organization working for the preservation of horseshoe crabs.

Horseshoe Crab

Horseshoe crabs partying after hours.

Ten Thousand Friends

(And Some Human Party Crashers)

AS A COLLEGE STUDENT, I NEVER ATTENDED AN ORGY. OH, sure, I heard about certain "celebrations" that had taken place over spring break down in Mexico, or the occasional initiation party along Fraternity Row, but I was certain they were more hyperbole than fact. Even in my current role as a college professor, I sometimes overhear inflated stories about bacchanalian weekends or wild end-of-the-academic-year festivals in obscure corners of the campus. But I have never been an observer of (nor certainly a participant in) a full-blown, Roman-style orgy where indiscriminate—and quite frequent—sexual encounters take place long into the night...and even into the following day.

At least, not until I went to Delaware.

Although it was late May, the air was crisp. A small group of us stood in informal clusters along a sandy parking area bordering Broadkill Beach. We watched a brilliant mass of solar hydrogen slowly creep down toward the western horizon, spreading crimson, saffron, tangerine, and fuchsia across the rippled waters of Delaware Bay.

Broadkill Beach is a long sweep of sand positioned two-thirds of the way down the eastern edge of Delaware and across from Cape May, New Jersey. Broadkill is part of the Prime Hook State Wildlife Management Area, an expansive preserve about ten miles northwest of the tourist hotels, T-shirt shops, and ubiquitous saltwater taffy stores that flank the boardwalk of the resort town of Rehoboth Beach. Houses here are few (condos are fewer), and people are a rarity along this seemingly deserted and forgotten stretch of sand dunes—each sprinkled with clumps of blue-green sea grass and the tracings of offshore winds.

We were an eclectic troop of teachers, businesspeople, housewives, artists, construction workers, plumbers, lawyers, ecologists, accountants, authors, and social workers. Led by Glenn Gauvry of the Ecological Research & Development Group, a wildlife preservation organization whose primary focus is the conservation of horseshoe crabs (you'll meet ERDG again in Chapter 11), we had signed up to witness one of nature's most spectacular rites of spring: an orgy of arthropods. The annual mating call had sounded, and tens of thousands of ancient creatures had heeded its siren echoes, scraping their way up out of the depths to frolic in front of wide-eyed voyeurs.

I guess if you want to have group sex, an isolated beach in Delaware is as good a place as any.

As we strolled along the beach, we watched transfixed as couples mated on any stretch of sandy real estate they could find. Almost alien in appearance, these "submarine tanks" plowed their way out of the water, up the beach, and into each other with all the delicacy of a frenzied herd of bull elephants. There were the usual twosomes and threesomes, and occasionally we would come across a foursome, a fivesome, and even one over-stimulated sixsome.

KEY FACT

The biggest and oldest female horseshoe crabs may weigh up to ten pounds.

Cameras clicked and notes were scribbled as we traipsed through rippling waves to watch these critters perform. Oblivious to our presence, each crab was totally absorbed in a ritual propelled by tides and temperatures and hormones…forces nearly as old as time itself.

Occasionally, Gauvry would pause and proffer some instruction on the biology, anatomy, or physiology of these ancient critters. At one juncture, he gathered up a lonely male, turning it over to reveal features of its anatomy. He pointed to the underside and identified each of the six pairs of appendages. He told us how the horseshoe crab uses the first pair (the *chelicerae*) for placing food in its mouth (it particularly favors marine worms and small clams). The next pair of appendages is called the *pedipalps*, and these are the first ambulatory legs. In the adult male, the *tarsus* (final segment) of these legs is modified as a grasping appendage (a "boxing glove"), allowing

Glenn Gauvry shows off a horseshoe crab's anatomy.

males to clasp females during spawning—a unique coupling that will receive considerably more attention later in this book. The rear legs are the "pusher legs," which are used for both terrestrial and underwater locomotion.

Gauvry swept his hand toward the tail and the five pairs of branchial appendages with book gills on their inner surfaces. He told us how the horseshoe crab uses these both for propulsion (when swimming) and "breathing." Similar to the gills in a fish, the book gills are membranes that allow oxygen to pass through while keeping water out. We posed a few questions ("What's the shell made of?," "How long do they live?," and "What is *that* thing?"), and our brief biology lesson was over. Ever so gently, Gauvry placed the uncomplaining "specimen" back onto the beach right side up. The over-hormoned crab lost no time in scuttling off to seek a ready female.

By now, the sun had slipped below the thin line separating sky and sea, and we were bathed in the pale light of a resplendent moon. Flashlights clicked on and headlights flickered as we continued down the beach, carefully sidestepping the panoply of single-minded creatures that scurried and scuttled and clasped and fertilized in a mating ritual both silent and frantic.* From time to time, we would encounter a horseshoe crab unceremoniously somersaulted onto its back by an unexpected wave. One of us would gently reach down and flip the hapless creature right side up, whereupon it would continue its journey up the sand or back into the waiting arms of the bay.

Each of us moved silently over the sand, occasionally crouching down to watch the circus of arthropods before us or sharing a comment with another member of the troop. Like the constant budding of amoebas, we would divide into small groups of threes, fours, and fives, reassemble, and then divide again—carefully observing the action on the beach, relating an observation, or gathering a seashell or two for display on the living room coffee table. Conversation was muted as we listened to the scraping and clatter of horseshoe crab shells rubbing against each other in the still air.

Up and down the beach were thousands of female crabs, each with one or more males attached, and each engaged in an evolutionary dance—a cosmic tango—as old as time itself. While we were temporary, these crabs were part of the permanence of nature, a constant coming and going that transcends human time.

---

* During spawning, males will grasp onto females with all the passion and ardor of a sailor home from a six-month deployment. No amount of twisting, turning, or somersaulting by the intensity of the waves will separate a mating pair of horseshoe crabs.

For millennia after millennia, these crabs and their ancestors have been locked in an eternal embrace, passing their genes from one generation to the next. Each of us knew we were brief witnesses to a perpetual spectacle that has been taking place since…well, since almost forever—a spectacle full of awe and mystery and the passion of persistence.

It is, I hope, a never-ending story.

AT THIS JUNCTURE IN OUR JOURNEY, IT IS IMPORTANT TO MAKE A clarification: I am not a scientist, just a significantly-past-middle-age-balding-with-streaks-of-gray-former-surfer-dude-now-professor-of-education who has never lost his childhood curiosity for the magic and mystery of the ocean. My childhood was spent along the shores of southern California, where I grew up slipping and sliding through the tidepools of Little Corona, snorkeling over kelp-rich patches of sea life, bodysurfing long, cresting waves off Newport Beach, and gathering an array of strange critters into various cardboard boxes hidden in the back corners of our garage. I was fascinated by any creature that came from the sea, including the clams lodged in the mucky sand in front of our house on the bay, the invertebrates that clung to the underside of my tiny sailboat, or the sand bass that would greedily grab a fishing hook cast into the placid waters of Newport Harbor. Occasionally, there would be a hair-raising tale about a great white shark sighted off the Balboa Pier that would find its way onto the front page of *The Daily Pilot* newspaper and into the mind of a very impressionable young boy.

As I grew older, I never lost my childhood fascination with the sea; once salt water courses through your veins, you can never separate yourself from it for very long. Although I now live in a semi-rural region of south central Pennsylvania, I am still drawn to the sea. My wife and I often escape to the shores of New Jersey, the beaches of Delaware, the coastline of Virginia, the surf of California, and the volcanic sands of Hawaii—much as salmon are drawn upstream in their annual migration. We particularly enjoy the secluded places, places without the hustle of tourists or the din of motorized watercraft. It is there that we stroll along the edge of a rising tide, discover non-franchised restaurants where the chef knows better than to overcook halibut or undercook scallops, and where the sunsets echo off a pitcher of margaritas set on the sun-bleached deck of a rambling seaside hotel. As a writer of science for both children and adults, I am able to sustain my obsession with sea life of every stripe and color and continue my maritime adventures in tropical waters, warm bays, languid harbors, and on distant beaches.

Horseshoe crab spawning is an evolutionary dance almost as old as time itself.

WHETHER YOU LIVE IN OREGON, NEW MEXICO, LOUISIANA, SOUTH Dakota, West Virginia, New Hampshire, or any of the other forty-four states—or even in Canada, Mexico, or one of a hundred other countries— you may be surprised to discover (as I was) how much horseshoe crabs are a part of your life. Indeed, for many readers, this book may well be their first introduction to these mysterious creatures—their first look at an animal that has beaten the environmental and evolutionary odds and survived for longer than 99 percent of all the animals that have ever been.

And should you need further reason to continue this scientific journey, here are two pieces of information you may find interesting: first, horseshoe crabs are probably the single most-studied invertebrate animal in the world, and second, three Nobel Prizes have been awarded to scientists who did some, part, or all of their research on an aspect of the horseshoe crab's physiology.

WE'LL BEGIN OUR SCIENTIFIC ROAD TRIP BY VISITING ONE ROGER N. Parker of Golden, Colorado, and learn how a creature he has never met literally saved his life—and perhaps yours as well. Next, we'll take a voyage back in time to learn about the natural history of horseshoe crabs and why they have persisted for millions of years. Then, in Chapter 3, you'll get a short geography and history lesson (no final exam is required) about the Delaware Bay—a place that's not so primordial, but that harbors the world's largest concentration of these ancient creatures.

In Chapter 4, we'll examine some of the recent history of horseshoe crabs and how they have been exploited and maligned by generations of humans. We'll devote two chapters to the biology and anatomy of these animals and some of their unbelievable physical features, including the fact that they are the only known animal to have ten eyes (none of which can wink).

As you've already seen, one of the most incredible spectacles in nature is the spawning of the horseshoe crabs along the eastern seaboard of the United States every spring; we'll explore this phenomenon in considerable detail in Chapter 7. Tangentially, we'll see how horseshoe crabs are crucial to the lives of the great flocks of migrating shorebirds that pass throughout the Atlantic flyway each year. From there we'll take a close look at the growth and development of horseshoe crabs from egg to adulthood—a process fraught with unimaginable perils.

In Chapter 10, we'll take a short vacation to western Florida, where we'll meet some fascinating individuals, human and otherwise. Afterward, it's back to southern Delaware to learn how one environmental organization, ERDG, is working to preserve and protect these amazing animals. In Chapter 12, I'll introduce you to one of the most amazing scientists you'll ever meet, ninety-two-year-old Dr. Carl Shuster, who has been studying these critters for more than half a century. Then we'll all go back to school at a three-day conference called Green Eggs & Sand, where we'll pick the brains of some of the most knowledgeable people in this field.

KEY FACT

The horseshoe crab does not have an immune system—it does not have antibodies to fight infection.

We'll end the book on a philosophical note: a reexamination of the value of these creatures in all our lives, and why they're worthy of preservation. Finally, you'll be invited to join me on a visit to a secluded beach in southern New Jersey for one last horseshoe crab orgy.

IN THE UNDERGRADUATE SCIENCE COURSES I TEACH, I ALWAYS DEFINE a scientist as "someone who asks questions, and then goes out and tries to find the answers." For me, the perfect scientist is a four-year-old child—an incessant chatterbox who is always asking "why" questions ("Why is the sky blue?," "Why do birds fly?") A four-year-old is a bottomless well of queries and has an endless passion to discover how the world works.

Like any four-year-old, I, too, have an innate curiosity. I enjoy learning new subjects and exploring new venues. I'm fond of topics that have little to do with my career as a professor of education, but which provide me with experiences I might not otherwise have. For me, the writing life is a voyeuristic experience—looking around the corner, peeking at distant sites, gazing at the incredible, and poking into someone else's business.

Parts of this book have been drawn from interviews with and research by folks more learned than I. I had the great pleasure of speaking with some of the most dynamic people in the field—the movers and shakers of horseshoe crab-ology, so to speak—and they generously volunteered their answers to the great questions surrounding this enigmatic animal. They were patient and instructive, holding my journalistic hand when necessary and sending me off on research ventures far beyond my original queries.

But I also took the author's prerogative to detour into new territory, observing horseshoe crabs with a layman's eye—an eye unfettered by formal scientific protocol or decorum. Serious zoologists and untenured assistant professors of biology may "pooh-pooh" this work for its digressions and narration, its anecdotes and musings, but this book is not for them. It is for all the former four-year-olds who still have a raft of unanswered questions about the universe in general or about this particular ocean creature. It is for the unabashedly inquisitive and the unashamedly ignorant, myself included. I learned much on this journey, and I hope this book provides you with insights, perceptions, and a few truths about a critter that is as much a part of our lives as *American Idol* or mocha lattes.

CHAPTER 1

Mr. Roger N. Parker of Golden, Colorado, Lives Another Day

How Horseshoe Crabs Saved His Life (and Yours, Too)

ROGER N. PARKER* IS AN ALL-AMERICAN FAMILY MAN. HE AND his wife, Cindy, have been married for twenty-seven years, have two grown children (Ben and Clarice), one slightly mangy family dog, a cat who sleeps the day away under the living room couch, a hefty mortgage, and two cars: a 2008 Toyota Yaris and a 2002 Subaru Outback. Their home in Golden, Colorado, is a two-level ranch house in a small development. It is nearly twenty years old, needs a new roof, has no room in the garage to park the cars ("Too many 'boy toys,'" laments Cindy), and was completely repainted—gray with maroon trim—three years ago.

Roger's neighborhood is a typical American suburb. The trees are neatly trimmed, the lawns are always mowed, and the streets are quiet, except for the occasional weekend party down at the Taylors or the noise from the Crenshaws' garage as their son Tyler rebuilds the engine in his 1957 Chevrolet.

Roger works as an accountant for a large manufacturing firm in Denver. He has been there for twenty-one years, makes a salary in the neighborhood of $85,000 per year, and has great benefits. Cindy volunteers at the Denver Museum of Nature and Science, takes private art lessons from a respected artist in the city, and transports the kids to soccer practice and flute lessons

---

* Roger is a fictional character. What he experiences, however, is similar to what thousands of real people experience every year.

each week. Every summer, they take a two-week driving vacation to a destination somewhere in the West. Last year the family visited Arches National Park and Zion National Park in Utah; in years past, they went to the Petrified Forest and the Grand Canyon, as well as Glacier and Yellowstone National Parks. (The rear of the Subaru has bumper stickers from all those places.)

Roger is fifty-eight years old and just under six feet tall, and he has a couple of extra pounds around his midsection (Okay, let's be honest, he has a lot of extra pounds around his midsection) and a full head of dark brown hair. He has hazel eyes, a booming laugh, and a sense of humor second to none. He loves chocolate chip ice cream, drives just a little too fast on Interstate 70, and has all the Eagles' albums. He helps coach the local Little League team and drops by to see his eighty-four-year-old mother in Aurora every other Saturday. He cheers for the Denver Broncos, savoring the good years and trying to forget the bad ones.

When Roger was in high school and college, he was on the cross-country team. He used to run six to eight miles every day, entered several 10K races during the year, and was in great physical condition. But married life and the constant demands of work slowed him down. He loves to eat out at steakhouses and frequently grabs lunch at local fast-food restaurants. He not only added the extra pounds, he also filled his arteries with fats and triglycerides. Males in the Parker family have always had a history of heart disease, and Roger inherited the bad genes his ancestors had been passing down through the generations. Both his father and his paternal grandfather died young of heart attacks, and so when he felt some shortness of breath, Roger decided "an ounce of prevention is worth a pound of cure."

He scheduled a visit with his family doctor, Maria Gonzales. Dr. Gonzales suggested a consult with a noted cardiologist, Lawrence Maggart. Dr. Maggart told Roger he needed a full cardiac workup. Two weeks later, Roger was sitting on an exam table back in Maggart's office. Cindy was squeezing his hand tightly. Maggart was known for being both blunt and direct, and he wasted no time in telling Roger that he had a defective heart valve that needed to be replaced. Roger gulped, held down his emotions, and scheduled the surgery. Then he went home, opened a "cold one," and watched reruns of *NCIS* for the rest of the evening.

The cardiac tests Roger went through indicated he had a mitral valve regurgitation—a leaking or backflow of blood through the valve between the left upper heart chamber (atrium) and the left lower heart chamber (ventricle). If serious, this condition can eventually result in heart failure.

On the morning of the surgery, Roger was given general anesthesia and wheeled into the operating room. Dr. Maggart made a large incision in

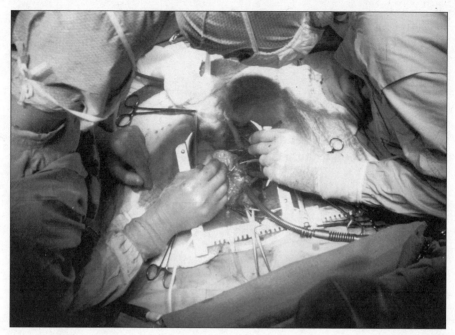

Open heart surgery.

Roger's chest, spread his ribs, and placed him on a heart-lung machine. Over the next four hours, Maggart removed Roger's damaged valve and replaced it with an artificial (prosthetic) one.

The surgery was an unqualified success, and before long Roger found himself back home. After a period of recuperation, with everyone in the family and neighborhood taking care of him (except for old man Nelson, who always forgot to mow the back lawn), Roger was eventually able to return to work. He slowed his pace, took a little less work home every weekend, and started thinking about changing his unhealthy diet (although giving up hot dogs and beer at Broncos home games was going to be a challenge). He began working with a physical therapist to develop an exercise program of light weights and walking. The future looked good.

Roger had many individuals to thank for his successful surgery: Dr. Maggart, of course; the army of nurses who took care of him at the hospital; his family who stood by him throughout the entire ordeal; friends and neighbors who rallied to trim the hedges, paint the shutters, and take out the garbage while he was convalescing; and his associates at work who pitched in to cover his assignments while he was out.

He didn't know it, but he also should thank a crowd of marine creatures living 1,687 miles away in a sheltered bay on the East Coast.

PLEASE GRAB A PEN OR PENCIL AND COMPLETE THE FOLLOWING QUIZ
(it's okay to write in this book). Place a checkmark in the box if a statement
is true for you:

☐ I have been to a hospital.

☐ I have been to a medical clinic.

☐ I have received medication from my family doctor.

☐ I have received an injection.

☐ I have taken a prescription drug.

☐ I wear contact lenses.

☐ I have had some form of surgery.

☐ I have had stitches for a wound or surgical incision.

☐ I have had a part of my body (e.g. knee, hip, heart, etc.)
   replaced or repaired.

☐ I have received some form of vaccine.

If you checked any of the boxes above and are still alive to read this book,
then you have horseshoe crabs to thank. In other words, were it not for the
horseshoe crab, many of the items you checked above could have been life-
threatening or downright fatal. And were it not for horseshoe crabs, our friend
Roger N. Parker of Golden, Colorado, would, most likely, not be alive today.

Let's be absolutely blunt: the horseshoe crab saved Roger's life. It has
probably saved yours, too!

Believe it or not, horseshoe crabs have probably saved the lives of an astronomical number of people on this planet. And, guess what? The horseshoe crab will continue saving your life, the lives of your family members,
and the lives of millions of other people every day. They're like Indiana
Jones, Wonder Woman, and Superman put together.

TO UNDERSTAND WHY HORSESHOE CRABS ARE SO IMPORTANT TO your everyday health (and Roger's), we need to go back in time.

In the early part of the twentieth century, people who received fluids intravenously (directly into the vein) were often developing high fevers. Studies were conducted proving that these fevers were the result of bacterial contamination. Physicians quickly realized that they were often making people sicker than they needed to be, because they were injecting bacteria into them along with the intravenous fluids.

Then, in the 1920s, Florence Seibert developed a test in which a rabbit would be injected with a pharmaceutical, and if over a period of time the rabbit spiked a fever, that meant the product was contaminated (it also meant the demise of the rabbit, but this was long before rabbits formed unions and protested those unfair labor practices). Dr. Seibert was testing for *pyrogens*— that is, any of a group of substances that cause body temperature to rise. If a medical product contained any pyrogens, a fever could result, possibly followed by shock and even death.

In 1942, the U.S. Food and Drug Administration (FDA) approved the rabbit pyrogen test. It tests for endotoxins, which are toxins (poisonous substances) associated with certain gram-negative bacteria. You may be familiar with gram-negative bacteria such as E. coli and salmonella—both of which can make you quite sick or quite dead. For many years, the rabbit test was the only practical pyrogen test.

It seemed as though another, more rabbit-friendly test was needed. At this point, I'll turn the story over to Thomas J. Novitsky:

In the 1960s, Dr. Frederick Bang, a Johns Hopkins researcher working at the Marine Biological Laboratory in Woods Hole, Massachusetts, found that when common marine bacteria were injected into the bloodstream of the North American horseshoe crab, *Limulus polyphemus*, massive clotting occurred. Later, with the collaboration of Dr. Jack Levin, the MBL team showed that the clotting was due to endotoxin, a component of the marine bacteria originally used by Dr. Bang. In addition, these investigators were able to localize the clotting phenomenon to the blood cells, amebocytes, of the horseshoe crab, and, more importantly, to demonstrate the clotting reaction in a test tube. The cell-free reagent that resulted was named *Limulus* amebocyte lysate, or LAL. The name LAL is extremely descriptive: Limulus is the generic name of the horseshoe crab, amebocyte is the blood cell that contains the active components of the reagent, and lysate describes the original process used by Levin and Bang to obtain these components. In Levin and Bang's process, amebocytes, after being separated from the blue-colored plasma (hemolymph), were suspended in distilled water where they lysed [ruptured] due to the high concentration of salt contained in the amebocytes versus the absence of salt in the distilled water. Surprisingly, this same process with some minor modifications is still used today to produce LAL.

In the late 1970s, draft guidelines were published for the use of LAL in testing blood products, vaccines, syringes, and other medical equipment. Then, in 1987, the FDA issued official guidelines for pharmaceutical companies that allowed them to use LAL in place of rabbits for testing all drugs and medical devices. Finally, rabbits were (for the most part) released from their scientific bonds of indentured servitude and could return to their cute, furry, and very placid lives.

At this point in our discussion, you may be wondering how an LAL test is performed. Once again, I'll relinquish the podium to Dr. Novitsky:

A laboratory reconstitutes [a] vial of freeze-dried LAL with endotoxin-free water. An equal amount of reconstituted LAL, usually 0.1 ml, is then added to the sample solution in a small, glass, endotoxin-free test tube. The mixture is then incubated at 37°C for one hour. At the end of this time, the mixture is examined for gel formation by gently inverting the tube. If sufficient endotoxin was present in the sample, a firm gel, one that can withstand inversion of the tube, is formed. Knowing the sensitivity of the LAL then allows the investigator to determine the quantity of endotoxin in the sample. If the sample is found to contain an amount that exceeds the limit set by the FDA, the sample fails and the lot of pharmaceutical product must be rejected. The U.S. FDA currently requires the LAL test to be performed on all human and animal injectables as well as medical devices used to deliver these injectables. In addition, many implantable devices and artificial kidneys used for renal dialysis also require an LAL test.

Every LAL manufacturer is required to be licensed by the FDA, and the FDA also regulates the procedures they use for bleeding horseshoe crabs. The horseshoe crabs are collected live from offshore areas and immediately brought to the bleeding facility. Only healthy, uninjured horseshoe crabs are used; those with the slightest injury are automatically rejected. The rejected horseshoe crabs are put into separate containers for eventual release back into the ocean.

The horseshoe crabs are cleaned and disinfected. Each one is carefully bent backward along a hinge bisecting its back. Imagine bending over and not quite touching your toes, and you'll have an idea of what each horseshoe crab now looks like. Each "V-shaped" animal is gently wedged (back end first) into a length of bleeding stock (two one-foot by four-foot painted boards formed into a sideways "V" shape). The horseshoe crab is placed into the V so that its arthrodial membrane (located in the center of its back hinge) is exposed.

The membrane is swabbed with alcohol, and a needle is inserted through the membrane into the creature's heart. (The elongated heart of a horseshoe crab lies just under the axis of the shell.) The horseshoe crab's blue blood drips into a small sterile glass jar containing some anticoagulant solution, which protects the cells from opening (lysing) prematurely. Once a jar is filled with blood, it is centrifuged, or spun out, using a machine that looks like a small version of the Scream Machine at your local county fair, and the amebocytes separate to the bottom. The horseshoe crab's blood is blue (in oxygen) because of a copper binding protein, *hemocyanin*, in the blood that absorbs oxygen.* A large horseshoe crab may yield as much as twelve ounces of blood, but only one ounce of that will be amebocytes. The blue plasma is decanted, and the amebocytes are lysed in distilled water, as noted earlier. The resulting liquid is further refined to make it more sensitive, freeze dried for long-term stability, and packaged and sold to pharmaceutical companies. It is now known as *Limulus* amebocyte lysate—LAL, or just lysate, for short.

KEY FACT

Processed horseshoe crab blood is worth more than $15,000 a quart.

REMEMBER ROGER? HIS HEART IS NOW FULLY FUNCTIONAL, AND although he has to reduce his intake of medium-rare steaks and potato chips and exercise just a little bit more than he is used to, his doctor has told him that he can live a full life, filled with grandchildren, lazy days on tropical beaches, and the peace of mind knowing that he has beaten his hereditary odds.

And he owes it all to horseshoe crabs.

---

* The term "blue blood" (translated from the Spanish phrase *sangre azul*) may have originated in medieval Spain. It was most likely used to distinguish the noble or aristocratic classes (whose superficial veins appeared blue through their untanned skin) from the working classes (who had those golden tans).

The source of LAL.

IT'S A GIVEN IN MEDICINE THAT EVERYTHING USED IN A SURGICAL
procedure should be clean and sterile. While that's something we assume
today, it wasn't always the case back in the "good old days," when patients
were thrown on a table, held down with ropes and straps (as there wasn't any
anesthesia, restraint was the only way to prevent patients from leaping off
the operating table and dashing out the door), and chopped with all sorts of
instruments, including saws, meat cleavers, axes, or any other cutting tool
that was handy. If the operation took place in a barn, say, during the battle
of Gettysburg, then the tools used might be farming implements. Suffice it
to say, the surgical procedures of years gone by left quite a bit to be desired.

Today, however, surgeons like things nice and clean. They typically don't
like nasty microbes crawling around the operating room or across your
body. No matter how good the surgeon might be, those tiny little critters can
mess up all her good work and cause the patient to go home in a body bag
rather than in the front seat of the family car. That's always bad for public
relations and repeat customers.

So everything in an operating room must be washed. And because water
is easily contaminated by gram-negative bacteria, and hence endotoxins, it
is not surprising that LAL tests are conducted on water. You wouldn't want
all those scalpels, spreaders, and other tools to be washed with impure water, would you? Especially if they were going to be used on Roger or, most

importantly, on you. If there are endotoxins in the water, then the things washed in that water would tend to be pyrogenic. That's not good!

Roger had several drugs injected intravenously during his surgery. You can only imagine the consequences if some of those drugs had not been tested for levels of contamination before they were injected into Roger's bloodstream. The water used to formulate those drugs, as well as other critical ingredients, is also tested by LAL. For the sake of patients' health, almost everything that is put into a body must be tested prior to the "putting."

You will also recall that Roger's surgeon placed an artificial device inside his heart. By this point in the chapter, you would not be surprised to learn that implanted devices such as heart valves can also harbor harmful levels of endotox-

KEY FACT

LAL is used by the food industry to test for bacteria in canned food.

ins, which could cause some serious problems, including possible rejection of the device; so they, too, must be tested prior to implantation. Also tested were the various implements used in Roger's surgery—things like syringes, catheters, and needles. Although these devices are manufactured in sterile conditions, they must be checked with LAL.

I think we can probably agree that LAL is pretty important stuff. But LAL isn't even the only medical contribution made by horseshoe crabs. During the surgery, the doctor wisely decided to close up the gaping opening in the middle of Roger's chest so all that stuff inside wouldn't fall out when he stood up. Surgical closures are usually done with sutures. The sutures (stitches) used in Roger's operation were coated with chitin—a substance obtained from the shells of horseshoe crabs. It has been discovered that chitin-coated sutures can dramatically enhance the healing process.

TRAFFIC WHIZZES BY ME AS I WAIT IN THE LEFT-HAND TURNING lane of U.S. 15 South to swing onto Biggs Ford Road and toward the tiny hamlet of Walkersville, an eye-blink of a town in the rural reaches of western Maryland. Just on the outskirts of town is a sprawling cluster of undistinguished and whitewashed buildings that house Lonza Pharmaceuticals, one of three firms in the United States (the others are Associates of Cape Cod in Woods Hole, Massachusetts, and Charles River Endosafe in Wilmington, South Carolina) that manufactures LAL. I am here to interview Maribeth Janke, marketing manager for Lonza's endotoxin detection product line. Janke's Ph.D. is from the University of New Hampshire, where her dissertation was titled "Initial characterization of coagulin polymerization and a novel trypsin inhibitor from *Limulus polyphemus*." Her dissertation demonstrated how similar horseshoe crab blood coagulation is to human blood coagulation. She would be my guide through the amazing world of LAL.

Before our interview, Dr. Janke took me on a tour of the Lonza facilities—a beehive of hallways and specialized labs, with humans swarming around the rooms. She was quick to tell me that because LAL is a biologic, the FDA regulates everything involved in the manufacturing process. The FDA is keen on the concept of sterility, and sterility is a constant throughout the facility. As you might imagine, there are explicit protocols for the manufacturing process, and government officials (with thick glasses, equally thick clipboards, and a predisposition to frowning) visit approximately every two years.

Janke led me through a series of rooms where LAL is formulated, produced, and tested. She cautioned me about the proprietary nature of the entire process, and for that reason I am not allowed to tell you everything I saw or heard. Although I can't reveal the precise procedures used in the various stages of LAL manufacture and was not permitted to take any photos, Janke invited me to hand copy a chart posted outside one of the production rooms. The chart summarizes the various stages of LAL manufacture into a handy flowchart (figure 1.1).

After touring the facility, we retired to Janke's office, a small room filled with scientific reports, documents, and hefty books with titles such as *Encyclopedia of Rapid Microbiological Methods, Volumes 1–3; Endotoxins—3rd Edition*; and *The Bacterial Endotoxins Test: A Practical Guide*. Not exactly bedtime reading.

Janke told me that Lonza's primary customer base is pharmaceutical companies or biotech companies that make injectables or parenterals (according to the Merriam-Webster Collegiate Dictionary a parenteral is something "introduced otherwise than by way of the intestines"), or anything that comes in contact with the bloodstream or cerebral spinal fluid. Makers of implantable devices—such as knee replacements, stents, or pacemakers—and dialysis clinics are also customers. Janke pointed out that, "If a company makes something that is sterile, or free of live bacteria, then they will be testing for endotoxins as well."

I mentioned our friend Roger, and Janke informed me that if he had an IV bag and anything was injected into the IV bag, all of those liquids would have been tested. His replacement valve would have been tested, as well as

Figure 1.1. The various stages of LAL manufacture

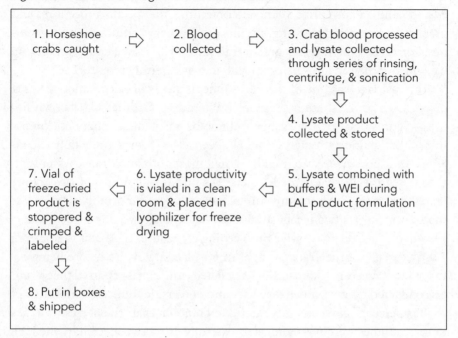

the needles and syringes used throughout the operation. Even the surgeon's gloves would have been tested.

I ask Janke why she considers LAL to be such an important advance over the earlier rabbit test. She proceeded to take me back through the history of pyrogen testing and the fact that rabbit testing killed a lot of rabbits. Fortunately, according to Janke, "there is not much rabbit testing going on because of LAL." LAL, it turns out, is much more sensitive to endotoxins than the rabbits were, and that fact alone has virtually (although not entirely) eliminated the rabbit pyrogen test.

Horseshoe crabs have been around for hundreds of millions of years (rabbits have a considerably shorter ancestry), but their blood clotting system is similar, in many ways, to ours. Janke put it in more passionate terms when she said, "They have kindly donated their blood to us, and it's our turn to make sure we take care of them. So the significance is that [horseshoe crabs] are helping make products that we use safer. The rabbits, I'm sure, are very happy to be retired."

The LAL manufacturing industry is regulated *ad nauseam.* Janke told me that the FDA regulates the industry (the horseshoe crab collection process is overseen by the Atlantic States Marine Fisheries Commission) in terms of the number of horseshoe crabs they can bleed, how they are to be transported and handled both prior to and after bleeding, the specific procedures and practices used during bleeding, sterility and sanitary conditions in the facilities, horseshoe crab tagging, and overall safety. Horseshoe crabs can only be bled once each year, and their mortality rate is carefully monitored.

This last fact was one of the most difficult pieces of information to track down. Each of the three horseshoe crab bleeding facilities has its own figures—figures that are proprietary and not for public dissemination. Companies with high mortality rates would be seen as less "environmentally friendly" (or less "horseshoe crab friendly") than those with lower rates. As a result, the figures are closely guarded secrets. The film *Crash: A Tale of Two Species* (2008) reported, "LAL manufacturers have measured mortality rates of less than 3 percent. Yet two recent studies estimate that between 10 percent and 15 percent of crabs do not survive the bleeding procedure...." That is to say, from 3 to 15 percent of the crabs brought in for bleeding expire before being returned to the ocean. Thomas Novitsky (cited earlier) has reported that "studies conducted by government agencies and universities indicate a mortality of 10 to 15 percent." Novitsky was careful to point out that "the horseshoe crabs in these studies were not handled as carefully as those collected by the LAL industry." When I asked Janke about horseshoe crab mortality rates (post-bleeding), she told me, "A specific paper said 15 percent, although some people are saying more. We [Lonza] say, in our hands, it's less; it's single digits."

KEY FACT

LAL cannot discriminate between living and dead bacteria.

In gathering material and conducting research for this book, I was not surprised to discover that large segments of the American population have never heard of horseshoe crabs. A local newspaper reporter called me up during the writing of the book to interview me about another book I had recently written. When she asked what projects I was currently working on, I told her about this one. Her response—"Horseshoe crabs, what the heck are they?"—was tinged with surprise and wonder. Other folks I encountered across the country in the past year also expressed either complete ignorance or surprise about these prehistoric wonders. Janke told me a story about one of her colleagues at Lonza who, when he gets on a plane for a long flight, purposely asks the person next to him, "Well, what do you do?" "He figures they'll eventually ask him what he does, and then, for the next eight hours, he can tell them all about horseshoe crabs," she said.

Thus, it was with a certain sense of authorial curiosity that I asked Janke why the average person should know or care about horseshoe crabs. She said that most "people assume that if they are being treated or having some sort of surgical procedure, that the things that are being used to treat them are sterile, are clean, that there is quality built into those procedures, and that [an operation, for example] is not going to make them sicker." In short, there's an inherent trust between the public and the medical profession. Janke believes the general public should realize that horseshoe crab blood, and the LAL that's made from it, assists pharmaceutical and medical device companies to make their products safer for us to use. The horseshoe crabs, according to Janke, help us by donating their blood, not because they want to, but rather because it has been proven to be one of the most reliable and accurate measures for detecting pyrogens and preventing illness and death in the human population.

Interestingly, Janke is also an advocate for alternative technologies that may eventually replace the need to bleed horseshoe crabs.* "We [should] retire them now and look into other ways to test for endotoxins that don't need the blood of an animal," she told me.

Retiring horseshoe crabs...*hmmmmm*. I get this vision of a long row of horseshoe crabs in sunglasses reclining in wooden rockers on the front porch of Sunny Beaches Retirement Home, a pepperoni pizza on the table and a cold Corona clutched in each of their pedipalps.

I probably shouldn't tell Roger about that vision (at least the pizza and beer part).

---

* Just as I was completing this chapter, I received a press release issued by the National Science Foundation. The NSF reports that "...researchers at the Department of Chemical and Biological Engineering at the University of Wisconsin-Madison have found what may be a more effective way to test for endotoxins that involves liquid crystals, the same material used to make some flat screen computer monitors and televisions."

Horseshoe crabs have been spawning on beaches for nearly half a billion years.

CHAPTER 2

Long Before the Dinosaurs

Yes, They've Been Around a While

ASK MOST PEOPLE HOW OLD THEY ARE, AND A PREDICTABLE psychological reaction will occur. They will feign either a complete lack of mental awareness or the first signs of senility. Or they will engage in a behavior practiced by politicians who have sent photos of themselves in various states of undress around the Internet—they will lie, fib, misrepresent, fake, conjecture, tell stories, invent half-truths, and perjure themselves. Indeed, ever since the invention of language, human beings have been loath to reveal their true age.

We are a culture of fibbers when it comes to our ages. But, we are not alone in this propensity to ignore our birth certificates and manipulate years for the sake of making an impression. This is a cultural constant that has taken place in every century and every civilization since the dawn of history. Stories about legendary centenarians, age-defying potions, and eternal retirement spots have been told around campfires and shared at community gatherings for tens of thousands of years.

In ancient times, people didn't subtract years from their true age—they added them. Longevity stories were an essential element of almost every culture. The longer humans lived (or thought they should live), the more connected they were to the spirits of their ancestors. As the stories of long-livers were passed down from one generation to the next, a few years were added here and there in order to extend the storyteller's genealogy further back

25

into the past. In Japan, emperors' ages were inflated in a blatant attempt to extend Japanese history back in time beyond that of Europeans. The ancient Romans, always looking to demonstrate their superiority, frequently cited such examples of longevity as Nestor, who allegedly lived for 300 years, or Tirasis of Thebes, who supposedly lived well into his six hundreds. Apparently, religiosity is a major determinant of human longevity—Saint Servatious, a bishop around AD 300, was rumored to be 375 years old when he died, while LP Suwang, a Buddhist saint in Thailand, lived to be either 200 years old (according to some) or well past his five hundredth birthday (according to others).*

In many primeval cultures, old people were a rarity, and when some village elder exceeded the norm, he or she was revered and celebrated in song, dance, and story. These village elders were a source of pride and admiration for a village, and tales would evolve about how they achieved a long life— stories that were spiced up in order to outdo the fibs perpetuated by neighboring villages. Since most stories from the countryside were shared as part of the oral tradition, facts were of small consequence, and ages into the triple digits were often reported (and enhanced).

It wasn't until the twentieth century, and our growing regard for accuracy and precision, that questions of human longevity were finally subjected to logical and scientific analysis. Although there were stories about Russians living past 160, Britons sipping tea until the ripe old age of 185, and Indian swamis living past 200, these claims were often an attempt to demonstrate that philosophy, spirituality, or meditation had more of an effect on one's lifespan than did heredity, lifestyle, or plain luck.

ALTHOUGH HUMAN BEINGS MAY BE GENETICALLY PREDISPOSED TO fib about their age, the planet Earth cannot. Rocks never lie, and a geological analysis of rocks has pinpointed the earth's age at just about 4.55 billion years. At first, ice and rock particles swirling around the young sun smashed together, eventually forming the planet. As the earth's surface slowly cooled,

---

* Currently, throughout the world, the average life expectancy of all humans is 67.2 years. The country with the highest overall life expectancy is Japan at 82.6 years (79.0 for men and 86.1 for women). The country with the lowest life expectancy is Swaziland at 39.6 years (39.8 for men and 39.4 for women). According to a list prepared by the United Nations, the United States currently ranks thirty-sixth, with an average of 78.3 years (75.6 for men and 80.8 for women).

over the first seven hundred million years or so of its existence, ours was an alien world without water, oxygen, or life. But there were changes—big changes—to come.

This timeline (figure 2.1, next page) shows the various eras and periods of time into which scientists divide the earth's history. These divisions help us talk about the timing of events in the natural history of this planet in a language that everyone can agree on.

Now, let's take a little journey back in time and examine (very briefly) each of the major eras and some of the events that took place in each one.

The Precambrian era makes up about seven-eighths of the earth's history—a total of approximately four thousand million years. A number like that is too much for most of us to comprehend. But let's dip into a book by John McPhee—*Basin and Range*—and take a look at how he illustrated this time span. Stand with your arms held out to each side and parallel to the floor. Let's let the extent of the earth's history be represented by the distance from the tip of the middle finger on your left hand to the tip of the middle finger on your right hand. Now, if someone were to run a file across the fingernail of your right middle finger, the time that humans have been on the earth would be erased. Using the same analogy, the distance from the tip of your left middle finger, across your chest, to a place right around your right wrist would represent the Precambrian era. (Okay, you can put your arms down now.)

The enormous length of the Precambrian era allowed several important biological, geological, and chemical events to take place. These included the rise and movement of the first tectonic plates, the infusion of oxygen into the atmosphere, and the evolution of eukaryotic cells (cells with a nucleus, which make up all animals, plants, fungi, and protist microorganisms). It was only toward the end of the Precambrian era that complex multicellular organisms, including soft-bodied marine creatures, began to appear.

The next era in the history of Earth is called the Paleozoic. This was an era of tremendous and incredible growth in the number, diversity, and complexity of animal life. The oceans swarmed with primitive arthropods called trilobites, which are now-extinct relatives of the horseshoe crab. Clams, snails, and other marine creatures inhabited the shallow waters of inland seas, as did members of the subclass *Xiphosurida*, a group of creatures that included the earliest members of the horseshoe crab family. Later in the era, primitive plants began to appear on land, and the first jawed fishes developed.

This era would have been the joy of any serious gardener, because this is also when complex plant life appeared. Huge ferns and forests of "scale

Figure 2.1. Geologic Time Scale*

PERIOD	MILLIONS OF YEARS AGO	CHARACTERISTIC LIFE
CENOZOIC ERA "Time of Recent Life"		
Holocene	0.01–0	Modern times. Mankind dominates land. Horseshoe crabs continue to thrive.
Pleistocene	2.6–0.01	Ice age mammals, including early man, dominate.
Pliocene	5.3–2.6	Climate is cool. Mammal life is similar to present day.
Miocene	23–5.3	Grass-eating, running mammals are widespread.
Oligocene	33.9–23	Mammals begin to look like modern types.
Eocene	55.8–33.9	Mammals are widespread.
Paleocene	65.5–55.8	All kinds of new mammals develop. Horseshoe crabs continue to thrive.
MESOZOIC ERA "Time of Middle Life"		
Cretaceous	145.5–65.5	Largest variety of dinosaurs. Dinosaurs and many marine organisms become extinct.
Jurassic	201.6–145.5	Giant dinosaurs are abundant. First toothed birds, conifers, and cycads are also plentiful.
Triassic	251–201.6	Dinosaurs evolve from thecodont reptiles. Primitive mammals appear.

* Adapted from Walker, J.D., and Geissman, J.W., compilers, 2009, *Geologic Time Scale*: Geological Society of America, doi: 10.1130/2009.CTS004R2C.

PERIOD	MILLIONS OF YEARS AGO	CHARACTERISTIC LIFE
PALEOZOIC ERA "Time of Early Life"		
Permian	299–251	Mass extinction of many invertebrates and armored fish. Horseshoe crabs survive and thrive.
Carboniferous	359–299	Massive forests of fern trees dominate. First reptiles develop. Several horseshoe crab species (*Bellinurus, Euproops, Liomesaspis, Valloisella, Paleolimulus, Rolfeia,* and *Bellinuroopsis*) are alive.
Devonian	416–359	Fish and sharks are abundant. First amphibians and primitive land plants appear. Early horseshoe crabs (*Kasibelinurus*) live in shallow seas.
Silurian	444–416	Jawless and armored fish abound. First land plants evolve. Early horseshoe crabs (*Bunodes, Limuloides, Pastemakevia, Pseudoniscus,* and *Cyamocephalus*) are abundant.
Ordovician	488–444	First vertebrates appear. Marine invertebrates with hard parts abound. Earliest ancestors of horseshoe crabs (*Lunataspis*) appear.
Cambrian	542–488	First shelled animals evolve. No evidence of life on land.
PRECAMBRIAN ERA	4,600–542	Most of Earth's history. Simple marine organisms only.

trees" dominated the landscape. The first winged insects and assorted varieties of reptiles made their appearance. And the first cockroaches—four inches long, no less—made their entrance onto the land and eventually into kitchen cabinets all around the world.

There were six major continental landmasses during the Paleozoic Era. Over time, these great, amorphous continents crunched together in a one collective supercontinent known as Pangaea.*

The Paleozoic ended with the proverbial bang, as they say—a massive extinction that may have been precipitated by tremendous volcanic activity or wide-scale glaciation (the exact causes are still unknown). This extinction, which forms the border between the Permian and Triassic periods, was so widespread that as many as 50 percent of all animal families and 95 percent of all marine species were eliminated over a period of a few million years.

The Mesozoic Era (which included the Triassic, Jurassic, and Cretaceous Periods), or the "Time of Middle Life," was also the time of the dinosaurs. These "terrible lizards" rose during the Triassic, thrived during the Jurassic,[†] and were gone by the end of the Cretaceous—a total span of about 165 million years. Two of the oldest known dinosaurs were *Eoraptor,* a fast-running predator who had some herbivore teeth, and *Herrerasaurus,* a bipedal (two-footed) carnivore ten to twenty feet in length with curved sharp claws. Both of these early dinosaurs have been discovered in Argentina in rocks that are 228 million years old. At the other end of the dinosaur timeline is *Arenysaurus ardevoli* ("Sand dinosaur"), a muscular, swimming, duck-billed species discovered in 2009 in Spain. It apparently lived just a few thousand years before the end of the Cretaceous.[‡]

KEY FACT

Horseshoe crabs first appeared 445 million years ago; dinosaurs appeared only 250 million years ago.

---

* Contrary to popular belief, Pangaea was not the only supercontinent in Earth's history. Many geologists believe several others appeared and disappeared prior to the formation of Pangaea. Pangaea is, however, the best known.

† The title of the 1993 film *Jurassic Park* (and the book by Michael Crichton) was actually a misnomer. Most of the dinosaurs featured in the movie and book did not exist until the Cretaceous Period.

‡ By comparison, the earliest humanoids appeared about four million years ago and modern humans—*Homo sapiens*—originated in Africa about two hundred thousand years ago. In short, dinosaurs lived for 164,800,000 years longer than humans have been around. Or,

The Mesozoic Era ended with a massive extinction—all of the dinosaurs and about 50 percent of all the marine invertebrates were eliminated. There are several theories for what caused this extinction, but the most plausible seems to be a massive asteroid impact near the Yucatán peninsula. Extinctions rarely happen all at once; rather, they typically take place over long slices of time. According to the fossil record, we know dinosaurs died out over a period of hundreds of thousands of years. This is very fast in geological terms, but still many generations of dinosaur lives. It seems likely that massive volcanoes in India, in tandem with the catastrophic aftermath of the Yucatán explosion, ensured their extinction. The dinosaurs didn't entirely disappear, however: today's birds are their direct descendants.[§]

The Cenozoic Era is sometimes known as the Age of Mammals. With the demise of the non-avian dinosaurs, mammals, which had been small, began to expand in both size and diversity. Marine mammals such as whales and porpoises appeared, and a wide variety of land mammals spread across the continents.

Flowering plants diversified and spread, insects grew in abundance, greater numbers of fish inhabited the oceans, and birds filled the skies. The continents were slowly moving into their present positions, separating themselves from the supercontinent Pangaea. As a result, several animal species were geographically separated—which increased their biological diversity—and the animals we know today were able to migrate to the farthest reaches of the globe. The last ice age occurred approximately 110,000 to 10,000 years ago.

SO WHERE DO HORSESHOE CRABS FIT INTO ALL THESE PREHISTORIC events? Well, they got their evolutionary start about half a billion years ago. Horseshoe crab shells are made of chitin, a cellulose-like compound that decomposes very rapidly and doesn't readily turn into fossils. In spite of this, scientists have discovered horseshoe crab fossils that date back to the Silurian Period, more than four hundred million years ago.

Recently, however, a team of Canadian scientists discovered rare, new horseshoe crab fossils in 445-million-year-old rocks in central and northern Manitoba. Palaeontologist Dave Rudkin from the Royal Ontario Museum,

---

to put it another way, for every year of human existence, dinosaurs roamed the earth for 325 years.

§ Birds are scientifically classified as theropods ("beast feet"), a group that also includes, among other dinosaurs, *Tyrannosaurus rex*.

working with colleagues Graham Young of the Manitoba Museum in Winnipeg and Godfrey Nowlan at the Geological Survey of Canada in Calgary, gave these remarkable new fossils the scientific name *Lunataspis aurora*, meaning literally "crescent moon shield of the dawn." Although they are more "primitive" in several aspects than present-day horseshoe crabs, the resemblance is unmistakable.

These fossil horseshoe crabs were recovered in the course of fieldwork on ancient, tropical seashore deposits. Their discovery provides an important link to their modern descendants found along seashores of the eastern United States and the Indian Ocean. This is particularly significant, explains Rudkin, in "understanding how horseshoe crabs adapted to this ecological niche very early on, and then remained there through thick and thin—[giving] us insights into how ocean and shoreline ecosystems have developed through deep time."

To many scientists, horseshoe crabs are affectionately known as "living fossils," simply because they have remained relatively unchanged anatomically for more than 400 million years. They were around long before the dinosaurs ever set foot in a Colorado floodplain or on an Argentine plateau.

Some of the earliest ancestors of today's horseshoe crab might have been sea scorpions. These animals existed from about 425 to 230 million years ago, primarily during the Cambrian and Ordovician Periods. Like modern-day horseshoe crabs, the front of their bodies had a rounded design. The second part of their body, unlike modern horseshoe crabs, was comprised of several interlocking pieces hinged together. This undoubtedly gave it enormous flexibility as it searched for prey or escaped from its enemies. Some sea scorpions also had sharp tail spines quite similar to the horseshoe crab's tail (the *telson*).

One of the anatomical features that differentiated these ancient relatives from today's horseshoe crab species was that its walking legs extended beyond the perimeter of the carapace. In other words, its legs stuck out from the sides of its shell. Most sea scorpions also had pincers at the end of the front pair of walking legs, which would have been useful for grabbing and holding onto prey.

Sea scorpions also varied tremendously in size, ranging from a tiny six inches (about the size of your average hamster, not counting the tail) all the way up to a gargantuan nine feet in length (about as long as an adult female alligator, including the tail). Sea scorpions shared other similarities with today's horseshoe crabs, including the ability to grow a new set of lenses for their compound eyes whenever they molted, book-like gills, and the ability to mash their food with the shoulders on their walking feet. A distant

A fossilized horseshoe crab ancestor.

relative of the sea scorpion eventually evolved to become the first land scorpion, which subsequently evolved into the first spiders.

Many scientists believe horseshoe crabs are the closest living relative of the ancient and geographically diverse trilobite. Trilobites (meaning "three lobes") first appeared in the early Cambrian Period, about 562 million years ago. These creatures were some of the most successful of all the early animals, roaming the seas for well over 270 million years (about a hundred million years longer than the dinosaurs).

We know a lot about trilobites, because unlike early horseshoe crabs, they had a mineral exoskeleton composed of calcite and calcium phosphate that fossilized easily. As a result, they left a much more extensive fossil record.

About seventeen thousand species of trilobites have been identified throughout the world. This diversity of species also meant a diversity of lifestyles. Some trilobites were predators, hunting down small marine creatures. Others were scavengers, feeding on the flotsam and jetsam that accumulated along the ocean floor. Some were filter feeders, and others fed on tiny bits of plankton. Trilobites ranged in size from 0.04 inches long up to more than two feet. Like horseshoe crabs, their bodies were divided into three distinct sections: the first part (the "head") was known as the *cephalon*; the second part (the "body") was known as the *thorax* (similar to the middle section,

Trilobites were a relative of horseshoe crabs. Their fossils are found worldwide.

also called the thorax, of modern day insects); and the third part (or "tail") was known as the *pygidium*.

Trilobite fossils have been discovered worldwide, and they may be one of the most diversified creatures ever. Some of the better-known locations for trilobite finds include the Burgess Shale in British Columbia, Canada; the Maotianshan Shales in China; and the Hunsrück Slates in Germany. Trilobites are also known as index fossils, because they allow geologists to date the age of the rocks in which they are found.

WE'VE TALKED QUITE A BIT ABOUT FOSSILS, SO LET'S BACK UP FOR A few moments here and learn a little more about what fossils are and where they come from. Interestingly, much of what we know about ancient creatures, including trilobites, sea scorpions, and horseshoe crabs, depends on the fossils they left behind. It's difficult to have a conversation with a creature that has been dead for more than 400 million years, but even in their silence, the fossils these ancient beasts left behind can tell us much about their lives.

Technically speaking, fossils (from the Latin *fossus*, which means "having been dug up") are the preserved remains or traces of animals, plants, and other organisms from the remote past. Many paleontologists will tell you a preserved specimen is called a "fossil" if it is more than ten thousand years old. Interestingly, people have known about prehistoric fossils for a long time. Writings of Chinese druggists dating from around 3000 BC contain the earliest known descriptions of fossil bones. These bones, sometimes referred to as "dragon bones," were (and still are) ground up for use in a variety of traditional Chinese medicines. The Greeks and Romans often displayed fossilized bones in their temples. We do not know what animals these bones came from, or their age, but even the ancients recognized them as remains of creatures that did not exist anymore.

That said, it's important to remember that fossilization is an exceptionally rare biological occurrence, because most components of formerly living things tend to decompose relatively quickly following death.*

Here's a basic fact of life (or death): most living things vanish after they die. Immediately upon death, a formerly living organism is subjected to an incredible menu of forces that—depending on temperature, the

---

* Here's a little known fact: in the tropics, a human body can be reduced to just a skeleton in two weeks or less (with the undivided assistance of organ-destroying bacteria, voracious insects, and various carnivorous critters both large and small).

availability of oxygen, the cause of death, the depth of burial, access by scavengers, wounds, humidity, rainfall, body size and weight, the surface on which the body rests, and, sometimes, even the food in the organism's digestive tract—eventually reduce it to nothing.

The fossils most prized by scientists, because they tell us so much about the distant past, are the skeletons of prehistoric animals. For the moment, let's suppose that an animal died tens of millions of years ago. Usually other animals—scavengers—would feed on its body, tearing its flesh and gnawing its bones. The remains may be subjected to various environmental factors that would hasten the breakdown and decomposition of the body. But once in a while, good fortune might intervene. Mud, gravel, or sand might get to the body first, quickly burying it under several layers of sediment.

KEY FACT

According to the *New York Times*, a team of British and Australian geologists in western Australia has discovered what may be the world's oldest fossils—single-celled organisms 3.4 billion years old.

That quick burial is critical, because in order for an organism to be fossilized, the remains need to be covered by sediment as soon as possible (fossils only occur in sedimentary rock). The sediment (often from a flash flood, river deposits, or other natural event) creates an anaerobic environment, in which oxygen is kept away from the dead organism. Oxygen tends to enhance the decay of organic materials, destroying body parts before they can fossilize. A lack of oxygen, however, retards spoilage. Thus, the longer a dead body can stay in an oxygen-deprived condition, the better the chances for it to fossilize.

Time passes…a very long time. Over many years, centuries, and millennia, sediments build up on top of sediments. This constant buildup slowly compresses the lower layers into various forms of sedimentary rock, such as sandstone, shale, and limestone. In that extended time, water seeps through cracks in the rocks and slowly dissolves body parts, such as bones, which may be replaced by minerals carried in the water. Gradually, most of the original material is replaced by stone. On very rare occasions, even dung may be mineralized and transformed into fossils known as *coprolites*.*

---

* In conducting research for another book—*Walking with Dinosaurs: Rediscovering Colorado's Prehistoric Beasts* (Boulder, CO: Johnson Books, 2012)—I had the pleasure of interviewing Karen Chin, a paleoscatologist with the University of Colorado. She is one of the

It's important to remember that paleontologists seldom find completely fossilized animals. Generally, only the hard parts of living things survive. These include bones, teeth, shells, and the woody parts of plants. Other fossils, known as trace fossils, are not parts of animals or plants at all, but rather animals' or plants' imprints left in mud that hardened before the prints disappeared. These may include footprints of dinosaurs wandering along a shoreline, impressions of the leaves of an ancient conifer that grew in the Rocky Mountains when the Rocky Mountains were at sea level, or impressions of the bodies of long-dead invertebrates such as sea scorpions, trilobites, or horseshoe crabs.

TIME, NOW, TO RETURN TO OUR ANCIENT (AND VERY FOSSILIZED) friends. At this point I'll turn the discussion over to noted horseshoe crab expert Carl N. Shuster, Jr. (whom you'll meet in Chapter 12), and Lyall I. Anderson:

> By the beginning of the Mesozoic era, some 245 million years ago, horseshoe crabs had essentially the appearance of the extant [modern-day] species. Further back in geologic time, into the Paleozoic era (245 to 570 million years ago), the species are still recognizable as horseshoe crabs, but they were much smaller and varied more from the extant body plan. Two major groups have been recognized: the Xiphosurida, in rocks of the Carboniferous and Permian; and the Synziphosurines, which range in age from the Ordovician to the Devonian…. The major difference between the two is whether the midpart of the body was essentially a solid piece of fused segments, as in the Xiphosurida, or was composed of articulating segments, as in the Synziphosurines. In function, the most obvious difference was the greater control of various functions within the deeper vault of the solid piece versus the ability to roll up in the geologically older group.

The *xiphosurans*[†] (Greek for "sword-tailed ones") have undergone relatively

---

world's leading experts on dinosaur coprolites. By studying fossilized feces, she can determine not only what a prehistoric creature ate, but how it ate, where it lived, how it behaved, the climate and geology of the area in which it lived, and tons of other information about its habits and life.

† Many of the early xiphosurans (e.g. *Weinbergina, Euproops*) are listed in figure 2.1 according to their geologic time period—from Ordovician through Carboniferous.

few changes, evolutionarily speaking, over the hundreds of millions of years since. Most of the changes have been to their external anatomy (they have lost most of their segmentation and increased overall in size) and to their habitat (now living exclusively in a marine environment).

Although we know much about these ancient creatures, there is still much more to learn. Professors Anderson and Shuster underscore this when they state:

> The origin of the extant species is not known, but they or their antecedent species might have migrated from their original center of abundance when the Mesozoic shallow seas where Europe now stands became land. One ancestral type moved westward, giving rise to *Limulus* [see below], while the type(s) giving rise to three species went eastward. That may have happened, but there is also the possibility that the lineage leading to *Limulus* may have been established much earlier in its part of the world, while...related species gave rise to the Indo-Pacific horseshoe crabs. Further morphological study and comparison of these Mesozoic fossils is required to test this particular hypothesis.

Today there are four species of horseshoe crabs (or "living fossils"). One species lives along the Atlantic coast of North America, and three live in Indo-Pacific waters. They include:

- *Limulus polyphemus*. The "American" or "Atlantic" horseshoe crab ranges from Maine southward along the Atlantic seaboard to Florida, around the Florida peninsula, and along the Florida Panhandle. There is also a small population on the edge of the Yucatán peninsula in Mexico. This is the species on which we will concentrate our attention throughout this book.

- *Tachypleus tridentatus*. The "Japanese" horseshoe crab, this is the only species found in Japanese waters. This is an endangered species, mainly because of the construction of dikes and artificial barriers in many coastal areas and extensive pollution in others.

- *Tachypleus gigas*. The "Chinese" horseshoe crab, this species is found primarily in the Bay of Bengal and throughout several Indonesian islands.

- *Carcinoscorplus rotundicauda*. The "Indonesian" horseshoe crab, this species frequents mangrove swamps. It, too, ranges from the Bay of Bengal eastward into the Indonesian islands.

It is astounding to me that horseshoe crabs have survived for such an extended period of time. Like a persistent relative who always shows up at the annual family reunion, horseshoe crabs seem to be a "forever" critter— one that has endured long and changed little. That they have been around for thousands of millions of years, and that they may eventually outlive humans, is truly an evolutionary success story. They are survivors of the first order, and though they will probably not be contracted for a reality TV show that places contestants in tropical locations to see if they can "outwit, outplay, outlast" each other, they will certainly stand (or crawl) as one of the most enduring of creatures.

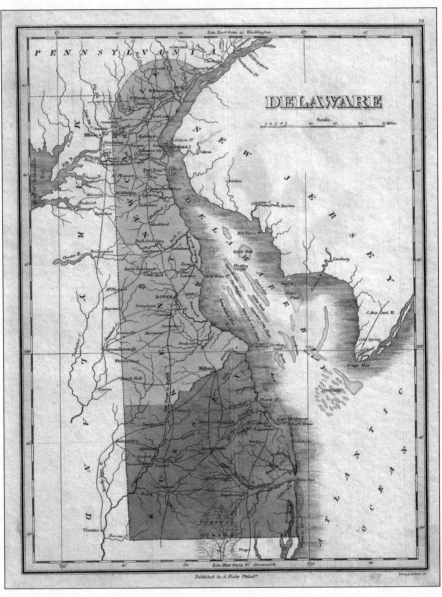

An 1827 map of Delaware and the Delaware Bay.

CHAPTER 3

Lord De La Warr's Bay

A Short Course in Geology and History

IMAGINE A MOUTHWATERING, TASTE-TEMPTING, GENUINE HOME-
made cherry pie. Think about that oh-so-sweet pie as it's baking in the
oven. Smells are wafting through the kitchen, down the hallway, and out
into the garden. The pie gradually turns a rich golden brown, and after about
thirty minutes a small rift—a crack—begins to appear in the crust. Over the
course of the next ten minutes or so, the rift grows a little longer and just
a little wider. A lava-like glob of cherry filling pops out of the crack, cascades over the fluted edge, and drips onto the bottom of the oven. Minute by
minute, additional blobs of cherry lava bubble up like thickened primordial
ooze. By the time the pie is ready to be pulled from the oven, the crack has
grown wider and longer, and the pie is oozing filling like mad.

The scenario above is one I share with students in my Teaching Elementary Science courses, particularly when we begin our discussions of plate
tectonics, volcanism, and the early history of the earth. Its imagery is immediate and sensory. Most important, it is a memorable (not to mention delicious) way to begin our journey into the past.

I tell students that the earth is not a static entity. It is constantly in motion,
forever sliding, shifting, moving. Tectonic plates continuously grind their way
over and under each other, earthquakes rip through the earth's crust daily,
volcanoes belch molten lava from subterranean bowels (just like our cherry
pie), and wind and waves sandpaper Earth's fragile surface time and time

again. The planet changes; it is never exactly the same from one day to the next, and certainly not from one eon to the next. It is constantly evolving.*

From 280 to 230 million years ago (the late Paleozoic Era until the late Triassic), the continent we now know as North America was contiguous with Africa, South America, and Europe. They were all part of an enormous supercontinent known as Pangaea. Then, as part of an enormous crustal dance, this supercontinent began to break up sometime in the early Mesozoic Era (between 251 and 65.5 million years ago). It was like a colossal cosmic fork cutting into a slice of our cherry pie, separating this wedge of geological dessert into distinct parts. As one section slowly separated from the other, metaphoric cherry filling oozed and seeped from the crack, and a temporary valley formed between the segments.

In the evolving Earth, an enormous fissure developed between Africa, South America, and North America, gradually ripping Pangaea apart. This cleaving began when magma (the cherry filling) welled up through a weakness in the crust, creating a volcanic rift zone. Powerful eruptions spewed great masses of ash and volcanic debris across the landscape as the severed continent-sized fragments of Pangaea slowly—ever so slowly—diverged.

Then, sometime during the Jurassic Period, 199.6 to 145.5 million years ago, the Atlantic Ocean began to form between North America and Europe. To carry our geological metaphor one more step, let's imagine some vanilla ice cream melting into the rift zone (the sea) between our two slices of cherry pie. The Eurasian Plate and the North American Plate continued to separate. Between them was a plate boundary, now known as the mid-Atlantic ridge,† that provided the raw volcanic materials for the expanding ocean basin. Somewhat later, South America and Africa also drifted apart (look at a map of the world and you will see how they might fit together, even today, like two gargantuan jigsaw puzzle pieces or, if you will, two oversized portions of slightly deformed cherry pie).

Meanwhile, what is now North America was ponderously slipping westward, away from the rift zone. The thick continental crust that made up the

---

* The U.S. Geological Survey estimates that several million earthquakes occur in the world each year. Many go undetected because they hit remote areas or have very small magnitudes. The National Earthquake Information Center now locates about fifty earthquakes each day, or about twenty thousand a year.

† This ridge now extends from a point northeast of Greenland to the Bouvet Triple Junction in the South Atlantic, a distance of approximately 6,200 miles. It is the longest mountain range in the world.

A delicious cherry pie (does not contain horseshoe crabs).

new East Coast slowly collapsed into a long series of fault blocks that roughly parallel today's coastline. Then, as the edge of North America moved away
from the volcanic rift zone, it began to subside beneath the new Atlantic
Ocean. This plate boundary became the trailing edge of westward moving
North America.

At the same time, sediments such as sand, clay, and gravel were eroding
from inland highlands and being carried east and southward by numerous
rivers and streams. These sediments (colored sugar sprinkles or a dusting
of cinnamon, perhaps) gradually covered the continental margin, burying
it under layers of sedimentary and volcanic debris thousands of feet thick.
Today most of the rock layers—those that lie beneath the coastal plain and
its fringing continental shelf—tilt gently toward the east, sloping down into
the Atlantic Ocean.

Even nine thousand years ago, what we now know as the Delaware Bay
was still not there; it had yet to form. However, at that time in Earth's history, a geological process known as *transgression* was taking place. Transgression is a combination of crustal subsidence (a decrease in elevation often caused by geological faulting, earthquakes, or groundwater issues) in
concert with a rise in sea level caused by melting glaciers and/or tectonic
movements in the earth's crust. In short, the land was going down and the

sea was going up (sea levels were rising at an estimated rate of about one inch per decade).

The waters along the Atlantic seaboard continued to rise until approximately 3000 BC, then they stopped. The rising sea overtook the ancient Delaware and Susquehanna river valleys, transforming them into what are presently the Delaware and Chesapeake Bays. Finally, Earth, perhaps tired from all its geological labors, rested (if only momentarily), and the cartological boundaries of the Delaware Bay settled into their present-day configuration.

And the cherry pie? It is finished!

FOR GEOLOGISTS, THE PAST IS PRETTY CUT-AND-DRIED. THE EARTH preserves and records its changes as sedimentary deposits, glacial etchings, and volcanic upheavals. It's not so easy for historians, because human beings have a tendency to ignore some things, fudge a few events, or fail to write things down when they happen. (Imagine, if you can, a time before Twitter.) Thus, some of the human history of the Delaware Bay is perhaps more speculation and story than fact.

I've always been fascinated by the word "discovered." As in, "A new leech species with ferociously large teeth was recently discovered [in 2010] in Peru." Or, "Researchers reported [in 2011] that a simple chemical cocktail can coax mouse muscle fibers to become the kinds of cells found in the first stages of a regenerating limb." Scientific discoveries like these can be verified with experimentation or validated by following scientific protocols.

KEY FACT

Approximately 70 percent of the oil shipped to the eastern United States passes through the Delaware Bay.

In historical circles, however, the word "discovered" is sometimes subject to simplification or manipulation. This is particularly true when we're talking about very large things, such as a large piece of geography (e.g. a state, a country, or a continent). Who was the first one to have discovered a new territory? It depends on who's writing the history (or who's publishing the textbooks). If a conqueror is writing, then that chunk of real estate will have been "discovered" by that conqueror. Those who may have inhabited the land for the previous several centuries, hunted game across vast stretches of the territory over millennia, or farmed large areas to sustain their villages during several generations may not have any historical claim to the land, even though they were there first. The victors may be there after the fact—way after the fact—but they write the history.

That said, we know the area around the Delaware Bay has been inhabited by generations of Native Americans since at least 8500 BC. The earliest visitors were primarily migratory hunters dependent on abundant populations of wildlife such as rabbits, deer, waterfowl, and bears. Sometime around 1200 BC, those people began to settle down and establish villages. These settlers left behind archeological evidence in the form of stone cooking tools, along with an abundance of shellfish remnants that suggests these early peoples relied partly on the bay for their nourishment. Later, after 800 BC, agriculture and farming became more integrated into the lifestyles of the Native American tribes living in the area, leading to more permanent encampments.

Settlements led to increasing trade between villages. However, for many reasons (climatological changes, soil fertility), this trade seemed to slow down around 900 AD. Many tribes developed into seminomadic hunter-gatherers, building woodland villages during the winter months and coastal enclaves during the summer. When the Europeans arrived in the sixteenth century, most Native American tribes were highly dependent on the natural resources of the environment for their sustenance.*

And so, given that Native Americans had already been living there for centuries, who discovered the Delaware Bay? Although we don't have absolute records, there seems to be some agreement that the earliest European explorations of the Delaware coastline were made around 1526 by Spanish and Portuguese sailors. The first *recorded* discovery of what was to be known as the Delaware Bay was by Henry Hudson, the English explorer who devoted his life to a search for the Northwest Passage, a fabled shortcut across the top of North America to the riches of the Far East.

In 1608, Hudson desired to command a third expedition to the New World. Unfortunately, he was unable to find any British backers. This was probably because of his failure to find the Northwest Passage on his previous two voyages (it seems that bankers then, as now, like to get a little return on their investments). So he left England and approached the Dutch, and on January 8, 1609, he signed a contract with the Dutch United East India Company that stated in part:

---

* When Europeans arrived, it has been conservatively estimated that the population of Native Americans in this area was approximately eight thousand individuals.

The above named Hudson shall, about the first of April, sail in order to search for a passage by the north, around the north side of Nova Zembla, and shall continue thus along that parallel until he shall be able to sail southward to the latitude of sixty degrees. He shall obtain as much knowledge of the lands as can be done without any considerable loss of time, and if it is possible return immediately in order to make a faithful report and relation of his voyage to the Directors, and to deliver over his journals, log-books, and charts, together with an account of everything whatsoever which shall happen to him during the voyage without keeping anything back; for which said voyage the Directors shall pay to the said Hudson, as well for his outfit for the said voyage, as for the support of his wife and children, the sum of eight hundred guilders; and, in case (which God prevent) he do not come back or arrive hereabouts within a year, the Directors shall further pay to his wife two hundred guilders in cash; and thereupon they shall not be further liable to him or his heirs, unless he shall either afterwards or within the year arrive and have found the passage good and suitable for the Company to use; in which case the Directors will reward the before named Hudson for his dangers, trouble and knowledge in their discretion, with which the before mentioned Hudson is content.

In April, Hudson and his crew of twenty men set out on his ship, the *Half-Moon*, sailing under the Dutch flag. Unfortunately, freezing weather and ice almost precipitated a mutiny (the same thing happened on Hudson's previous two voyages). Hudson wisely decided to change direction and head into warmer waters. In July 1609, he passed Newfoundland and Nova Scotia. Later that month, members of the crew landed in what is now Maine, trading with Native Americans near Penobscot Bay. Four days later, the *Half-Moon* dropped anchor at George's Harbor, where Hudson made his first visit to the New World. While there, he made contact with some local Native Americans (referred to in the ship's log as "savages").

The *Half-Moon* eventually sailed southward as far as the Cape of Virginia. Returning northward, Hudson and his crew entered what was later to be known as the Delaware Bay on August 28, 1609. He did not come ashore (he decided the bay was too shallow to explore fully), but he reported that the area seemed to be a good location for settlement. Hudson decided to name this body of water the *South Bay*, although it was north of the considerably larger Chesapeake Bay. After a short visit, Hudson sailed on. He later entered what is now New York harbor and began his explorations of the river that would be named after him.

Hudson made many discoveries along what is now the eastern seaboard of the United States. These discoveries gave the Dutch "permission" to claim a major chunk of the New World (which they referred to as New Netherlands) as their own. You see, Holland, at the time, was a power on both the sea and in commerce, and the Dutch were interested in advancing their economic influence. Numerous explorers were sent to New Netherlands in an effort to secure vast riches from the Far East. It was hoped, at least briefly, that both the Delaware Bay and the Delaware River would be shortcuts to India. Turns out, they were not.

In March 1610, English sea captain Samuel Argall, along with the newly appointed Virginia governor (a title earned for life), Lord Thomas De La Warr, set sail for the Virginia colony (it was Argall's second voyage to Virginia). They arrived at the James River settlement on June 10, 1610. De La Warr was able to save the increasingly disillusioned colonists there (they had just survived the First Anglo–Powhatan War and the "Starving Time" of 1609–1610) from abandoning the colony and heading off to Newfoundland.

Thomas De La Warr was the son of Thomas West, the eleventh Baron De La Warr. Educated at Oxford, he served in the English army and eventually became a member of the Privy Council, a formal advisory group to the throne. After assisting in the reorganization of Jamestown, De La Warr appointed Argall as his deputy and returned to England after having only served two years as Virginia's governor. In one of history's enduring ironies, it has been proven that De La Warr never ventured north beyond Virginia, yet the Delaware Bay, the Delaware River, a Native American tribe, and the state of Delaware have all been named after him.

In 1616, Captain Cornelius Hendricksen, aboard a boat called *Onrust* (Dutch for "Restless"), entered the Delaware Bay. His brief record of this exploration is interestingly written in the third person:

> He hath discovered for his aforesaid Masters and Directors certain lands, a bay and three rivers, situate between 38 and 40 degrees. And did there trade with the inhabitants; said trade consisting of Sables, Furs, Robes and other Skins. He hath found the said country full of trees, to-wit: oaks, hickory, and pines, which trees were in some places covered with vines. He hath seen in the said country bucks and does, turkeys and partridges. He hath found the climate of the said country very temperate, judging it to be as temperate as that of this country, Holland. He also traded for and bought from the inhabitants, the Minques, three persons, being people belonging to this Company, which three persons were employed in

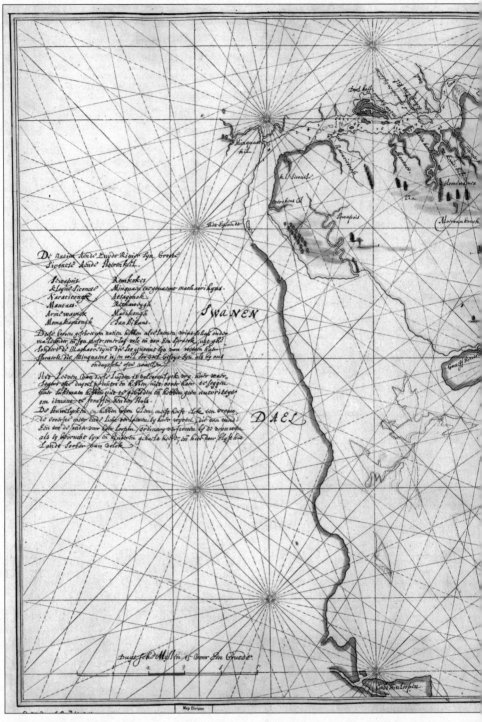

A map of the Delaware Bay created in 1639 by Dutch artist Johannes Vingboons.

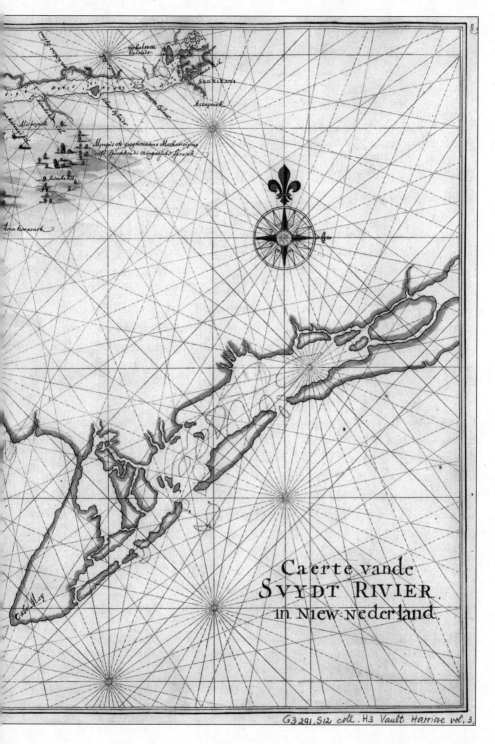

Caerte vande
SVYDT RIVIER
in Niew Nederland.

the service of the Mohawks and Machicans, giving for them kettles, beads, and merchandise.

As you'll note from the last sentence in the entry above, Captain Hendricksen relieved the Minques Indians of three prisoners. Apparently, these three men had fled a Dutch fort near Albany, New York. After wandering around in the wilderness for some time, they found themselves near the Delaware Bay and in the hands of the Minques. They must have been quite delighted by the appearance of some fellow Dutchmen willing to exchange a couple of kettles and beads for their freedom.

Since the Dutch were increasingly interested in profitable ventures throughout New Netherlands, several adventurers were sent over to establish commercial ventures. One of these was Peter Heyes, who commanded the ship *De Walvis* (The Whale) in 1630. The ship had a full complement of immigrants, as well as food, cattle, and numerous whaling implements (Heyes's sponsor, David Pietersen De Vries, had been incorrectly told that whales abounded in the Delaware Bay). History records that the partners planned to open a whale and seal fishery in addition to establishing a tobacco plantation.

In the middle of the seventeenth century, areas around the bay were not only claimed by the Dutch, but also by the Swedes as part of the New Sweden colony. Although the Dutch prevailed, they ran into several conflicts with the British, who were also interested in expanding their territorial interests. After wars (such as the Third Anglo-Dutch War) and treaties (such as the Peace of Breda), some degree of peace was eventually established in the area. Colonies such as Delaware, Virginia, New York, and Pennsylvania* were carved from this humongous territory. As the area was settled by Europeans, the city of Philadelphia grew upriver on the Delaware, becoming the largest city in North America in the eighteenth century.

Today, the Delaware Bay is a major estuary outlet of the Delaware River. The bay is one of the most important navigational channels and busiest waterways in the United States (the Mississippi River is the busiest). The bay,

---

* Pennsylvania was named not for William Penn, the founder of Philadelphia, but rather for his father—Sir William Penn. It seems as though Charles II owed a large debt (£16,000) to Penn Senior and offered one of history's largest land grants as repayment. It was named Pennsylvania ("Penn's Woods") in honor of Sir William. Penn the younger wanted the tract to be named "Sylvania," so that people wouldn't think he named it for himself. However, King Charles prevailed and, ever since, it has been called Pennsylvania.

approximately 782 square miles in area, is bordered by the states of New Jersey and Delaware. The shores of the bay are largely composed of salt marshes and mud flats, with a sprinkling of small communities. Aside from the Delaware River, the bay is fed by numerous small streams, and its lower course forms part of the Intracoastal Waterway. For centuries, the bay has served as an important breeding ground for many aquatic species, including oysters, shad, herring, and, as we know, horseshoe crabs.

THE DELAWARE BAY'S IMPORTANCE TO THE GEOGRAPHY OF THE Eastern seaboard and as a hotbed for the spawning of horseshoe crabs has not been lost on either cartographers or biologists. But one piece of the evolutionary pie has been frequently misinterpreted by the general public.

Let's take a slight left turn in our journalistic journey and make a very important point relative to the history of horseshoe crabs, particularly in the Delaware Bay region. I'm sure you recall, from the previous chapter, that horseshoe crabs have an evolutionary history spanning approximately 445 million years. By the same token, we've noted that the Delaware Bay is a locus for horseshoe crab spawning. You might, therefore, be tempted to put those two events on the same plate, as you would a slice of cherry pie and a dollop of vanilla

KEY FACT

More than half of Atlantic Ocean horseshoe crabs nest in the Delaware Bay.

ice cream. Unfortunately, that would be an evolutionary blunder. Simply put, horseshoe crabs have *not* been coming into the Delaware Bay for hundreds of millions of years.

You see, today's Delaware Bay was only formed after the most recent glacial period (a period of time lasting from 110,000 to 10,000 years ago). The bay is thought to have developed into a tidal estuary[†] sometime after that climatological event, at the most five thousand years ago. Given these facts, it seems likely that horseshoe crabs increased their spawning activities in the Delaware Bay gradually over the last three to five thousand years—just a moment ago, in the context of the 445 million years of their natural history. Where they did their spawning before the creation of the bay is still being investigated by scientists.

---

† An estuary is a partly enclosed coastal body of water (a bay, for example) with one or more rivers or streams flowing into it, and with a free connection to the open sea.

The Delaware Bay is an ideal habitat for the horseshoe crab.

However, there is one question we can answer: Why is the bay such an ideal location for spawning horseshoe crabs? To answer that query, we should examine some of the environmental conditions horseshoe crabs enjoy.

First of all, horseshoe crabs do best in a relatively short range of oceanic temperatures. Because most of the largest specimens of the American horseshoe crab have been found between Georgia and Long Island Sound, we can safely conclude that the thermal environment in this region is ideal for horseshoe crab development, growth, and survival. We can take that one step further and conclude that horseshoe crabs do not inhabit the bone-chilling waters of, say, the Canadian maritime provinces because the water is not warm enough, or the warm-water season is too brief.

But why is *Limulus* not found further south than the broad continental shelf off Yucatán? There is no easy answer to that question, but some scientists suggest that subtle variations in tidal conditions, the increased slope of the continental shelf, and other environmental conditions may be partly to blame for the paucity of horseshoe crabs in the South Atlantic.

You certainly know that excess salt in your diet can have some serious medical implications. The same thing holds true for horseshoe crabs; that is, the salinity, or salt content, of seawater has an impact on populations of *Limulus*. Just like Goldilocks's three bears, horseshoe crabs prefer a salinity level that is not too salty, not too fresh, but just right. The Delaware Bay is a relatively large estuary, with 720 square miles of surface area and 128 miles of shoreline. About 98 square miles (or 13.5 percent of the total area of the bay) consists of shallow water areas with an overall depth of less than six feet. This results in a range of salinity levels, from ocean saltwater at the mouth of the bay to one-quarter salinity at the mouth of the Delaware River. Interestingly, *Limulus* can survive quite nicely in that range of salinity levels—from quarter-strength (eight parts per thousand) to full-strength seawater (thirty-five parts per thousand). Therefore, we could say the Delaware Bay's salinity is perfect for horseshoe crabs.

Population surveys have determined that the area available to *Limulus* is much greater than just the Delaware Bay, however, because many of the larger-sized juveniles and adults move out of the bay and onto an area of the continental shelf that extends nearly thirty-one miles beyond its mouth. The continental shelf borders North America from Maine all the way to the middle of Florida (remember the geology lesson earlier?). This extensive underwater area is a gradually sloping, shallow water plateau that was the margin of the continent in more ancient times. The shelf is composed primarily of sand and is rarely more than 200 meters deep. This shallowness is conducive to horseshoe crab distribution, because crabs prefer waters less than 150 feet in depth. If we flip that around, we could also say that great depths tend to restrict the distribution of horseshoe crabs, and as a result, the extensive, shallow continental shelf is ideal for horseshoe crab habitation.

The continental shelf and the Delaware Bay are also habitats favorable for large populations of marine invertebrates, especially mollusk species such as the surf clam—one of *Limulus's* all-time favorite foods.* Other continental shelf creatures, such as marine worms, are also favored by *Limulus*. In short, the continental shelf provides a gastronomic extravaganza for horseshoe crabs.

The Delaware Bay offers another factor favorable to horseshoe crabs' annual mating rituals: calm waters. Without calm water, horseshoe crabs would have a very difficult time spawning. Specifically, they are most likely to spawn when the waves are less than one foot in height. Higher waves tend to diminish the number of males in a spawning group; the waves push and pull the horseshoe crabs in several different directions. As a result, many of the unattached males are swept away

KEY FACT

Near-shore areas may contain more than one billion gram-negative bacteria per milliliter of seawater.

from a receptive female, leaving one male attached to one female—never a good thing for horseshoe crab spawning purposes (more on this in a later chapter). Waves in the Delaware Bay are usually considerably less than one foot high.

You probably don't often hear the term "tidal amplitude"—the difference in elevation between low and high tides in a body of water—but it's an important one from the perspective of horseshoe crabs. Beaches bathed twice daily by tides with amplitude varying by several feet (four to five feet is typical in the Delaware Bay) have been found to be the most advantageous for horseshoe crab egg development. It seems this variation in tidal amplitude enhances the mixture of moisture, warmth, and oxygen necessary for the successful incubation of *Limulus* eggs. The Delaware Bay, as it happens, has the appropriate variation between high and low tides.

---

* Not only is the Atlantic surf clam prized by horseshoe crabs, it has been equally prized by generations of human consumers for its sweet flavor. Its meat is used in clam strips, sushi, and clam chowder. It is also known by other names such as "hen clam," "bar clam," and "skimmer."

The Delaware Bay, then, is an ideal housing development for horseshoe crabs. While it doesn't have tennis courts or a clubhouse with a swim-up bar, it has water of the right temperature and salinity, of the right depth, with the right amount of wave and tidal action. It also has lengthy sandy beaches favorable for the incubation of horseshoe crab eggs and extensive intertidal areas where juveniles can forage and survive. In short, the bay boasts a unique combination of ecological factors working in concert to assure a most favorable living and breeding environment for horseshoe crabs. It's a perfect place for this equally unique creature.

The manner of their fishing.

John White illustrated Native American fishing methods in 1585. There are two horseshoe crabs at bottom right and men fishing with spears in the background.

CHAPTER 4

From Fertilizer to Bait

Taking Advantage of an Ancient Creature

NAMES. WE ALL HAVE THEM. SOME OF US REALLY LIKE OUR names, and others question what our parents were thinking. Names identify us (and perhaps scar us) for our entire lives.

Consider the playground taunting and teasing that might occur if the original definitions of the following names were ever made public:

- Cade ("round, lumpy; barrel-maker")

- Byron ("place of the cow sheds")

- Mallory ("luckless")

- Travis ("toll collector")

- Logan ("hollow")

- Bernard ("brave bear")

- Chelsea ("landing place for chalk")

- Isaac ("he will laugh")

- Cameron ("crooked nose")

- Julian ("down-bearded youth")

- Bethany ("house of figs")

- Brody ("muddy place")

- Maria ("bitter")

Please be advised that if you happen to work with a "round, lumpy, barrel-maker," a "place of cow sheds," or a "down-bearded youth," you might want to keep your onomastic (from the Greek *onoma* meaning "name") knowledge to yourself. Some things are just better left unsaid.

Unlike parents, scientists want to be sure the names they give to organisms are precise and unique. There's no sense having an inappropriately named critter, or two different creatures both with the same name. So, there are very specific rules they have to follow.

You know how there's always some kind of governmental agency telling you how to do things? For example, there's always someone telling you when to pay your taxes, what you need a license for, how to build according to code, when you need a passport, etc. Scientists have their own regulatory agencies telling them what to do, including when they want to name an animal or plant. This is true for critters long since dead, such as dinosaurs, as well as any newly discovered creature that has wandered into our lives and needs a name so it can be reported accurately in the papers ("Two-Headed Prehistoric Reptile (*Dualcraniumasaurus rex*) Terrorizes Florida Town").

This agency is the International Commission on Zoological Nomenclature (ICZN), which governs the creation of scientific names of nearly all animals (certain Florida Everglades creatures are exempted). The ICZN specifies that each animal must have a two-part scientific name (often in Latin,*

---

* Latin is often referred to as a "dead language." Language death, also known as language extinction, is a condition where "the level of linguistic competence that speakers possess of a given language variety is decreased, eventually resulting in no native or fluent speakers." Some linguists estimate that 90 percent of the 6,912 living languages now spoken around the world will become extinct within the next hundred years. How many languages have died since humans began speaking? Well over six thousand. (Anyone remember Cumanagoto, Ubykh, or Zarphatic?)

which is, of course, the language of science) that is the same throughout the world. The first, more general part of any scientific name is the name of the genus to which the organism belongs. A genus is a group of one or more closely related species thought to have evolved from a common ancestor and sharing many characteristics.

The second part of a scientific name is the species name. A species is a group of organisms that breed naturally with one another and do not breed with other such groups. The ICZN states that "a generic name must be a singular Latin noun in nominative case and…the species epithet must be linguistically constructed as a modifier of that noun." For example, here are the scientific names of a few creatures you already know:

- Yellowfin tuna: *Thunnus albacares*

- Pig: *Sus domestica*

- Cat: *Felis catus*

- Giraffe: *Giraffa camelopardalis*[†]

- Hippopotamus: *Hippopotamus amphibus*

- Robin: *Turdus migratorius*[‡]

- Green sea turtle: *Chelonia mydas*

- Koala: *Phascolarctos cinereus*

- Great white shark: *Carcharodon carcharias*

In many cases, animals are named for their physiological or anatomical features, their geographic range, or a distinguishing feature. Here are a few examples:

---

† In the fourteenth century, Europeans believed giraffes were a cross between a camel and a leopard (they were known as "camelopards").

‡ *Turdus* here is the Latin word for "thrush." That is probably not what you first thought it meant.

- *Danaus* (sleeper) *plexippus*: Monarch butterfly

- *Delphinus* (dolphin) *delphis*: Common dolphin

- *Phoca* (seal) *vitulina* (harbor): Common seal

- *Ursus* (bear) *americanus* (who lives in America): American black bear

- *Panthera* (the yellowish animal) *leo* (lion): Lion

And so it is with the American horseshoe crab. Prior to the mid-1700s, this marine creature was known by several different common names. These included "swordtail crab," "saucepan crab," "king crab" (frequently spelled "King Crabb"), "piggyback crab," and "horsefoot crab"—its most common common name. According to some scholars, it was referred to as "horsefoot" simply because its shape and the shape of a horse's foot were similar. It wasn't until 1758 that it acquired its scientific name, *Limulus polyphemus*.

I am certain that the biologists who first named this critter meant well, but they were not very kind. *Limulus* means "a little askew or odd." And the critter's species name, *polyphemus*, is the name of the Cyclops of Greek mythology.* Living with a moniker that means "odd creature with one eye" for hundreds of millions of years is, indeed, a burden I would not want to carry throughout my evolutionary history.

In more modern times, the horseshoe crab has acquired a broad array of other names. Here's a chart of some *Limulus* monikers from around the world:

- *Kabutogani* (Japanese)

- *Belangkas* (Malaysian)

---

* Polyphemus was a man-eating giant with a single eye set in the middle of his forehead. He loved the sea nymph Galateia, but since she was not into one-eyed men, she spurned his advances. When he discovered her in the arms of another, he unceremoniously crushed the suitor beneath a rock. The hero Odysseus later found himself trapped in Polyphemus's cave. Angry at the intrusion, the Cyclops began to devour Odysseus's men. However, Odysseus, ever the clever one, plied the Cyclops with cheap wine, and while the giant slept Odysseus pierced his single eye with a burning stake. The blinded Polyphemus tried to sink Odysseus' escaping ship with rocks, but failing in the attempt, begged his father Poseidon to avenge him.

- *Rama-lakhania* (Hindi)

- *Cangrejo cacerola* (Spanish)

- Learning fish

- Pan crab

- Piggyback crab

- Helmet crab

- Stinky crab

Now that we've given it a name, let's consider how the American horseshoe crab (*Limulus polyphemus*) may have been used by early humans.

Unfortunately, we have little hard evidence about how the horseshoe crabs in and around the Delaware Bay were used by early Native Americans, for two reasons. First, the early settlers in the bay area did not leave any written records of their lives, their settlements, or their habits. Second, because chitin, an organic material and the primary substance of which horseshoe crab shells are composed, tends to deteriorate quickly over time, there are no physical remains of tools, artifacts, or utensils that may have been made from these shells by tribes inhabiting the shorelines of the Delaware Bay. Thus, we are left with a certain degree of speculation and inference, given what we know about how other cultures used components of their environment to survive.

However, when the first Europeans came to these shores, they recorded their observations of native tribes, including, among other things, how they employed horseshoe crabs. There are records of native peoples supposedly using the telsons (tails) of horseshoe crabs as spear tips. They apparently lashed the telsons to the ends of long poles and used these spears to fish coastal waters ("...they put the hollow tail of a certain fish like a sea crab onto their reeds or long rods for a point..."). A fisherman would stand in a boat or dugout canoe with spear in hand. Upon sighting a fish, he would throw the spear into the water and—he hoped—into a fish. Said speared fish would then become dinner, and the spear could be reused to obtain another fish.

One of the early visitors to the New World was the artist John White, who would later become governor of the "Lost Colony" settlement on North

Carolina's Roanoke Island.* In 1585, White produced a work of art that not only illustrates native fishing methods, but also clearly depicts an example of *Limulus* in the lower right section of the painting (page 56). The illustration also shows, in the far background, natives fishing with spears.

Seventy-five of John White's original drawings of the New World are now in the British Museum, bound together as "The Pictures of Sundry Things Collected and Counterfeited According to the Truth, in the Voyage Made by Sir W. Raleigh, Knight, for the Discovery of La Virginea, in the 27th Year of the Most Happie Reigne of Our Soveraigne Lady Queene Elizabeth."

Although historians are not certain, it seems reasonable to infer that the carapaces (shells) of horseshoe crabs may have been used to bail out leaky canoes. As you can imagine, canoe technology in the fifteenth or sixteenth century was not as sophisticated as it is today, which meant a lot of leaky boats. Because they didn't have L. L. Bean canoe repair kits handy, people who traveled by canoe had to fend for themselves. The horseshoe crab carapace became, therefore, a most convenient tool.

One can only imagine the other uses a horseshoe crab carapace would have served in a primitive society, but they might include a water basin, a soup or salad bowl, a cooking vessel, or a very distinctive head covering. You may wish to conduct your own experiments by taking a mixing bowl out of your kitchen cupboard and imagining all its various uses.

Just as most of what we know about native use of *Limulus* has come from early European chroniclers, it was those same naturalists who gave this creature the moniker "king crab" (or "King Crabb") because of its physical similarity to the edible crustaceans—crabs and lobsters—with which they were more familiar. (It wasn't until 1881 that horseshoe crabs were scientifically kicked out of the crab family, *Crustacea*. But by then, the name "horseshoe crab" had been firmly cemented in the minds of the public, and they have retained the misnomer ever since.) "King" was obviously a reference to the fact that they are considerably larger than true crabs.

One of the English chroniclers of that time was Thomas Harriot (also spelled Harriott, Hariot, or Heriot), a highly respected mathematician and astronomer. In an account of a voyage to the New World in 1590, Harriot refers to these marine organisms as "Seekanauk" (a Native American name for horseshoe crab). He specifically states that they "are a kind of crusty shell

---

* White would also later become the grandfather of Virginia Dare, born August 18, 1587, on Roanoke Island. She was the first English child born in America.

fish, which is good meat, about a foot in breadth, having a crusty tail, many legs like a crab, and her eyes in her back."

Reading Harriot's words—"which is good meat"—I pondered whether this "shell fish" would have been a significant source of food for Native Americans. I pored through stacks of research, but I was only able to locate a single document, issued by the University of Delaware College of Marine and Earth Studies and the Sea Grant College Program under the auspices of the Mid-Atlantic Sea Grant Programs and the National Oceanic and Atmospheric Administration. This report succinctly describes Native Americans' use of horseshoe crabs and states in part, "Indians who inhabited our shores many years ago were the first to recognize the importance of the horseshoe crab. They ate the meat found in the *opisthosoma*, which contains the muscles that move the horseshoe crab's tail, and possibly some organs in the *prosoma*, the front, semicircular part of the horseshoe crab." Whether the "meat" was barbequed, boiled, fried, steamed, roasted, grilled, braised, or sautéed prior to its consumption is unknown. Unfortunately, I could not locate any additional verification of this practice.

> **KEY FACT**
>
> Thomas Harriot founded the English school of algebra and was once described as "the greatest mathematician that Oxford has produced."

I did, however, come across a blog post from Malaysia[†] that addressed horseshoe crab consumption in the South Pacific. The author writes:

> We have been warned never to eat horseshoe crab because eating the wrong organ of the horseshoe crab can make us 'mabuk' or get a high.[‡] So, hubby and I have hardly touch it [*sic*]. However, many seafood restaurants do display horseshoe crabs in their tanks. Since they sell it, we try it. Actually, the horseshoe crab has no edible parts except the eggs or roe. Though it looks

---

† (http://www.malaysiabest.net/2009/03/22/have-you-eaten-a-horseshoe-crab-before/)

‡ An article (*Poisoning from eating horseshoe crab and its prevention and treatment*) by Li X. Liao of the Fisheries College of Zhanjiang Ocean University, Zhanjiang, China, unequivocally states that, "…it has been discovered that the major cause of the poisoning on eating Horseshoe crab in south region along the seacoast of China was taking tetrodotoxin from [horseshoe crabs] by mistake…. The effective prevention measures are not eating Horseshoe crab, especially the young ones. The treatment of the poisoning from eating Horseshoe crab is similar to the treatment of tetrodotoxin by removing the toxins from body."

huge, there are no fleshy parts like crabs. What is served is the roes. The restaurant told us we can either have the horseshoe crab grilled and eat the roe or they can take the grilled roe and make kerabu mango with it. The underside of the horseshoe crab has lots of greenish/orangey roe. I remembered the roe should be orange but ours are more green than orange. Anyway, after eating the gory stuffs [*sic*], I didn't die or I wouldn't be blogging, eh?

While humans are not typically consumers of horseshoe crabs, several species of seagull are. It has been observed that two species of gull, the herring gull and the great black-backed gull, often dine on overturned horseshoe crabs in addition to feasting on their eggs (Chapter 8 describes the many birds that enjoy the epicurean smorgasbord of horseshoe crab eggs). Outfitted with powerful bills, these two gulls rip apart the book gills and other soft areas on the underside of a stranded and upended horseshoe crab and consume the viscera and other soft organs, leaving the legs and carapace behind.

FOR THE NEXT PART OF OUR HISTORICAL SOJOURN, WE'RE GOING TO leave the Delaware Bay for a while and travel northward to Maine to climb aboard Samuel de Champlain's boat. Champlain (1567–1635) was a French navigator, cartographer, draughtsman, soldier, explorer, geographer, ethnologist, diplomat, and chronicler. He began exploring North America in 1603 and was the first European to explore and describe the Great Lakes, eventually publishing several maps of his journeys and accounts. Champlain is frequently memorialized as the "Father of New France," and there are many places, streets, and structures in northeastern North America that bear his name or contain monuments established in his memory. The most notable of these is, of course, Lake Champlain, which straddles the border between the United States and Canada.

Champlain noted that the native peoples along the Maine coast used horseshoe crabs to manure their corn crops. One or more horseshoe crabs would be placed into the ground around corn stalks. The natives had discovered that adding these sea creatures to their plantings significantly increased their yield of corn—apparently one of the earliest uses of organic (marine) fertilizer. The natives of this region also constructed a rudimentary hoe from the carapace of horseshoe crabs. While we don't know for certain, there is some speculation that these practices eventually worked their way down the Atlantic seaboard and were embraced by native peoples in and around the

Delaware Bay. We are left to guess whether this practice was shared with any of the early colonists.

By sometime in the mid-1800s, farmers throughout the Middle Atlantic region had adopted the practice of using horseshoe crabs, in whole or in pieces, as a form of plant fertilizer. Indeed, several testimonials celebrate the efficacy of these creatures as a ready source of soil nutrients:

- "The dead bodies of the [horseshoe crabs] themselves are hauled up in wagons for manure, and when placed at the hills of corn, in planting time, are said to enrich the soil, and add greatly to the increase of the crop." (1840)

- "Mr. Springer of Dyer's Creek, with a compost of 7,000 crabs, 20 loads of muck, 2 coal-pit bottoms, 7 or 8 loads of hay, and manure applied on 6 acres of sandy loam, raised 151½ bushels of wheat." (1887)

- "On land which would not grow wheat at all up to that time, crops of 20, 25 and even 30 bushels to the acre have been raised by the use of these crabs composted with earth." (1908)

The decades after the Civil War, often referred to as the Gilded Age, were an era of rapid economic and population growth in the United States. It was during the Gilded Age that the modern industrial economy was initiated. The 1870s and 1880s saw the U.S. economy grow at the fastest rate in its short history. Wages, wealth, and production all increased rapidly. Big corporations rose and prospered as business operations became more sophisticated and better managed. By the time the twentieth century rolled around, the United States led the world in per capita income and industrial output. Towns and cities grew and expanded, employment soared, and prosperity was on the rise.

This was also an era of agricultural expansion. Larger tracts of land were cleared and made available for farming. Farming methods improved and crop yields increased as science played more of a role in agriculture. One of the elements necessary to "power" these burgeoning farming operations was a cheap source of fertilizer. Farmers had used horseshoe crabs as fertilizer for generations, but growing agricultural demands required production on a much larger scale.

Initially, horseshoe crabs were collected by hand from beaches during the spring spawning season. Large armies of workers would scour the beaches along the Delaware Bay, picking up horseshoe crabs and tossing them into wagons. The wagons were then transported to large wooden bins constructed along the shore. Thousands upon thousands of horseshoe crabs would be piled into the bins, creating, as you might imagine, a stench that would hang in the air for quite some time. The size of the harvests was limited solely by the number of horseshoe crabs that could be collected manually.

The introduction of "pounds" along the New Jersey shore greatly increased those harvests. These pounds were a combination of netting, wire-covered poles, and wooden boards that extended from the high-water line on the shore to the low-water level at low tides. When the tide ebbed, the horseshoe crabs that had been spawning left the beach and were guided by an arrangement of wire and boards into a pen at the end of a pound. The crabs entered the pound via a ramp, falling off at the end into a crib. Fish were also caught in these pounds, but as the water ebbed, they were able to swim back out through narrow, vertical bars that stopped the horseshoe crabs. The pounds were emptied daily at low tide, and the captured horseshoe crabs were loaded onto a skiff or a horse-drawn wagon and pulled ashore. They were then, as in earlier days, piled inside large wooden containers on the shoreline and left to die and dry.

An assortment of horseshoe crab fertilizer factories was scattered along the New Jersey and Delaware shorelines. In most cases, the carcasses of dead and dried horseshoe crabs would be taken to a nearby fertilizer plant, where they were pulverized by a grinding mechanism—similar to the electric blender in your kitchen—and then passed through heated passageways to dry further. The resulting product was then collected, bagged, and distributed nationally. Because horseshoe crabs were mistakenly thought to be crustaceans (a misconception we'll deal with in the next chapter), the fertilizer shipped out of these factories was called "cancerine," which, literally translated, means "derived from crabs."

At this point, you may be wondering what all this harvesting was doing to the population of horseshoe crabs in the Delaware Bay. Were there enough in the bay to keep those factories supplied?

Trying to determine exactly how many horseshoe crabs were harvested over the years is a tricky proposition. That's because recordkeeping was not always very precise, and because various stakeholders—the local government, the state government, federal fishery agencies, the fertilizer factory people, fishermen, and more—were involved in this commercial enterprise and their respective numbers don't always agree. Different entities used different counting procedures in tabulating these thousands—indeed millions—of marine creatures.

Having said that, figure 4.1 represents a very rough estimate of the number of adult horseshoe crabs harvested in the Delaware Bay over more than a century. Please keep in mind that these numbers only represent a portion of the total adult population. As Carl Shuster once stated, "While there is no sound estimate of the peak numbers of *Limulus* that existed in the Delaware Bay area at some time in the past, as in Colonial days, the adult fraction of that population must have included several millions, perhaps tens of millions." Shuster points out that it would be "difficult to conceive how over four million could be harvested in one year in the 1870s" if the total population in the Delaware Bay wasn't several times that number.

Looking at the chart, I notice two trends. One, for more than half a century, more than a million horseshoe crabs per year were harvested from the Delaware Bay for use as fertilizer. I'm no mathematician, but that seems like a lot of *Limulus* pulled from the waters of the bay. Or, we can look at it this way: if we assume that the average adult horseshoe crab is approximately twelve inches wide and up to two feet in length including its tail, then one million horseshoe crabs laid side by side and end to end would cover an area of approximately 45.91 acres. That's the area of 35.32 professional football fields, 95.35 Madison Square Gardens, or 851.42 average American homes. You must admit, that's a lot of *Limulus* lying around and smelling up the beaches.

Second, you'll also note that there was a substantial decline in the number of horseshoe crabs harvested from the waters of the Delaware Bay from

Figure 4.1. Historical Delaware Bay horseshoe crab harvests

DECADE	AVERAGE NUMBER OF HORSESHOE CRABS HARVESTED ANNUALLY
1871–80	4,300,000
1881–90	1,693,000
1891–1900	1,231,000
1901–10	1,826,000
1911–20	2,310,000
1921–30	1,563,000
1931–40	797,000
1941–50	286,000
1951–60	115,000
1961–70	42,000
1971–80	274,000
1981–90	923,000
1991–2000	422,000

the beginning to the end of this time frame. This was because of a combination of factors, including the development of alternative fertilizer sources; the very pungent and malodorous smells that would emanate from the storage bins and factories as the result of dying, dead, and decaying horseshoe crab bodies; the growth in human population along the bay, and their desire not to live with the aforementioned stench; and finally, an overall drop in the population of *Limulus* caused by overharvesting.

WHILE THE NEED FOR HORSESHOE CRABS AS FERTILIZER DECLINED IN the twentieth century, there wasn't a significant decline in the need for horseshoe crabs overall.

From the 1800s through the end of the 1900s, the harvesting of horseshoe crabs from the Delaware Bay was a thriving and substantial industry. Jobs were created (smelly, stinky jobs, but jobs nonetheless), and fertilizer barons became wealthy. This industry encircled the Delaware Bay and was as much a part of the culture as horse-drawn carriages, hoop skirts, Model-T cars, and pocket watches. But, as you saw in the figure 4.1, the numbers of harvested horseshoe crabs declined across the years and across the bay. As the fertilizer industry waned, the population of horseshoe crabs in the bay began to rebound; more animals were seen spawning on more beaches. It looked as if a recovery was in progress. But before that recovery could establish invigorated levels of *Limulus* in the bay, a new industry emerged—one equally dependent on an adequate supply of horseshoe crabs for its existence and survival.

At this juncture in our story, let's take a little side road off the horseshoe crab highway and look at a development a little further out in the ocean. During the latter years of the twentieth century, ocean stocks of various types of fish were in decline, largely because of overfishing. Lower numbers of fish were being pulled from the ocean, and smaller fish were being loaded into boats and sent to market. As a result, various states and other official bodies began enacting laws and regulations to reduce the number of fish taken from the ocean so that the extant stocks could replenish themselves.

Suddenly, many fishermen and watermen found themselves in an economic quandary. They desperately needed other seafood markets in order to sustain themselves and their families, and so many turned to what had been much smaller markets for the American eel and whelk (or conch).

While many of us may find the thought of consuming eels somewhat less satisfying than, say, a sizzling medium-rare filet mignon at the local steakhouse, the consumption of eels is more prevalent than you might imagine.

Eel with garlic.

Although not traditionally found in American cuisine, eels are quite popular in many Asian cultures and throughout Europe. They have numerous nutritional benefits:

- Eels are high in vitamins A, B1, B2, B12, D, and E.

- The consumption of eel meat decreases cholesterol, lowers blood pressure, and reduces the risk of developing arthritis.

- Eels promote good eyesight, normal brain development, and nervous system function.

- Eating eels reduces the risk of cardiovascular disease and lowers triglyceride levels.

- Eel is believed by the Japanese to be a culinary cure for lethargy. They say it helps people regain stamina sapped by heat or other causes.

- Eating eel has been shown in certain studies to significantly reduce the chances of the development of type 2 diabetes among certain groups.

- A 7.2 ounce fillet of eel has only about 375 calories.

Most of the eels harvested along the eastern seaboard of the United States have been sent to Europe and Asia. There is also a small market in North America primarily directed at immigrants from other countries. In addition to the wild eel harvest, the 2005 Census of Aquaculture reports that three eel farms, one each in Maryland, New Jersey, and Pennsylvania, are in operation. And fishermen have reported that horseshoe crabs are far and away the best bait to use to catch eels.

Horseshoe crabs are also used as bait in the Delaware Bay whelk pot fishery industry. Domestically, whelk meat is sold principally in ethnic markets in the northeastern United States, whereas international consumption is concentrated in Asia. Whelk fishing has grown substantially over the years, primarily because of the rules and restrictions placed on other fisheries. Several Canadian provinces are stepping up efforts to produce raw whelk meat for markets in Korea, Japan, and China. Just as in the eel industry, whelk fishermen typically used whole horseshoe crabs (one female or two males) to bait each pot.

For many years, the eel and whelk markets were relatively small and largely unregulated. They were closely tied to horseshoe crabs, because *Limulus* was the bait of choice for capturing these seafood delicacies. Then, in the latter part of the twentieth century, the eel and whelk markets—particularly in Asia—expanded exponentially. More people wanted more eel, and more people wanted more conch. This could only mean one thing: a rapidly expanding need for horseshoe crabs as eel and whelk bait.

During the last decade of the twentieth century, large boats dredged the bottom of the Delaware Bay during horseshoe crab spawning season, gathering thousands at one time. Large refrigerated tractor-trailers lined the roadways flanking the bay to collect masses of horseshoe crabs and haul them away to New York, Massachusetts, and Virginia. It was a time for making lots of money, and anyone with access to a flatbed truck or a large transport vehicle could make a considerable sum of cash in a short amount of time.

So, just as the fertilizer industry was declining and the horseshoe crab population was on the rebound, the crabs-for-bait pressure was added to the mix. Many environmentalists believed the mass harvesting of egg-laden females, in particular, would have a significant negative effect on overall horseshoe crab populations...perhaps for many years. And migrating shorebirds, which depend on horseshoe crab eggs for their survival, could also be threatened.

As a result, there was growing conflict between the watermen, who needed the horseshoe crabs for bait, and the environmentalists and birders, who

were concerned about decline in the horseshoe crab and shorebird populations. And let's not forget the biomedical industry, which needed horseshoe
crabs for LAL bleeding. By the mid-1990s, it was clear that the horseshoe
crab "industry" had to be managed to ensure the survival of the species, as
well as the survival of all the constituencies that depended on this prehistoric creature.

As public pressures increased throughout the 1990s, there was a growing
need for a horseshoe crab management plan—a plan for a species that had
not previously been subjected to any form of regulation. It was clear that
whatever regulation or legislation resulted would have profound impact on
the livelihood of commercial fishermen, several species of migratory shorebirds, and the horseshoe crabs themselves. As months and years passed and
populations of spawning horseshoe crabs throughout the bay region were
increasingly affected, the state of Delaware requested a coast-wide Horseshoe Crab Fishery Management Plan (FMP) that would ensure the sustainability of the population and promote the needs of several user groups.

Eventually the Atlantic States Marine Fisheries Commission (ASMFC)
adopted an FMP that included a state-by-state quota system. They also established an extensive reserve off the coasts of Delaware and New Jersey that
would provide vital habitat protection for the development of sub-adult horseshoe crabs in an area that had previously been heavily harvested by trawlers.

Despite the new regulations, the debate did not diminish. Environmentalists were concerned about dwindling populations of shorebirds and felt that
there should be harvesting moratoriums. The fishermen disputed the scientific data on declining horseshoe crab populations. Because their harvests had
already been cut back, they felt that additional restrictions would only add to
their economic woes. There seemed to be no quick and easy solution.

AT THAT POINT, A "MAGIC BULLET" ARRIVED, BY VIRTUE OF A MOST
fortuitous invention. But to understand that invention, we need to take yet
another side trip; we need to look at how horseshoe crabs were traditionally
used as bait.

When watermen fish for eel or conch, they would typically take a whole
male or half a female horseshoe crab and place it on a spike inside a fishing
pot, which was tied up underwater. The smell of the horseshoe crab would
attract the targeted catch. Once trapped, however, the eel, conch, or whatever other creature wandered in was free to eat the bait, making it ineffective
for catching more animals.

One fisherman, Frank Eicherly, began experimenting with putting the horseshoe crab in a plastic mesh bag that was fastened to the bottom of the conch pot with bungee cords. Eicherly discovered that the bag didn't diminish the lure of the bait, but it did significantly prevent its consumption. He also found that he used less bait, changed it less frequently, and was therefore able to reduce his need for horseshoe crabs by as much as 76 percent. (Imagine reporting to your boss that you were able to reduce the company's expenses by 76 percent.)

Several groups, including the Ecological Research & Development Group (ERDG is the primary horseshoe crab preservation group in the world), the Virginia Institute of Marine Sciences Sea Grant program, and Delaware's Department of Natural Resources and Environmental Control, quickly picked up on this innovation. Tests were run, experiments were conducted, and studies were commissioned that confirmed the feasibility of using bait bags to reduce the demand for horseshoe crabs. In quick order, mandates were passed and policies were enacted requiring the use of bait bags by the conch industry. The bags were subsequently manufactured and distributed free of charge to watermen by ERDG. ERDG reports that "...bait bags are now in use by conchers up and down the coast, resulting in substantial declines in horseshoe crab bait use."

KEY FACT

Currently, fishermen pay between 50 cents and one dollar for each horseshoe crab they use as bait.

The issues, however, have not all been resolved. In the early part of the twenty-first century, scientists noticed a significant decline in populations of migrating shorebirds. Some studies indicated that these birds were not gaining the weight they needed during their annual Delaware Bay stopover (because of insufficient quantities of horseshoe crab eggs) and were unable to complete their migratory journey and breed. Other studies conducted in both the Arctic and South American ranges of the shorebirds also verified significant declines in viable populations.

As you will discover in Chapter 8, migrating shorebirds are highly dependent on horseshoe crabs for their survival. By the same token, the horseshoe crabs depend on the actions and practices of human beings for their survival. Thus, the connections and interrelationships between these three constituencies are often tenuous, fragile, and evolutionary. The results of any human mandates or legislation, however, may be permanent and irrevocable, and the consequences not easily predicted. It is

Use of bait bags is minimizing the number of horseshoe crabs used for bait.

conceivable that Mother Nature may be the final arbiter—irrespective of what we want.

Horseshoe crabs have been around for a very long time, and they have proven themselves to be useful to human beings and to other organisms. It remains to be seen whether they will be able to continue their multifaceted role in the decades and centuries to come. We'll address those possibilities in subsequent chapters; for now, we need to take a look at the basic construction and design of these most engaging creatures.

There's a lot going on under the horseshoe crab's shell.

CHAPTER 5

Horseshoe Crab-ology 101

All That Anatomy and Physiology Stuff

I WAS A CHILD OF THE 1940S AND 1950S, A TIME WHEN NUCLEAR energy was in its infancy and the power of the atom bomb was the great dread. A figurative mushroom cloud hovered over us like an ominous thunderhead. Photographs of the devastation of Hiroshima and Nagasaki were regularly splayed across magazines and shown on TV documentaries, causing us to worry about not only the bomb itself but also the long-lasting effects of nuclear radiation.

People in my southern California coastal neighborhood and across the country were quick to erect fallout shelters—deep underground, concrete-reinforced bunkers filled with shelves of canned food, caches of water, and all the other things a family of four would need to survive a two-week period immediately following a nuclear attack. Fallout shelters sprang up in the corners of basements or were discreetly buried beneath the backyard swing set. The idea was to get as much mass as possible between us and the radio-active aftereffects of a cataclysmic atomic detonation.

During my formative years, I was in love with B-grade science fiction movies. I would scrape, scrounge, beg, borrow, and (almost) steal coins from my parents, sisters, and friends just to be able to sit in the balcony at the local movie theater to watch the latest radioactive creature attack a small band of campers, or some horrible mutant life form take over the bodies of farmers in Iowa, or perhaps a prehistoric oversized reptile knock over a couple of office buildings after emerging from a million-year slumber.

One classic science fiction film that took advantage of the consequences of rampant radiation was *Attack of the Crab Monsters,* a 1957 movie pro-

duced and directed by Roger Corman ("The King of B Movies") about the aftermath of an atomic explosion. Made on a total production budget of $70,000, it was distributed as the main feature on a double bill with the movie *Not of This Earth.* The poster for the film shows an enormous Dungeness crab (I think) grasping a scantily clad blonde maiden in its oversized right claw. The crab is baring a full set of dentures and seems eager to consume the writhing, screaming, and obviously terrified young maiden with her strategically torn and slightly revealing swimsuit.

This film was one of a plethora of 1950s sci-fi movies in which horrible monsters were created or weird prehistoric creatures were awakened from extended hibernations. In many cases, the "beast" wasn't so much the creatures themselves as the atomic fear that spawned them.

I can still remember sitting in the theater, an ice-cold Coke clutched in one hand and a box of Raisinettes in the other, full of anticipation. I didn't want to miss even one of the sixty-two minutes of this incredible movie about some creatures bent on destroying a South Pacific island, or at least showing a bunch of uncomprehending human beings that crustaceans deserve some respect, too.

As the movie opens, a deep baritone voice proclaims:

"You are about to land in a lonely zone of terror...on an uncharted atoll in the Pacific! You are part of the second scientific expedition dispatched to this mysterious piece of coral reef and volcanic rock. The first group disappeared without a trace! Your job is to find out why! There have been disturbing rumors about this strange atoll...frightening rumors about happenings way out beyond the laws of nature..."

The movie indeed opens with a group of scientists landing on a remote Pacific island to search for a previous expedition that disappeared, and to continue research about the effects of radiation from the Bikini Atoll nuclear tests on the island's plant and sea life. During the landing on the island's beach, one of the boats flips and an apparently uncoordinated sailor falls into the surf. After a brief tussle with some underwater thing, he is pulled out, only to be missing his head. It is now obvious that this is not Maui, but some really strange tropical destination that actually *consumes* tourists shortly after they arrive.

Two of the characters have a portentous conversation:

Hank Chapman*: Well, you remember that first big H-bomb test—the one that blew Elugelab Island right out of the ocean?

Seaman Ron Fellows: Well, who'd forget that?

Hank Chapman: A tremendous amount of the radioactive fallout came this way. A great seething, burning cloud of it sank into this area, blanketing the island with hot ashes and seawater. Dr. Weigand's group is here to study fallout effects at their worst. Dr. James Carson is a geologist. He'll try to learn what's happening to the soil. The botanist, Jules Deveroux, will examine all the plant life for radiation poisoning. Martha Hunter and Dale Brewer are biologists. He works on land animalism, while she takes care of the seafood. Dr. Karl Weigand is a nuclear physicist. He'll collect their findings and relate them to the present theories on the effects of too-much radiation.

Unfortunately, the floatplane that transported the team explodes and leaves them all marooned, and their radio equipment is rendered temporarily useless by severe weather. Undaunted, they begin conducting experiments on what is now a rapidly shrinking atoll. "And why is it rapidly shrinking?" you ask. Well, that's because a cast (the scientific group name for a gathering of

---

* Hank Chapman was played by actor Russell Johnson, who would later achieve fame as "The Professor" on *Gilligan's Island*.

crabs) of mutated, man-eating, and very ticked-off crustaceans are destroy-ing the atoll with a series of crab-induced earthquakes. (Really!) In addition, the apparently voracious giant crabs are also consuming the atoll chunk by chunk.

Then the scientists make an astounding discovery. To their horror, they learn that these mutant crabs ate the earlier group of scientists, and they have gained intelligence by absorbing the minds of their victims. What's more, the crabs can now communicate with our now very scared group of scientists using the voices of their recently consumed predecessors. Ah, the plot thickens!

Dr. Karl Weigand: The matter that the crab eats will be assimilated in its body as solid energy, becoming part of the crab.

Martha Hunter: Like the bodies of the dead men?

Dr. Karl Weigand: Yes, and their brain tissue, which is, after all, nothing more than a storage house for electrical impulses.

Dale Brewer: That means that the crab can eat his victim's brain, absorbing his mind intact and working.

Dr. Karl Weigand: It's as good a theory as any other to explain what's happened.

In quick succession, a giant crab attacks the scientists' house, strange clack-ing sounds are heard, a small group discovers a series of underground caves, the radio transmitter is destroyed by some unknown entity, and scientist Jules Deveroux is viciously attacked by one of the insatiable crabs, who makes short work of one of his hands.

Later, while another expedition explores the underground caves, three of the cast (the human cast) are subjected to those insidious clacking noises. Once again, a giant crab appears from offstage and begins a seemingly un-provoked assault on the three men. It is eventually subdued, and the men retrieve one of its claws (radioactive crabs, as you know, always have detach-able claws) and return to the house, where Martha Hunter makes a startling discovery:

Martha Hunter: It looks like we're on the verge of a blessed event.

Dr. Karl Weigand: What's that? What's that?

Martha Hunter: Or is this the one you killed?

Dr. Karl Weigand: No, it is still alive! We did not kill it.

Martha Hunter: Notice the belt of yellow fat around the base of the shell. It would indicate that she's in a very delicate condition. Pretty close, too. I for one should not like to be around to hear the patter of so many tiny feet.

The plot gets even thicker. After some more crab-induced earthquakes, sizeable chunks of the island falling into the sea, several physical and mental encounters with the oversized crabs, a search for the source of a mysterious oil leak, and the consumption of one more scientist by one more cave-dwelling mutant crab, we come to the climatic scene of the film…which I will save for the end of this chapter.

WERE YOU, GOOD READER, TO VIEW *LIMULUS POLYPHEMUS* FOR THE first time on some stretch of Delaware beach or Florida sandbar, you, too, might be inclined to slap the moniker "crab" on this ancient and curious beast. You would be doing what European explorers of the sixteenth and seventeenth century did—give it a name that is both misleading and inappropriate.

According to the basic rules of biology, the horseshoe crab is not a crab at all. Most people (but few biologists) are surprised to learn that horseshoe crabs have few features in common with the more familiar—and certainly more delicious—marine crustacean we might call a "true crab." Oh sure, it scuttles along the sand, it has a hard shell, it has leg-like appendages with claws, and it lives in shallow offshore waters like a crab. But a crab it is not.

It's not a crab, because its anatomy is more dissimilar from that of a crab than similar.

KEY FACT

Unlike true crabs, horseshoe crabs have no antennae.

In fact, you may be surprised to learn that the horseshoe crab's closest living relatives, biologically speaking, are spiders and scorpions. Yes, you may have some of the horseshoe crab's relatives in the dark corners of your basement, or you may have seen them scuttle across the desert floor on your last trip to Arizona. Still, you may be inclined to counter that if it looks like a crab, walks like a crab, and has appendages like a crab, then it certainly must be a crab.

No, no, no! Let's take a look at the basic distinctions between horseshoe crabs and true crabs: a true crab has antennae and mandibles (or jaws); as we will soon discover, a horseshoe crab does not. True crabs also have five pairs of legs, including a front pair with claws, whereas horseshoe crabs have seven pairs of appendages, five of which have claws.

At this point in our discussion, it becomes necessary for us to digress just a little to discuss an element of the biological sciences known as taxonomy. If we went back and asked some ancient Greeks hanging out on a street corner in ancient Greece, they would tell us that the word *taxis* means "arrangement" and *nomia* means "method." Taxonomy is the practice and science of classification, the words we use to identify a particular organism as different or unique from every other organism.*

Now, if we were to ask your neighborhood taxonomist about the American horseshoe crab, the primary subject of our book, he or she would grab a taxonomic textbook and map out the taxonomy for our friend detailed in figure 5.1.

As you may have noticed in the chart, horseshoe crabs belong to a unique and very distinctive phylum,† the arthropods. Arthropods are invertebrate animals having an exoskeleton (external skeleton), a segmented body, and jointed appendages. Included within this phylum are four classes of animals: insects, arachnids, crustaceans, and merostomata. Figure 5.2 (page 82) shows how those classes would look in chart form (with a few examples of each).

---

* Wikipedia further clarifies and ensures that the term "Taxonomy" is absolutely crystal clear by telling us that "...a taxonomy, or taxonomic scheme, is a particular classification arranged in a hierarchical structure. Typically this is organized by supertype-subtype relationships, also called generalization-specialization relationships.... In such an inheritance relationship, the subtype by definition has the same properties, behaviors, and constraints as the supertype plus one or more additional properties, behaviors, or constraints." Got that?

† A phylum is defined in two ways: it is a group of organisms with a certain degree of morphological (the form or shape of an organism) or developmental similarity, or a group of organisms with a certain degree of evolutionary relatedness. In the animal world, there are thirty-six phyla, including *Chordata* (animals which are either vertebrates or one of several closely related invertebrates), the phylum to which humans belong. Other members of the *Chordata* phylum include hagfish, sea squirts, and some Paleozoic jawless fish, among many others.

Figure 5.1. American Horseshoe Crab Taxonomy[1]

TAXONOMY	NAME	MEANING
Kingdom	*Animalia*	Animals
Phylum	*Arthropoda*	Joint-legged animals
Subphylum	*Chelicerate*	Animals with no jaws
Class	*Merostomata*	Mouth surrounded by legs
Subclass	*Xiphosura*	From the Greek *xiphos* meaning "sword" and *ura* meaning "tail"
Order	*Xiphosurida*	Sword-tailed animals
Family	*Limulidae*	One living member: *Limulus*
Genus	*Limulus*	From Latin, meaning "somewhat oblique, odd, or askew" and referring to the sideways placement of the compound eyes.
Species	*polyphemus*	From the Greek name of the mythical Cyclops and a reference to the simple eye on the front of the shell.

1 The three Asian species of horseshoe crabs—*Tachypleus tridentatus, Tachypleus gigas,* and *Carcinoscorplus rotundicauda*—are in the Merostomata class, but each have a somewhat different taxonomy.

Horseshoe crabs are distinctive in the fact that they have their own class (*Merostomata*) within the arthropod phylum. *Merostomata* (from the Greek *meros,* meaning "thigh," and *stoma,* meaning "mouth") are animals that have the bases of their legs surrounding their mouths.

As I'm sure you are beginning to see, the horseshoe crab is almost totally unlike any other creature, including the true crab. The horseshoe crab also has some unique anatomical features that distinguish it from every other creature in the world. Let's take a look.

Figure 5.2. Arthropods

INSECTA (1,000,000 species)	**ARACHNIDA** (70,000 species)	**CRUSTACEA** (26,000 species)	**MEROSTOMATA** (4 species)
Crickets	Spiders	Lobsters	Horseshoe crabs
Ants	Scorpions	Crabs	
Wasps	Mites	Shrimp	
Moths	Ticks	Barnacles	

A HORSESHOE CRAB PLOWING ACROSS A STRETCH OF SAND LOOKS similar to a World War II army tank stuck in first gear. Its architecture seems unsuited for land travel as it fitfully stops and starts, lurches and lunges across the beach. But put this critter in water and it frolics like an underwater ballerina. Its adeptness is due in large measure to a distinctive body design that has changed very little in the last 445 million years.

Back in Chapter 2, we talked about how 445 million years ago the earliest horseshoe crabs were similar in shape to ancient critters known as trilobites and sea scorpions. As you'll recall, those marine creatures had several freely articulating mid-body segments. Through time, those segments eventually consolidated into the three-piece exoskeleton of today's horseshoe crab (which we'll discuss momentarily). A major structural characteristic of those early species was the concave and vaulted undersurface of their front and mid-parts—something we don't find in many marine organisms. As we'll see in just a few paragraphs, many scientists consider this a significant evolutionary design.

Let's do something bold. Let's pluck a horseshoe crab from the waters of the Delaware Bay and take a look at him. We'll call this specimen "Hank" (figure 5.3), although it has both female and male characteristics.

At first glance, Hank looks like an army helmet slipping along the edge of the ocean. From above, Hank's body could be described as "tank-like" or "helmet-shaped." That's not a bad thing and is in fact one of the evolutionary factors that may have helped Hank's species survive as long as it has. One of the first things we notice about Hank is that his body has three main parts. The first part (the "head") is known as the *prosoma*. (If you took your breakfast cereal bowl, flipped it over, and cut it in half, it would look very

Figure 5.3. Hank shows off key bits of the horseshoe crab's anatomy.

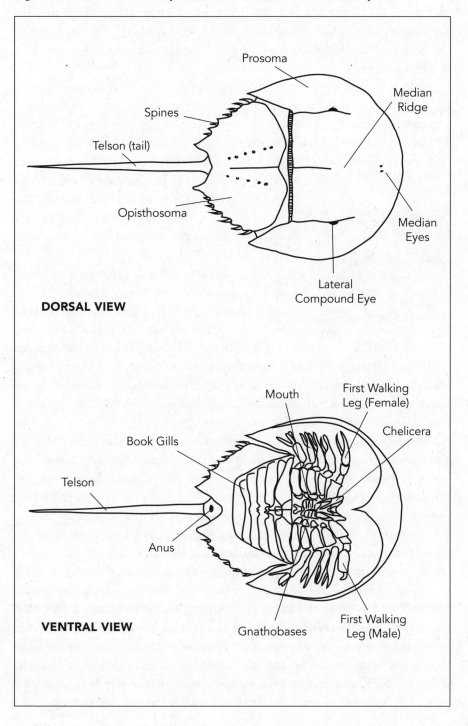

DORSAL VIEW

VENTRAL VIEW

similar to Hank's prosoma.) The prosoma is also sometimes called the *cephalothorax*. The thorax of an animal (in insects, it's where their wings and legs are attached) is defined as "a division of an animal's body that lies between the head and the abdomen," which means that Hank has his head and chest fused together.

Look carefully, and you'll notice that one of the most distinctive features of Hank's prosoma is the location of several of his ten eyes. Actually, you can only see five of those eyes. Two other rudimentary eyes are virtually invisible to the naked eye (your naked eye, that is), an additional two eyes are on the underside of his body, and his tenth eye is along his telson. We'll look deep into Hank's eyes in Chapter 6, but for now know that he can see as well at night as during the day, has eyes that track the time of day, and has light receptors along the length of his tail.

KEY FACT

The curved shell allows horseshoe crabs to plow through undersea muck and mud in search of buried food.

The bowl-shaped prosoma also forms a protective roof over the portion of Hank's body that contains the bulk of his organ systems. Within this vaulted structure, the actions of the appendages (the legs) are largely protected from outside disturbances, such as any nearby predators. The prosoma also serves to protect organs such as Hank's tubular heart, which is about half of his body length, roughly bisected by the hinge near the middle of his body.

The *opisthosoma* is the second part of Hank's body, between the prosoma and the long tail (the *telson*). The opisthosoma is distinguished by a series of moveable spines on both sides. These large spines help Hank feel his way along the bay or ocean bottom. They also contain receptors that provide Hank's central nervous system with critical information, including any shifts or alterations in the surrounding ocean currents or significant increases or decreases in the temperature of the water.

Equally important, the opisthosoma provides protection for Hank's breathing apparatus, the book gills. Book gills, as their name suggests, are arrayed like the pages of a book. Horseshoe crabs have thousands of book-gill leaves, which aerate their blood (known as *hemolymph*), help move sperm-laden water over any eggs during spawning, and serve as paddles to help Hank swim around his marine environment. They also assist Hank in controlling his heartbeat and respiration. The first pair of gills is fused and creates the *operculum*, a flexible flap that protects the next five pairs.

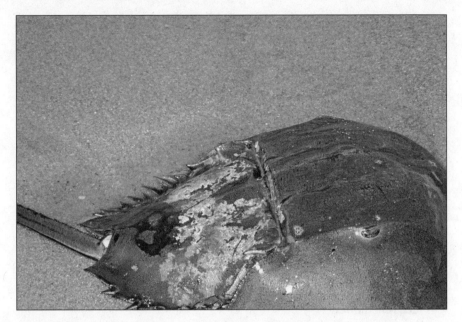

The carapace may be loaded with hitchhikers picked up along the way.

The prosoma and opisthosoma together form Hank's *carapace*, or outer shell. Depending on where Hank lives, the color of his carapace can range from light gray or tan to almost black. If Hank lives in the Delaware Bay or points north, then his carapace would tend to be dark; in the southern states, his shell would have a lighter color. If Hank is a senior citizen, somewhere between fifteen and twenty years of age, his carapace might include a few injuries, such as cracks and punctures. Hank's older girlfriends would also have some cracks and other assorted injuries, most likely incurred during mating.

Let's assume that Hank is one of those so-called senior citizens. As he ages and his growth rate slows, he stops shedding his shell, and it becomes a home for a striking variety of hangers-on. According to Dave Grant, the director of the Ocean Institute of Brookdale Community College in New Jersey, these freeloading hitchhikers could consist of any—or most—of the following:

- Barnacles

- Encrusting bryozoans

- Polychaete worms

- Flatworms

- Sand builder worms (which glue sand grains together for its home)

- Red beard sponges

- *Bugula* (a bushy bryozoan that is often dyed green and sold in florist shops as "Irish sea fern")

- Blue mussels

- Snail fur

- Sea stars

- Ghost anemones

- Scuds

- Red seaweed

- Hard tube worms

- Skeleton shrimp

- Sea lettuce

- Eastern oysters

- Sea strawberries

As Hank moves, water swirls around him, providing these organisms with food and oxygen. Researchers have found as many as three-dozen plant and animal groups—all freeloaders—living on the shells of *Limulus*.

Let's move to the end of Hank's body and take a look at that long spike-like telson. At first glance, it looks like a stinger, but a stinger it is not. It looks dangerous, and if you happened to step on it in bare feet and it was covered by pathogenic (infection-producing) bacteria from the bay floor, then that would be serious. Otherwise, it's basically harmless.

One thing you should not do is pick Hank up by his telson; it is not a convenient handle. Yanking on the telson could lead to damage to Hank's muscles, which might prevent him from turning over if he was flipped upside down by a wave. Said yanking might also result in its breaking in two, leaving you with a useless piece of chitin and Hank with a considerably shortened telson. If this doesn't upset Hank, it would certainly upset the author of this book.

Hank is capable of moving his telson up and down, using it as a lever to right himself if he has been flipped onto his back (for example, by the aforementioned wave action). If Hank had a shortened telson as the result of some injury, then he would likely not be able to turn over, twisting and turning with little success.

How long does it take an individual horseshoe crab (with a complete telson) to turn over? It most cases, a few minutes, but in other cases it might take hours, depending on factors such as the age, weight, and health of the individual and the length and condition of the telson. In rare cases, an overturned horseshoe crab will anchor itself on the beach by inadvertently thrusting its telson down into the sand. As you might imagine, this leads to some significant, if not downright impossible, challenges.

KEY FACT

A horseshoe crab can breathe for days on a beach as long as its book gills stay wet.

Now, let's slip underneath Hank and take a look at his appendages. Hank uses his first, relatively small set of appendages, known as the *chelicerae*, to push food into his mouth. Each of these has tiny claws at the end that allow Hank to manipulate food—clams and worms primarily—toward his mouth.

The next pair of appendages are the first ambulatory (or walking) legs, also known as pedipalps. In Hank's female companions, these legs end in typical claws. In Hank, however, the end of each leg is modified to form a grasping claw (shaped like a boxing glove), which he uses to latch on to the females during spawning. Females have two areas on the rear of their opisthosoma (on either side of the telson) that allow males to clasp during spawning.

The next three pairs of legs are used for walking and digging. All of the legs surround Hank's mouth, and each has small spines at its base that help Hank in grinding and crushing his food. Thus, when Hank moves his legs back and forth, the spiny bristles help push the food into his mouth. There

The horseshoe crab's mouth is surrounded by its legs, which push in food.

is a common misconception that Hank can walk and eat at the same time; not so! He can only do one action (eat or walk) at a time. Hank is not a multitasker.

The fifth pair of Hank's legs is used for locomotion. The ends of these legs also spread outward to give Hank leverage when he tries to push his way across the sandy bay bottom. This last pair of legs, sometimes called the pusher legs, does not have claws; instead they have four leaf-like processes. Hank's female companions use their legs when burrowing. It is the pumping of the legs that creates a sandy slurry during the egg-laying process.

Hank has an alimentary tract that begins with a soft mouth situated between the bases of his legs. When Hank eats, he moves his legs in such a way that any nearby food is moved closer and closer to his mouth. As food passes through his mouth, it enters a curving esophagus and moves forward through his brain (yes, through his brain) into a chitin-lined crop-gizzard (similar to a bird's). There the food is ground up into tiny pieces prior to digestion. At the end of Hank's alimentary tract is a short, chitin-lined rectum.

You can distinguish adult males from adult female horseshoe crabs in several ways. In general, the leading edge of the male carapace is more convex, its edges are more flared, and it is somewhat smaller than the female. You'll also recall that the first pair of legs in adult males has claws called claspers that are modified for reproduction (they clasp). These claspers are larger than the other claws; it looks as if someone has tied tiny boxing gloves to the ends of Hank's pedipalps.

The genital pores also differ between the sexes. Males use theirs to release sperm, and females use theirs to release eggs. In males, the genital pores are located at the peaks of hard, conical projections; in females, they are softer and appear as elliptical slits. To see the genital pores, you need to pull back the operculum and look really hard, which is not for everyone. At least the horseshoe crabs know the difference.

Several biologists contend that the horseshoe crab is a model of anatomical efficiency. The fact that it has been able to endure for hundreds of millions of years is certainly a testament to its physiological strength, if not beauty. We human beings should be so lucky.

LET'S RETURN TO OUR MATINEE OF *ATTACK OF THE CRAB MONSTERS*, and the always eye-popping conclusion to any good sci-fi movie: the death of the radioactive creature. Because we are approaching the end of the movie, it should come as no surprise that our once hardy band of scientists has now been reduced to three individuals, two men and one woman. This trio is caught in one more crab-induced earthquake that generates enormous landslides and gargantuan fissures in the fast-shrinking island. They scramble up onto the last remaining spit of land, which, conveniently, holds a large radio antenna. Soon after, the "big daddy" of the mutant crabs crawls up from out of the ocean and begins its attack. The trio throws a series of grenades (where did those come from?) at the creature with little success (chitin is pretty tough stuff). Finally, Hank Chapman climbs onto the antenna and pulls it over, causing it to fall on the larger-than-life crustacean and parboil it inside its shell (and giving Chapman the shock of his life). A crescendo of inspirational music floods the movie theater as the last two survivors embrace and stare at the distant horizon. The End.

Attack of the Crab Monsters, born of the fear and misinformation that was so much a part of the 1950s, took enormous liberties for the sake of a story. As kids, we didn't mind those liberties; they made the story a little more interesting, a little more engaging. We were well aware that very large and angry crabs with a taste for human flesh were no more believable than say, eating a satisfying meal in the school cafeteria. But they were fun nonetheless.

While anatomical and physiological liberties were taken in this movie and a host of other movies about mutant beings, I still can't quite figure out why no one demonized horseshoe crabs in a 1950s sci-fi flick. How come nobody saw the obvious advantages of casting horseshoe crabs as a strange alien life form invading a small coastal town, for example, and devouring rocket scientists, beautiful blonde debutants, and mystified police officers on their march to some mystical energy force just over the horizon. After all, horseshoe crabs certainly look and act like aliens, with their armored domes, their multiple appendages, their ability to chew with their legs, their fearsome-looking tails, and those ten eyes.

Yes, those ten eyes! Let's take a look.

CHAPTER 6

Can You See What Eye See?

The Creature with Ten Eyes

I AM STUMBLING DOWN A LONG HALLWAY. THE SIGHTS AROUND ME are fuzzy and indistinct. People pass by me, but they all look amorphous, without a defined shape or composition. I react wildly to shafts of light that come in through the windows. I'm not sure where I am going or where I'll wind up. I wonder if I'll be able to locate my car or drive the twenty miles home. I am half blind and more than a little unfocused. My eyes are watering, so I wipe them with the sleeve of my shirt. I bump into a handrail, grabbing hold to regain my balance. I'm more than a little uncoordinated and unsteady.

No, I'm not drunk. I've just had my annual eye exam.

If you've recently had an eye exam, then the feeling I described above was probably not unfamiliar. I am not fond of these annual events, during which someone in a white lab coat will be poking, peeping, and peering into my eyeballs with Machiavellian instruments and semi-barbaric tools—several of which, I am certain, are leftovers from the Spanish Inquisition. With each eye exam, I am further convinced that ophthalmologists and proctologists go to the same school; they just happen to concentrate on opposite ends of the human body.

An eye examination is a battery of tests performed by someone with a professional title that starts with an "O." These people may include ophthalmologists (specialists in medical and surgical eye problems, or the folks who perform operations on our eyes), optometrists (healthcare professionals who provide primary vision care, including sight testing and correction), or orthoptists (people who evaluate or treat disorders of eye movement, vision, or eye alignment in children and adults). All of these people work in the field of ophthalmology, which is a combination of two Greek words, *ophthalmos,* meaning "eye," and *logos,* meaning "word, thought, or discourse." Translated literally, ophthalmology could mean "let's think about the eyes." Since Greeks are not always literal (it must be the ouzo), ophthalmology really means "the science of eyes."

These "O" people will tell you that the typical eye exam is designed to "detect potentially treatable blinding eye diseases, ocular manifestations of systemic disease, or signs of tumors or other anomalies of the brain. Ideally, the eye examination consists of an external examination, followed by specific tests for visual acuity, pupil function, extraocular muscle motility, visual fields, intraocular pressure, and ophthalmoscopy through a dilated pupil. A minimal eye examination consists of tests for visual acuity, pupil function, and extraocular muscle motility, as well as direct ophthalmoscopy through an undilated pupil." I didn't realize so much could be learned from the aqueous orbs on either side of my nose.

Visual acuity, the most well-known eye function, is a measure of the eye's ability to see an in-focus image at a certain distance. The standard of normal visual acuity is 20/20 vision. If you have 20/20 vision, you have average or normal vision—not perfect vision, mind you, just average. The 20/20 designation means that you can see at twenty feet what the average person can see at twenty feet. Some people have vision better than 20/20, and some (like certain authors) have vision considerably poorer than 20/20. If one can see at twenty feet what a normal person can see at forty feet, then one has 20/40 vision. If someone can see at twenty feet what a normal person can see at a hundred feet, then that person has 20/100 vision.

To determine what your rating is, most eye doctors use the Snellen Chart (figure 6.1). This familiar chart has lines of letters that start out large at the top and end up small at the bottom. The 20/20 line is near the bottom of the chart. In a doctor's office, it is usually placed twenty feet away from you. If you can read the 20/20 line (without having memorized it beforehand or without corrective lenses), you have 20/20 vision.*

---

* In the United States you are considered "legally blind" if your best corrected visual acuity (using eyeglasses or contact lenses) is 20/200 or worse. The last line on the Snellen Chart is 20/5, which very few people have, but many animals, especially birds of prey, do.

Figure 6.1. The Snellen Chart

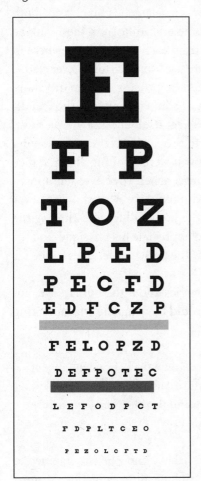

Let's suppose you can't read the letters on the 20/20 line, fourth from the bottom, but you can make out the letters on the 20/40 line above it. You therefore have 20/40 vision. If all you can see are the two letters on the second line (F, P), then your vision would be 20/200. The final part of the eye exam is the one where those damn eye drops are put into my eyes in order to dilate my pupils. Then, the "O" person uses a lighted instrument to look directly at my retina and other tissues in the back of my eye. The procedure is repeated in the other eye, while I experience something similar to a 1960s psychedelic torture test. I fully expect to hear acid rock emanate from the music system while a parade of long-haired, tie-dyed hippies parade before me shaking tambourines. Then I'm escorted to the door and left to stumble down the hall and out into the parking lot to locate my car in the bright sunshine.

KNOWLEDGE ABOUT THE EYE DID not come easily or quickly. Early physicians based a lot of their knowledge about the human eye on speculation, rather than observation. It may have been because there was some fear about cutting into eye tissue and releasing "bad humours," or it may have been because nobody really wanted to cut into an eye in the first place.

The ancient Greeks performed some of the first recorded studies of the human eye. Aristotle, a pretty smart guy hanging around Athens during the fourth century BC, dabbled in many different fields, including philosophy, science, and the arts. He was also one of the first to dissect the eyes of animals, although there is no record of which animals. I am sure that the good residents of ancient Athens kept their dogs and cats indoors whenever they saw Aristotle out for his afternoon constitutional.

As a result of his dissections, Aristotle discovered that eyes (human as well as animal) had three layers, and that there was a gelatenous fluid inside both orbs. He also speculated that there were three tubes leading from the eye to the back of the head, and that at least one tube from each eye met somewhere in the middle of the skull. What those tubes were used for, Aristotle never said.

Aristotle described what he thought was the process of human vision. He explained that the object being looked at somehow altered the "medium" (what we would call air) between the object itself and the viewer's eye. This alteration of the medium was thought to propagate in the eye, allowing the object to be seen. For example, let's say you were strolling along Venice Beach, California, minding your own business, when your eyes fell upon a young, muscle-rippling bodybuilder. According to Aristotle (who was never known to frequent the beach, by the way), the bodybuilder was altering the air around him, enabling you to see him and appreciate his physique. In other words, it's not what your eyes do, it's what the bodybuilder does to the air around him that allows you to notice him.

We owe much to Aristotle and his discoveries about the human eye, but no description of his experiments on eyes would be complete without citing the following excerpt from his writings:

> Why do such as weep much, urine but little? Because the radical humidity of a tear and of urine is of one and the same nature; and therefore where weeping doth increase, their urine doth diminish; and that they be of one nature is plain to the taste, because they are both salt.

I've always been a big fan of Aristotle, but now that I know he was inclined to taste both tears and urine as part of his physiological investigations, I must question a few of his scientific procedures.

It wasn't until the Middle Ages that Aristotle's ideas were turned inside out. It was commonly believed by many scientific theorists of the time that a viewer's eyes sent out a kind of invisible ray to an object. It was those rays, or emissions, that allowed vision to occur. Today we may find that information unusual or strange, but we need to remember that medieval science was often a haphazard collection of guesswork, speculation, and inferences, rather than empirical research. It's also important to remember that knowledge at that time was dictated in large measure by church authority (which forbade dissection, among other things).

During the European Middle Ages, several Islamic physicians published groundbreaking documents on ophthalmology. These included Ibn al-Haytham, who in 1021 wrote extensively on the anatomy of the eye; Ibn al-Nafis, who discovered new treatments for dealing with glaucoma; and Salah–ud-din bin Youssef al-Kalal bi Hama (popularly known as "The Eye Doctor of Hama"), who in 1296 wrote the most complete book on ophthalmology up until that time.

It wasn't until the seventeenth century that European physicians began to get a more realistic understanding of the eye's function and its various components. Two well-known physicists of the time, Johannes Kepler of Germany and René Descartes of France, made some of the most critical advances in understanding vision, although they were more concerned with the physics of light than with the physiology of the eye.

Kepler and Descartes independently discovered that it was the retina, not the cornea (as was previously thought), that was responsible for the detection of light. Kepler first proposed that the lens of the eye focuses images onto the retina. Several decades later, Descartes came up with a unique experiment that proved Kepler's optic conclusions were, indeed, correct. Descartes surgically removed an eye from an ox, then scraped the back of the eye to make it transparent. He then placed the eye on a window ledge, as if the ox were looking out of the window. Descartes then bent down and looked

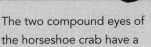

KEY FACT

The two compound eyes of the horseshoe crab have a range of about three feet.

at the back of the eye. Imagine his surprise when he saw an upside-down image of the scenery outside. He may well have shouted "*Sacré bleu*,"* "*Mon Dieu*" or some other appropriate French phrase of astonishment and excitement. Because of Descartes and his ox, scientists learned that seen images are inverted on the back of the eyeball as a result of being focused onto the retina by the eye's lens.

Thomas Young, who was both a physicist and physician in the early 1800s, also carried out a number of studies on the eye. His observations provided doctors with the specifics of how the lens focuses images onto the retina. In addition, his studies proved that astigmatism, for example, results primarily from an improperly curved cornea. As a result of Young's work, physicians developed a deeper understanding of several very common vision problems, including both nearsightedness and farsightedness.

---

* Literally translated, "*Sacré bleu!*" means "holy blue" and refers to the color associated with the Virgin Mary.

All this visual history is interesting, but if you really want to understand something about your eyes,* it's important to understand something about the eyes of horseshoe crabs. Research on their eyes has led to various discoveries about our own. We'll continue our history lesson in a while, but for now we need to take a short trip back to the beach (and, if you wish, those muscle-rippling bodybuilders) and look at horseshoe crabs.

IF YOU WANTED TO INVENT A TOTALLY WEIRD CREATURE FOR A forthcoming science fiction movie or YouTube video, you couldn't go wrong with a creature that has ten eyes. The average science fiction alien has two eyes (some with radioactive powers and some with dangerous ocular rays), but I would think that the addition of eight more eyes would certainly put your creature in a league of its own. Well, horseshoe crabs are in that league; they possess five times as many eyes as we do (see figure 6.2).†

The most recognizable are the two lateral compound eyes near the front of the carapace. These are the crab's largest eyes, and they are used primarily for finding mates during the spawning season. Each of the horseshoe crab's compound eyes has about one thousand receptors (technically termed *ommatidia*). The cones and rods‡ of these eyes are very similar in structure

---

* Here's some more fascinating information:
  - Each of your eyeballs is about one inch (2.5 cm) in diameter and weighs about a quarter ounce.
  - Males have slightly larger eyeballs than females.
  - There are more than 130 million special cells on the back of each eyeball to detect light and color.
  - The human eye can distinguish up to ten million different color shades.
  - Your eyes produce about eight ounces (one cup) of tears a year. If you live to be seventy years old, your eyes will have produced approximately four-and-a-half gallons of tears.
  - On average, you blink about fifteen times a minute.

† As I was working on one of the final drafts of this chapter, I happened to be talking on the phone one day with my six-year-old granddaughter, Isabelle, who lives in the north of England. I mentioned to her that horseshoe crabs have ten eyes. The phone was silent for a while and then she said, "I know why they have ten eyes, Pop-Pop." "Why?" I inquired. She replied, "They need two to look left, two to look right, two to look at the center, two to look up, and two to look down." Yes, I've already begun writing her letter of recommendation to Oxford.

‡ Rods translate light into monochromic values—everything from black to gray to white. Cones are the parts of the eye that convert light into color. There are three types of cones,

Figure 6.2. The horseshoe crab's ten "eyes"

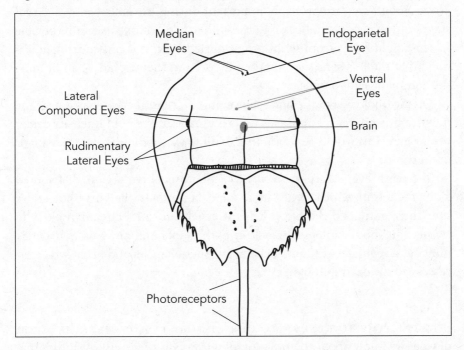

to the cones and rods in your eyes, except that they are around a hundred times larger.

Another two eyes on the crab's body, known as the *median ocelli*, lie next to each other near the midline of the carapace. These organs are most sensitive to the ultraviolet light from the moon and stars, sending signals to the brain that increase the efficiency and sensitivity of the lateral eyes in the dark. As a result, the crab's lateral eyes are much more sensitive to light at night. Thus, a horseshoe crab's vision—at least its vision of other horseshoe crabs—is better at night than it is during the day. The median ocelli and lateral eyes are the only eyes of the horseshoe crab that have lenses and form images.

The remaining "eyes" are primitive photosensitive organs. Three of them, the rudimentary lateral and the *endoparietal* eyes, are prominent in tiny horseshoe crabs less than a year old. It is thought that these eyes may provide very young *Limulus* with an ability to orient to light before their lateral and median eyes are fully developed. The rudimentary lateral eyes

---

one each of the primary colors of light: red, green, and blue. Humans have eighteen times more rods than cones.

are photoreceptors that become functional just before the embryo hatches. These simple eyes are probably important during the embryonic or larval stages of the organism, because even unhatched embryos seem to be able to sense light levels from within their buried eggs. It is only during adulthood that the less sensitive compound eyes and the median ocelli become the dominant sight organs.

On the underside of the horseshoe crab, two ventral eyes located near the mouth transmit neural messages to its brain about the light intensity under the animal. This would be useful in signaling whether it was right side up or upside down.

The tenth eye is actually a series of photosensitive organs distributed along the telson, which have a most important role in the horseshoe crab's life. Their output to the brain helps it synchronize its circadian clock (a twenty-four-hour biological clock in both plants and animals that determines and regulates certain biochemical, physiological, and behavioral processes*) to the day/night light cycle.

NOW IT'S TIME TO RETURN TO OUR HISTORY LESSON, BECAUSE MUCH of what we know about the function of our eyes is the result of studies that began more than seventy-five years ago on the large compound eyes of the horseshoe crab.

In the spring of 1926, H. Keffer Hartline was strolling along one of the many beaches on Cape Cod. He wasn't looking for seashells or loose change dropped by sunbathing tourists; he was hunting for an animal with a relatively simple visual system he could study. While walking along the edge of the water, he came across a large female horseshoe crab that was burrowing. As he bent down to look more closely at the horseshoe crab, he noticed something particularly interesting about her two lateral compound eyes.

Hartline first noticed that the receptors were large enough that he could see them without using a magnifying glass. The compound eyes provide the horseshoe crab with an enormous field of vision; in fact, horseshoe crabs are one of the few animals that can see to either side as well as ahead, behind,

---

* Human beings also have a circadian biological clock. Here are a few of the daily biological rhythms you may experience (these are averages, not absolutes for everyone): lowest body temperature, 4:30 a.m.; sharpest rise in blood pressure, 6:45 a.m.; high alertness, 10:00 a.m.; best coordination, 2:30 p.m.; highest blood pressure, 6:30 p.m.; highest body temperature, 7:00 p.m.

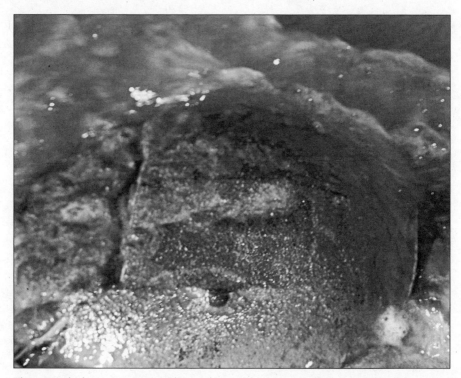

The retinal photoreceptors in horseshoe crab eyes are the largest yet discovered in any animal.

and above. Interestingly, the individual ommatidia of horseshoe crabs are the largest known retinal receptors in the animal kingdom. Hartline figured that if he could see those receptors so easily, he might also be able to easily record their electrical responses to light, and therefore study how those nerve signals provided the animal with vision.

Work on the eyes of horseshoe crabs consumed the next several decades of Hartline's life. He and his colleagues began making some startling discoveries about the eyes of horseshoe crabs and the relationship between their eyes and ours. Shortly after the end of World War II, Hartline was amazed to learn that increasing the amount of time that light falls on the horseshoe crab's retina reduced the eye's sensitivity. Leaving their eyes in darkness, however, increased their overall sensitivity. The connection with human eyesight soon was obvious, as this is a situation we often experience. For example, when we walk into a dark room, such as a movie theater, on a sunny day, it takes our eyes several minutes to fully adjust to the reduced light level. In essence, our eyes behave much the same as the eyes of a multimillion-year-old creature.

"I turned on the room lights, and the optic nerve response decreased," Hartline said as he recalled some of those early experiments on the *Limulus* eye. *Why should the response decrease when I increase the light intensity?* he asked himself. This was a phenomenon he had seen many times, but he had never appreciated its importance. Suddenly (in the mid-1950s), he saw its significance: illuminating receptors in the lateral eye can inhibit the responses of neighboring receptors. This is known as the concept of lateral inhibition—a concept that has proven to be a cornerstone of visual system organization in all animals, including humans.

For example, human vision is highly sensitive to borders and edges. According to Robert Barlow, "We enhance the contrast between light and dark areas in the visual field (a phenomenon known as simultaneous contrast). [In short,] contrast affects our perception of brightness. This ability of the human vision system could be explained by mutually inhibitory interactions in the retina." Interestingly, Hartline found physiological support for this concept in the visual system of horseshoe crabs—a species considerably less complex than we are.

KEY FACT

The horseshoe crab's compound eyes are primarily used for finding mates during the spawning season.

Besides his groundbreaking work on lateral inhibition (which, incidentally, assists horseshoe crabs in identifying potential mates, particularly in murky water), his research on horseshoe crabs provided vital information in helping us understand human eye diseases such as retinitis pigmentosa, which causes tunnel vision and can lead to blindness. In 1967, the Nobel Prize in Physiology or Medicine was awarded jointly to Ragnar Granit, H. Keffer Hartline, and George Wald "for their discoveries concerning the primary physiological and chemical visual processes in the eye."

ROBERT BARLOW WAS ONE OF HARTLINE'S STUDENTS IN THE 1970S, and he continued Hartline's work with horseshoe crabs in his role as the director of the Center for Vision Research at the StateUniversity of New York's Upstate Medical University in Syracuse. Barlow, like his predecessor, established himself as one of the preeminent researchers on human vision. Barlow discovered that horseshoe crabs were able to see better in dim, almost nonexistent light than in bright daylight. Beginning at dusk and ceasing at dawn, clock-generated neural signals increased the horseshoe crab's eye sensitivity as much as one million times over daytime levels. This provides an obvious advantage to the horseshoe crabs, which mate along the Delaware Bay beaches most actively during nighttime flood tides and at full and new moons.

Consequently, in the early 1980s, Barlow and his associates decided to test the role of night vision in horseshoe crab mating using a unique and compelling study. They created cement castings of female horseshoe crab shells, as well as other shapes, such as cubes and hemispheres, that were approximately the same size. The objects were painted black, gray, or white, to see whether contrast affected the males' behavior. The cement objects were then placed along the water's edge near Woods Hole, Massachusetts, in the late afternoon, and the scientists waited patiently for the evening high tide. At this juncture, I'll let Barlow take over the discussion:

> The experiment was a long shot.... We hoped no one would wander down to the beach to investigate. The last thing we wanted was to try and explain why serious scientists would be attempting to fool male horseshoe crabs with dummy females. Amazingly, as males came in with the tide, they began swarming around the castings of the female carapaces, especially the castings painted black. We were ecstatic, running up and down the beach like a bunch of kids, yelling to each other about how many males were around the submerged objects. It was truly a night to remember! There was no question that the female castings were the most attractive objects and the cubes the least. The black female castings, in fact, evoked the entire mating behavior of males: approach, mounting, and sperm release. As the tide receded, the males did not leave the immobile female castings and thus risked death by dehydration on the tidal flats. We took pity on these tenacious love-struck males, detaching them from the castings and placing them in the outgoing tide.

Barlow had unequivocally proven that vision plays a significant role in the horseshoe crab's behavior, helping males locate potential mates.

Barlow's research demonstrated that when males are on the lookout for females, they are searching for anything that has the general shape or configuration of a female horseshoe crab. If it's rounded and on a beach, there is a good likelihood that it's going to be a receptive female. In reality, it may be a rock, a pile of seaweed, a piece of driftwood, or some other rounded object. Having identified the shape as at least similar to a female, the male approaches and does what all love-struck males do.

Barlow was also interested in determining whether a twenty-four-hour clock affects human vision. His goal was to find out how vision is modulated, not only by circadian rhythms and signals from the brain, but also by blood glucose levels. During the Gulf War, U.S. Air Force pilots of Stealth F-117 fighters sometimes experienced fuzzy vision while flying at night, but their vision returned to normal when they ate a candy bar. Barlow's research suggested that their vision problems might result in part from a circadian decrease in blood glucose levels at night. Navy pilots during the Vietnam War had similar problems, and they found that breathing oxygen and consuming sugar improved their night vision. Because the eye and brain derive their energy only from blood glucose and oxygen, Barlow reasoned that optimal night vision would require high levels of glucose and oxygen. "We're studying vision, but the real goal is understanding how the brain works," he said. "We're really looking for the neural basis of behavior."

One of the more interesting experiments undertaken by Barlow and his associates involved mounting a camera, dubbed CrabCam, on male horseshoe crabs to record what they see underwater while they search for mates. Simultaneously, an electrode attached to a camera-bearing animal would take readings of the response of a single nerve fiber. On the computer, Barlow built a model horseshoe crab eye. When he showed the computer eye a digitized version of the underwater film taken with CrabCam, "the computed firing pattern of the optic nerve fibers contained robust signals about objects resembling potential mates, especially when they are moving. The image of a female *Limulus* virtually pops out of the background," Barlow said. "The accuracy of the computer eye's response is confirmed by comparing the response of a single optic nerve fiber in the computer eye with a corresponding nerve fiber in the animal's eye. The responses of the real fiber and the fiber in the model eye match so closely that the investigators are convinced they are learning how to listen in on conversations among neurons. We think we've found the neural code for vision, at least in the horseshoe crab."

The work by researchers such as Hartline and Barlow confirmed the horseshoe crab as an attractive proxy for human vision research, because the animal is large and hardy for an invertebrate, its retinal neurons are big and easily accessible, its visual system is compact, and its visual behavior is well defined. As Barlow put it, "The visual system of horseshoe crabs is simple enough to be understood, yet complex enough to be interesting."

IMAGINE IT'S 1958. IMAGINE SITTING IN A DARKENED MOVIE THEATER, a large soft drink clutched in one hand and a bucket of popcorn in the other. Imagine watching a movie trailer for a new film...a science fiction thriller with a deadly serious narrator—one who overemphasizes every word and reaches into the dark recesses of your mind with a really terrible case of overacting. Imagine the foreboding voice echoing through the deepest corners of the theater…the deepest corners of your mind. A horrifying voice that says:

"It fills the night with terror. For high on a mountainside, a mysterious creature strikes fear such as no human being has ever seen before.

The Crawling Eye.

It strikes without warning, wreaking death and destruction too horrible to behold…a force of evil that tortures its victims and hurls them mercilessly to the brink of murder and madness.

What is it? And, what does it crave…this creeping horror that hungers and thrives on human flesh…while it inhabits its own silent world that no man can penetrate. No one is safe from its spell of destruction—a cold, hypnotic stare striking fear into the hearts of all—creating a frenzied nightmare for those who behold it.

The unknown is closing in.

Relentlessly.

With a stranglehold of terror!"

Recall your first view of a horseshoe crab. You might have thought that this creature, too, was some mutant horror from a distant world. That might be particularly true when you consider the horseshoe crab's ten eyes. Although, collectively, these ten eyes are in no way comparable to the oversize ocular organ portrayed in the movie *The Crawling Eye* (1958), they are, nonetheless, unique in their own special way. Despite what its eyes may look like, a horseshoe crab is not a "creeping horror that hungers and thrives on human flesh."

Thank goodness!

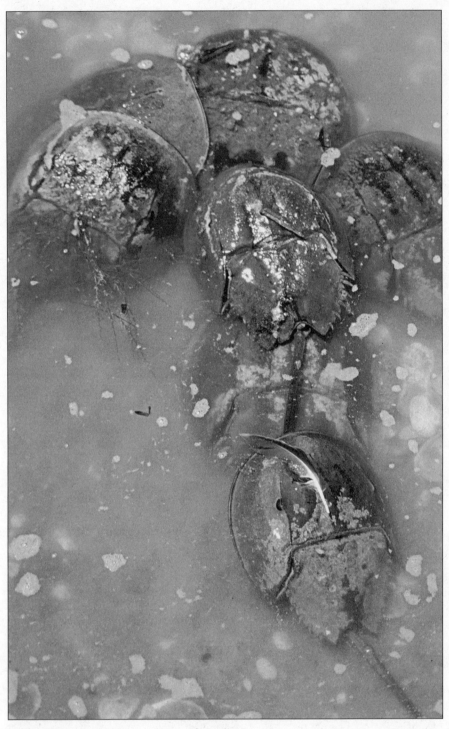

Horseshoe crab mating is a game of numbers.

CHAPTER 7

Ménage a Trois, Ménage a Quatre, Ménage a...Whatever

Reproduction Among the Arthropods

I N THE INTRODUCTION TO HER 2008 BOOK *BONK: THE CURIOUS Coupling of Science and Sex* (appropriately titled "Foreplay"), author Mary Roach* laments the stigma she encountered at neighborhood cocktail parties when talking about her research topic. For the book, she interviewed numerous sexologists, male and female prostitutes, married couples, and anyone else who could be swept into her journalistic web. She pored over innumerable research studies, read obscure books about obscure sexual practices, examined fetishes, investigated strange practices and the strange people who practiced them, perused doctoral dissertations ("On the Function of Groaning and Hyperventilation During Intercourse"), and even volunteered for a...well, a firsthand scientific "experiment" with her husband.

Early in the book, Roach makes a case for authors who delve too deeply, or get too involved, in the topics of their books. In talking about the research a brave cadre of scientists pursues regarding human sexual behavior, she says:

> People who write popular books about sex endure a milder if no less inevitable scrutiny. My first book was about human cadavers [*Stiff: The Curious Lives of Human Cadavers*], and as a result, people assumed that I'm obsessed

---

* I highly recommend Mary Roach's books *Stiff*, *Spook*, *Bonk*, and *Packing for Mars*.

with death. Now that I have written books about both sex *and* death, God only knows what the word on the street is.

In Chapter 1 of *Bonk*, Roach devotes a few paragraphs to a lightly funded arm of scientific research, animal sex. She talks about a little known pioneer in animal sexuality, Albert R. Shadle (1885–1963), who at one time was "the world's foremost expert on the sexuality of small woodland creatures." Indeed, you might want to consider a trip to Bloomington, Indiana, where you can stop by the Kinsey Institute for Research in Sex, Gender, and Reproduction and ask to listen to the multiple audio recordings Shadle made of "skunk and raccoon copulation and post-coitus behavior reactions."

All of which got me to thinking: is the study of animal reproductive habits a serious science or an element just on the outskirts of scientific protocol? Is it mainstream, or is it fringe? For the answers to those questions, I turned to Google. I started by typing in "animal sex," and I was amazed to turn up more than twenty-eight million sites advertising offerings such as "amazing free animal sex stories gathered at one special website!" and "free dog porn movies." I reconsidered my phraseology and typed "animal reproductive habits" (only slightly more than seven million websites popped up). I was immediately hit with the following: "The mating rituals of some animals are wonderfully bizarre. For example: Did you know that some insects' genitals explode during sex?" No, I didn't, but it occurred to me that this article could be successfully used in middle school abstinence education courses.

It soon became evident that Google was going to supply me with more research topics than I—or even Mary Roach—would ever have time to investigate. But in order to provide you with a complete picture of the lives and times of horseshoe crabs, I needed to delve into their reproductive habits. Once again, I returned to Google, typed in "horseshoe crabs reproductive habits," and turned up a mere fifty-four thousand entries. Although there clearly isn't as much interest in the mating rituals of multi-million-year-old creatures as there is in those of human beings or dogs, I did discover that the topic has not gone entirely unnoticed. After all, horseshoe crabs do exhibit some behaviors that are nothing short of amazing.

IMAGINE A FAMILY REUNION GONE HAYWIRE. IMAGINE ALL SORTS OF relatives, most of whom you've never seen before, showing up on your doorstep with strange kids and stranger food items. ("We'd thought y'all would like some possum meat for that there barbeque.") Every time you turn around, another car is pulling into the driveway and another load of distant relatives is clambering out to add their stories about Uncle Festis and Grandma Molly or the day the cows wound up on the front porch. Hundreds if not thousands of relatives keep pouring in—an unending stream of minivans, RVs, and battered station wagons, many held together by rust and bumper stickers.

The spawning of horseshoe crabs is like a family reunion on steroids. Tens of thousands of *Limulus* arrive, as though some invisible Pied Piper were calling them all out of the surf at one time. For most of the year, they inhabit the bottoms of bays and the slopes of the continental shelf feeding on marine worms and shellfish. Then, during a brief window of time, they creep and crawl out of the depths to do their thing.

For a few weeks in late spring and early summer, mature American horse-

KEY FACT

Each female may lay 88,000 eggs in a nesting season.

shoe crabs migrate to shore to spawn. An ancient siren call resonates across the Delaware Bay, reaching its peak during the high lunar tides around the full and new moons in May and June. The flurry of activity is most pronounced at night or in the low light hours around dawn or dusk. Some years there may be a plethora of horseshoe crabs congregating on the beach; other years may see a sharp decline in numbers. Most often the spawning takes place along sandy beaches in inlets and coves protected from waves. Factors such as weather, water temperature, and heavy surf can have a profound effect on where and when the horseshoe crabs beach themselves. After all, if you've been spawning for hundreds of millions of years, you've set some priorities about your reproductive habits.

The seasonal timing of this reproductive activity varies up and down the eastern seaboard. In the Delaware Bay and on Cape Cod, horseshoe crabs typically appear on beaches to spawn from about mid-May to mid-June. In Florida, spawning occurs year-round, but it tends to peak from March through May. Many horseshoe crabs spawn on the spring tides of the full and new moons, but this pattern is not absolute and is not valid in all areas where horseshoe crabs spawn. In the Delaware Bay and areas of Maine, for example, spawning coincides with the full and new moons at the beginning of the season, but not at the end of the season. On Cape Cod, spawning occurs in some areas every day during the breeding season, regardless of the lunar cycle, while in other areas it is associated with the new and full moons.

In addition to variations in their seasonal patterns of spawning, horseshoe crabs also show a great amount of variation in their daily patterns. Horseshoe crabs prefer to lay eggs during periods of high water, typically high tide. In the Delaware Bay, spawning is affected more by wave height than by tide height—when waves are too high, horseshoe crabs do not come to the beach. In Florida, on the other hand, there is a great deal of tidal variation, with some spawning activity at high tide and some throughout the entire tidal cycle.

During spawning, males often form a jagged and jumbled array of bodies in shallow water, patiently awaiting the females. You may be familiar with this reproductive strategy if you've ever been to a speed-dating event at a local coffee shop. Subsequently, the females approach the beach from the depths of the bay. As a female crosses the phalanx of males, one will typically attach himself to the rear end (technically known as posterior opisthosomal projections, or POP for short) of the female's carapace using his pair of boxing-glove-shaped pedipalps. As you recall from the previous chapter, males locate females using several visual cues. By the same token, they have also been observed latching themselves onto other objects that are decidedly not female horseshoe crabs, including rocks, driftwood, or the flotsam and jetsam that sometimes washes ashore after a storm.

As soon as a male attaches himself, he becomes very difficult to dislodge. Often he will continue to hold on to the female even when overturned by waves, and on occasion he will lose a claw rather than release his grip. The couple is now in *amplexus*, and the attached male rides above the female's telson and just over her rear end. Unfortunately, this coital position presents the male with a significant physiological inconvenience: he is now unable to eat.

Females don't escape unscathed, either. Older ones that have spawned numerous times show considerable wear from years of males holding onto them. Their POPs are frequently scraped or broken, and a "mating scar," or worn area, develops on the carapace. Because there are no horseshoe crab plastic surgeons, these dowagers of the sea must suffer quietly any resultant gossip about their looks.

Once a male latches onto a female, she tows him up on the beach. Occasionally, unattached females will emerge from the surf, at which point they may be pursued by one or more unattached males. Attached females will then select appropriate nesting spots, often near the water line. For the most part, females rarely approach the shore unaccompanied. Besides attached males, several unattached males (referred to as "satellite males") also come ashore. These satellite males eventually gather around one or more pairs in

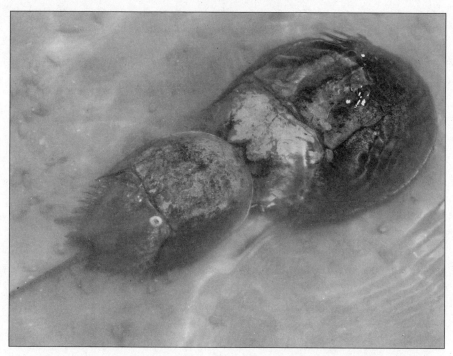

Horseshoe crabs in amplexus may stay attached for days or even weeks.

amplexus. Thus, it is not unusual for a single female to be surrounded by three, four, five, or more males. As a result, there are often more males than females at a spawning site.

How long does an attached pair stay attached? Good question. Often, a pair will stay attached for a few hours or a few days, but there have been reports of several sightings in which a pair remained together for several weeks. I have in my files a document that records one horseshoe crab pair in Florida that reportedly remained in amplexus for a total of fifty-one days!

After the paired horseshoe crabs come onto the beach, the female burrows into the sand near the water line to make a nest. She usually digs to a depth of about four to six inches. At the nesting site, she digs with her pusher legs to create a slurry of sand and water. She then releases her eggs from paired *gonopores* (a reproductive aperture or pore) located below the operculum on the underside of her body, then stirs the eggs into the sand and water slurry. At roughly the same time, the attached male releases his sperm from paired genital pores, also located under the operculum. The male's sperm, which are free-swimming, must travel at least seven to eight inches in order to fertilize the eggs. Apparently, they are excellent swimmers, because nearly all the eggs a female lays are fertilized.

As with so many other aspects of horseshoe crab biology, the method of fertilization is unusual. No other living arthropod uses this true external fertilization process. In all other arthropods, the sperm are transferred in packets or deposited in the body cavity of the female. Horseshoe crab sperm, however, travel in water exposed to the external environment, more like that of clams and marine worms.

After releasing one clutch of eggs, the female may move forward slightly and deposit another clutch. Each clutch takes an average of eight minutes to be released, and each female can lay up to fifteen clutches during one beach visit. Studies in Delaware found that females may lay between three and four thousand eggs per nest and can lay as many as 88,000 eggs per season. Quite frequently, so many horseshoe crabs are nesting that they dig up the eggs of those that nested before in the same location. Birds descend on this ecological smorgasbord to feast on the eggs (see Chapter 8).

KEY FACT

A horseshoe crab egg could fit inside this letter "O."

When nesting is complete, the attached pair returns to the water together, finding their way back by following the slope of the beach. During the spawning season, both males and females may bury themselves in the sediment off shore until it's time for the next nesting event. In one study, it was reported that 95 percent of tagged females spawned repeatedly, often on consecutive nights and frequently near the same spot on the beach.

After the eggs incubate for two to four weeks, larvae begin to emerge. A combination of churning wave action and digging and burying by other mating horseshoe crabs often frees them from their clusters and allows them to enter the water. After hatching, the larvae's lives consist mainly of foraging for food, growing, and dodging the numerous predators out to consume them. As horseshoe crabs grow, they gradually move into the deeper waters of the Delaware Bay or to the continental shelf. And when they reach adulthood, they, too, will begin their spawning migration, just as their parents did several years previously.

As you might imagine, beach nesting comes with some risks: the horseshoe crabs are exposed to the possibility of extreme temperatures while on the beach, moisture in selected beach areas may be insufficient for successful spawning to occur, or the crabs may be upended by wave action and subsequently stranded on the beach. Nevertheless, they're doing something right, or they wouldn't have survived for the past few hundreds of millions of years.

"I WAS DRAWN TO THE STUDY OF HORSESHOE CRABS BECAUSE I WAS just intensely curious about the mating behavior of this ancient, large invertebrate that crawls from the sea to spawn."

One of the most enthusiastic advocates of horseshoe crabs is H. Jane Brockmann, an animal behaviorist at the University of Florida. I caught up with Dr. Brockmann on a crisp November afternoon at a planning meeting of the Green Eggs & Sand educational initiative (see Chapter 13) at the St. Jones Reserve outside of Dover, Delaware. I wanted to talk about her extensive studies related to horseshoe crab reproductive strategies. It was an opportunity to pick the mind of someone who is, shall we say, a professional voyeur.

When Brockmann first arrived at the University of Florida in 1976, she began by conducting research on wasps. She also started taking students out to a field station on Seahorse Key, on Florida's Gulf Coast. Because she was teaching courses on animal behavior, she wanted her students to get some firsthand outdoor experiences, and the tiny island was an ideal location.

She led this field trip, which often took place around Easter during the new moon and full moon high tides, for many years. Because this was vacation time, the scheduling always brought groans and complaints from the college students. But, because of this timing, they were coincidentally able to collect fascinating data on the mating behaviors of the horseshoe crabs that just happened to frequent this tiny spit of land at the same time. In the late 1980s, Brockmann decided to start scheduling a weekend specifically devoted to horseshoe crabs—a weekend of specially designed experiments and lots of serious data collection.

About that same time, Brockmann "...sort of felt like I'd kind of taken the cream off the mud dauber wasp study; that I had done about as much as I could do with them, and I was kind of looking around for a new project." She realized that she had some interesting information on horseshoe crabs, much of it specifically related to their spawning behavior and the alternative mating strategies being used. For example, the fact that some males came in to shore attached to females while other males came in unattached raised some intriguing scientific questions.

She eventually applied for and received a National Science Foundation grant to conduct a long-term study of the alternative mating strategies exhibited by *Limulus polyphemus*. She continued to collect data on the populations at Seahorse Key and continued to encourage her graduate students to delve into some of the mysteries surrounding horseshoe crabs. She recently received another grant to work on females specifically (most of her previous work was with males), and that has been the focus of her research ever since.

At the time I spoke with Brockmann, I had been pondering the issue of egg laying. I knew that during a single visit to the beach, a female would deposit her eggs in several separate clusters on the beach. Most females lay an average of two to five egg clusters during a single visit, with a maximum of fifteen reported. Why, I asked, don't they lay all their eggs together? Why are they laid in separate and discrete clusters? Brockmann explained that no one really knows for sure, but there are a couple of possible explanations.

"One is that females are spreading the risk, so that if a predator comes on a cluster, it will not take all of her eggs," Brockmann said. Another possibility, according to Brockmann, is that egg development is affected by crowding; eggs that are at the center of a clump or in a larger clump develop more slowly than those at the edges or in smaller batches, so the female may spread out her eggs to increase their rate of development.

Females often re-nest several times during one tide, readjusting their location as the tide advances or recedes. "The same pairs of males and females may return to the same beach across several tides, remaining buried in the mud near shore between tides," Brockmann said. "Females usually complete their nesting for the year during one week [one tidal cycle] and do not return again until the following year." Males, however, return repeatedly (either attached to different females or unattached), which partially explains why there are more males at the nesting beach than females.

KEY FACT

Some scientists estimate that fewer than one egg out of 130,000 survives to adulthood.

I was equally curious about the sites a female chooses for her egg deposits. Are they random, or are females conditioned to select some spots as being more beneficial than others? Brockmann explained, "When a female chooses a place to nest, she is picking out a site where her offspring will develop for that important first month and even, perhaps, where they will spend their first year of life. Females have some sort of innate knowledge of the optimal conditions necessary to ensure a high survival rate for her offspring." If she chooses correctly, the offspring thrive; if she doesn't, they may be doomed before they even hatch. Brockmann has discovered that female nesting decisions are critical to offspring success, and therefore females that make sound nesting decisions are more likely to pass their genes (including their sound-nesting-decision genes) down to the next generation.

One might think that horseshoe crabs, like many other animals, would return to breed on the beaches where they were born, but Brockmann has shown that there is no direct evidence to support this idea. Her long-term studies indicate that adults return year after year to the same breeding beaches, but a few tagged individuals have been seen on other beaches in the same general area. She told me about one long-term tagging study in the Delaware Bay, which "found that many crabs move considerable distances, including from one side of the bay to the other." She was quick to point out, however, that there are still many unanswered questions about how horseshoe crabs find their natal beaches from far out at sea. "Do they use the sun or a magnetic compass like many other species of migrating animals, such as sea turtles? Do they use visual clues when in familiar areas? Or do they use odor cues, like salmon?" No one knows for sure.

I questioned Brockmann about global warming's effects on the spawning behaviors of horseshoe crabs. With her characteristic smile, she replied, "Sea level is definitely rising, and horseshoe crabs are very dependent on having good beaches for laying their eggs. There is a wide array of things that make a beach good, but they do need a beach or some kind of well-oxygenated sand in which to lay their eggs, and that's what this annual migration is all about. Of course, sea level rise has happened many times in the past, and horseshoe crabs, of course, have survived all of them, very nicely."

However, Brockmann went on to tell me that the current rise in sea level is different, because there is frequently development behind the beaches. If the sea level rises enough, it's going to flood those beaches. "In the past, that's been fine, because the beach sand was just moved further up the shoreline, resulting in beaches ten miles in from the previous shoreline," she said. "But people are not going to allow that to happen now. Raised land will be put up, and concrete blocks and walls will be erected, and eventually we're going to lose beaches simply because they won't be able to re-form as they have in the past." People will likely protect the developed land rather than the undeveloped beaches. "I'm from Florida," she said. "So, a good chunk of that state is going to be lost, and our beautiful beaches are going to be lost. It is definitely going to be difficult for both the shorebirds and the horseshoe crabs."

I WOULD WAGER THAT THE TOPIC OF POLYANDRY IS NOT ONE THAT comes up during your family dinnertime conversations. You can even shout "Polyandry!" in a crowded movie theater, and at the very most you'll get a

During mating, many male horseshoe crabs may surround a single female.

few people turning around and telling you to shush. Let's just say that the word is not casually bandied about in polite society.

By definition, polyandry is marriage between a woman and two or more husbands at the same time, and therefore is the opposite of polygamy, in which one man takes on multiple wives. Although an uncommon occurrence in Western cultures, polyandry is practiced, or has been practiced, in a variety of regions around the world, such as Tibet, the Canadian Arctic, Nepal, parts of China and India, Nigeria, Bhutan, Sri Lanka, and some Polynesian societies.

In the animal world, polyandry is a type of breeding adaptation in which one female mates with many males. Animals that practice this type of behavior include field crickets, certain types of frogs, marmosets, tamarins, gibbons, honeybees, and some birds of prey. Reasons for this behavior are many, but often center around the enhanced likelihood of fertilization and the prospects of more offspring.

Walk out on any beach along the eastern seashore during the spawning season, when hordes of horseshoe crabs are nesting, and you'll see hundreds if not thousands of satellite males crowding around spawning pairs. For the most part, the sex ratio on the beach varies markedly, but on some tides there can be twenty males for every nesting female. Jane Brockmann wondered why this was happening and what reproductive advantages it might convey.

"Here was a species with a highly male-biased sex ratio at the breeding site visibly competing with one another," she said, "but I wasn't sure about the goal of the competition. I also knew enough about these animals to realize that the males showed two different mating patterns, a phenomenon referred to as 'alternative reproductive tactics.' Two forms of mating for one sex is a bit mysterious from an evolutionary point of view, because one would expect that one or the other tactic would have higher success, and the less successful pattern would evolve out of the population. So, in evolution the maintenance of variability always requires a special explanation. This was a problem I had studied before, and I was eager to find another system in which I could evaluate hypotheses about alternative reproductive tactics."

Brockmann explained that unattached males come ashore to compete for fertilizations by engaging in what is known as sperm competition with attached males. Satellite males were known to release sperm, but scientists didn't know whether they fertilized any of the eggs. Brockmann and her colleagues answered the question by comparing the DNA of all the participants in a nesting group, a standard paternity analysis technique.

What she discovered was eye-opening. She learned that when the attached male was the only one present, he fathered all the offspring, "but when just one satellite was present, the attached male's success dropped to 51 percent, and the satellite fathered, on average, 40 percent of the progeny." The paternity of the remainder was unresolved. When more satellites were present, they did even better: in groups of two to four, satellite males fertilized an average of 74 percent of the eggs. "The average paternity of each satellite was affected by the presence of others: the success of two satellites spawning with a pair was higher than the success of three or four satellites," she said. So, when two satellites were present, they reduced the success rate of the attached male; as more joined the party, they reduced each other's success rates as well. Brockmann's research demonstrates that it is clearly advantageous for the unattached males to come ashore and compete for fertilizations with the attached males, rather than sitting out the dance.

In most species in which strong competition exists between males, larger males mate more often and with larger and more fecund females than do smaller males. This may be because females prefer larger males, or because larger males are more successful at male-male competition. "However," Brockmann said, "this is not true for horseshoe crabs; there is no correlation between the size of the female and the size of her mate." Furthermore, size is not associated with whether a male finds a mate or not; attached and unattached males do not differ in any measure of average size (carapace width, body weight or density, or claw size). "We also found that when females change mates between tides, the replacement male is not larger than the original male," she said.

So, what does determine whether a male becomes a main partner for a female or a satellite? Brockmann wondered about this as well. Researchers had assumed that pairings resulted from males simply grabbing the first female they encountered and coming ashore with her; if a male did not find a female, he came ashore unattached. However, Brockmann's analysis of hundreds of crabs led her to a different conclusion. "Unlike size, the age of the male crab [indicated by the color and condition of the carapace] was strongly associated with whether he was attached or unattached. The light-colored animals [the younger males] were more likely to be attached, and the darker, heavily fouled animals were more likely to be satellites," she said.

This was something I was able to observe directly on my visit to Cedar Key and Panacea, Florida (detailed in Chapter 10). Older males are more likely to be satellites while the younger bucks have a better chance of being Numero Uno.

FOR ABOUT 445 MILLION YEARS, HORSESHOE CRABS HAVE BEEN clasping and digging and laying and fertilizing and spawning and taking on multiple partners. They seem to be pretty good at it; the routine is efficient, the circumstances are ideal, and the participants are all willing and able. The result for any one pair is thousands of potential offspring. The result for many pairs is millions of potential heirs. In essence, we could say that horseshoe crabs have reproduction down to a science.

Not bad for a "living fossil."

CHAPTER 8

Free Food! All You Can Eat! Come and Get It!

The Birds and the Eggs

THERE IS AN ALL-YOU-CAN-EAT BUFFET RESTAURANT NEAR where I live that advertises an all-inclusive meal (less drinks) for the grand sum of $4.99. I am reasonably certain that this place has never been listed in the "Recommended Restaurants" section of any travel guide. (If you are planning to visit my town, let me know and I'll be happy to recommend a few places that have earned at least one star in someone's guide.)

In the interest of research, I stopped by there one day to sample their food. A pungent mixture of scents attacked my nasal passages as I pondered the microwaved slabs of meat, crispy strips of bacon, long flat things shaped like roadkill, lukewarm potato things, steaming pots of canned vegetables, pies overflowing with red or yellow corn starch, loaves of bread with gray crusts, and other assorted culinary adventures. I was reminded of food service back in my Coast Guard days, where we were often served large congealed lumps of dark brown stuff, massive accumulations of green-gray stuff, and heaping portions of reddish, orangish objects that possibly weren't quite dead.

Ah, what to choose?

I wanted to get a sense of what it would be like to be presented with a never-ending smorgasbord—platters and plates and pitchers and pots packed with a plethora of provisions (not to press the point)—waiting to be consumed by hordes of hungry diners. After all, this was research, and I needed to get a sense of what a gastronomic free-for-all was about. So I dug in.

Without going into the horrid details, I'll conclude this gastronomic an-
ecdote by telling you that the meal was an intestinal experience unlike any
other. The phrase "stick to your arteries" kept circulating in my head. Let's
just say that the pharmacy down the street was next on my research agenda.

While I have since permanently eschewed all-you-can-eat establishments,
animals in the wild don't have that luxury. Their survival is often dependent
on what they can locate, scrounge, or pilfer along life's highway. Sometimes
there is an abundance of food; at other times, locating sufficient food is a
desperate and demanding struggle. Then there are times when evolutionary
coincidences come together in a confluence that will amaze even the most
hardened of scientists. Such is the ecological relationship between battalions
of horseshoe crabs and never-ending flocks of migratory shorebirds.

IT IS EARLY MORNING AS I WALK OUT ON A DESERTED BEACH ALONG
the western edge of the Delaware Bay. The sun, just edging through last
night's cloud cover, sprinkles the sand with a few errant rays of sunshine. As
I gaze out over the beach, I can see clusters…no, hordes…no, armies of birds
swooping, swarming, dancing, and flittering across the vast sandy stretch.

I grew up a mere wing flap from San Juan Capistrano in southern California. Each year on March 19, St. Joseph's Day, the swallows return to San
Juan and begin rebuilding the mud nests that cling to the ruins of the old
stone church. The arches of the two-story, high vaulted chapel, ideal for
nest building, were left bare and exposed after the roof collapsed during the
earthquake of 1812. The town of San Juan Capistrano always takes on a fes-
tive air as scores of human visitors from all parts of the world gather to witness the miracle of the swallows' return.

What I am now witnessing on this stretch of Delaware beachfront re-
minds me of the swallows I saw in my youth, but here the birds are of every
stripe, color, and description. There is a constant blur of wings; a cacophony
of shrieks and calls; and crissing and crossing of flight paths as winged travelers dart through the pale blue sky and over the waves. With shrill squeals
and whistles, flock after flock of birds loops, glides, descends, and fights.
They claim territory for a few moments, then lose it to a new arrival. The
noise and frenetic activity make the beach seem like an avian insane asylum.
This is craziness—bird craziness—to the tenth power.

Crowded onto a long strip of beach that separates the waters of the Delaware Bay from the dunes of sand behind me is one of the largest gatherings
of birds in the world. These birds are on a quest. They are determined, they

Shorebirds crowd the Delaware Bay beaches at mating time looking for treats.

are pushy, but most of all they are hungry. They number a million or more, and they have been flying almost nonstop from their winter homes thousands of miles to the south—from remote beaches in Patagonia, Tierra del Fuego, and the furthest reaches of South America.

The local gulls are bullies; they crowd together, pushing and shoving against the great mass of their long-distance-traveler cousins. Long-billed dowitchers poke and root beneath the wet sand at the water's edge. Yellowlegs wade in the shallows searching for food. Red knots sweep across the sand like large flapping curtains randomly tossed over the landscape. Sandpipers dance in and out of the gentle waves, playing tag. Ruddy turnstones, sanderlings, plovers, dunlins, and willets all arrive—wave after wave after unending wave. One difference: this scene definitely does not have the gentility of San Juan Capistrano (tiny swallows are oh-so-much more polite).

They are here for the feast…the feast of horseshoe crab eggs.

These shorebirds are travelers with a purpose, like long-haul truckers on a cross-country route. Except that these winged travelers have come from the southern tip of South America and will eventually travel all the way to nesting grounds near the Arctic Circle. This is a long and exhausting journey each spring, and these birds have but a few precious places along the way to feed and rest. The timing of their journey is critical; the birds must reach the Arctic while the snow is melting to ensure their eggs will hatch in time for the annual insect hatch. Those insects constitute the primary diet of the young shorebirds. If the birds arrive too early, the insects are not there, and the newly hatched young have nothing to eat; if they arrive too late, the insects have departed—a mass exodus of food on the wing.

The Delaware Bay is a critical stopover point in the long-distance journey to the Arctic. Most of these birds have traveled night and day and day and night to arrive at the bay. After departing from near the bottom of the world, they make a single pit stop on the southeast coast of Brazil. After a brief rest, they take off for an unbelievable nonstop journey of five thousand miles over vast oceanic distances for the shores of the Delaware Bay. It is vitally important that the hungry birds find plenty of food when they arrive, or they will not have enough energy to complete their arduous journey to the vastness of northern Canada. Imagine traveling for five thousand miles hoping, just hoping, that there will be enough food at your destination. If there is, you live. If not…

In that regard, the Delaware Bay is a good choice for the birds because of a fortuitous ecological coincidence: the birds arrive upon these beaches in concert with the arrival of spawning horseshoe crabs. The shorebirds are lured here by an incredible banquet of little green eggs. Consider, if you will, the biological coincidence of these two species arriving at the same place at almost the same time, and within a very narrow window of opportunity. It is though a great script has been written, and the avian and arthropod actors are merely playing their ecological roles—as they have for thousands of years. It is nature's divine act of synchronicity.

KEY FACT

Three hundred tons of horseshoe crab eggs may be consumed by migratory birds.

The relationship of horseshoe crabs to the spring shorebird migration has only received extended scientific attention since 1981, when the New Jersey Audubon Society initiated a shorebird survey of Delaware Bay beaches. Approximately twenty different species of shorebirds bent on doubling their body weights were recorded cramming the Delaware and New Jersey shorelines. The study "…estimated that there were some 370,000 to 643,000 shorebirds on the New Jersey shore of Delaware Bay at the height of the migration, with perhaps double this number if the Delaware beaches were factored in." Additionally, the authors discovered that when these birds arrive they are literally down to bone, skin, and feather, having used up all their fat reserves and much of their muscle in flight.

Most of this activity occurs during the third or fourth week in May. Hundreds of thousands of migrating shorebirds arrive just as hundreds of thousands of horseshoe crabs emerge from the depths of the Delaware Bay to lay their eggs. Each female horseshoe crab deposits up to fifteen egg clusters during her spawning period, and each of those clusters will contain between three and four thousand eggs. Thus, each female can lay as many as eighty thousand eggs during a single spawning season.* Multiply that by a million or more horseshoe crabs, and you can see that the birds have the makings of quite an impressive banquet.

Most female crabs deposit their eggs approximately four to six inches below the surface of the sand. Although this depth is beyond the reach of most shorebirds, wave action and the heedless burrowing of other spawning horseshoe crabs move some of the eggs toward the sand's surface. It is these disturbed eggs that the voracious shorebirds rely on.

As you might imagine, eggs that remain buried in the sand have the greatest likelihood of survival. Eggs driven closer to the surface have the least likelihood of survival, both because of environmental factors, such as lack of moisture, and also because they are available for shorebird consumption. Another factor at play here is the length of the shorebirds' bills. The red knot, one of the most prevalent species of migrating shorebird, has one of the longest bills at an average of 1.3 inches. It can forage in moist sand and extract any eggs within 1.3 inches of the surface. Eggs buried deeper are beyond their reach, and thus considerably safer.

But the red knot is also an opportunistic feeder—happy to let others do its work. In this case, the workers are the other horseshoe crabs, who dig and scrape around the nests of early arriving females, disturbing and excavating previously laid eggs as they try to lay their own. A succession of spawning females, all nesting at approximately the same optimal spot on the beach, can release thousands and thousands of eggs from precursory nests. The more eggs released, the more eggs available for consumption.

In addition, one interesting study provided some evidence that the ruddy turnstone is able to excavate holes in the sand, and as a result, can reach clusters of eggs buried at depths of up to four inches. In general, the deeper

---

* For those who wish to compare horseshoe crabs with human beings, here are some relevant facts: A human female typically has about four hundred thousand potential eggs, all formed before birth. Only about 480 of those eggs will actually be released during her reproductive years. And, in case you were about to ask, your average chicken will lay about three hundred eggs in her lifetime.

eggs are buried the safer they are, but no egg is completely safe.

Gonzalo Castro, a biologist at the University of Pennsylvania, and his colleagues have done some interesting studies on the shorebird/horseshoe crab connection. Castro reported that "during the two to three week time period the birds stay on Delaware Bay, they undergo weight gains of at least 40 percent of their body weight." Castro and associates also estimated that "1,820,000 female horseshoe crabs are required to feed Delaware Bay's migratory birds. These calculations assume that shorebirds are feeding exclusively on horseshoe crab eggs." But as horseshoe crab researcher Mark Botton has pointed out, the birds "may augment their diet with other food sources, including invertebrates."

ALTHOUGH MORE THAN TWENTY-FIVE DIFFERENT SPECIES OF BIRDS may crowd the beaches of the Delaware Bay, four primary species use the bay as a stopover area during their northward migration. Red knots, semipalmated sandpipers, ruddy turnstones, and sanderlings make up approximately 95 percent of the birds that visit these shores. Let's take a closer look at each of these distinctive species.

The red knot has an average wingspan of about twenty inches (slightly longer than the distance from the tip of your middle finger to your elbow) and an overall length of approximately nine inches (slightly longer than from the tip of your middle finger to your wrist). Its back looks like a psychedelic checkerboard—a crazy assembly of mottled buff, streaks of black, and bits of white in a seemingly haphazard pattern. Its distinctive name comes partly from the fact that much of its head and all of its belly is robin red.

The red knot, one of the farthest ranging migrants in the animal kingdom, winters along the southern coasts of South America, primarily in Tierra del Fuego (Spanish for "land of fire"). It breeds in eastern Canada and on islands scattered across the Arctic Circle. Take a look at a globe, and you will quickly appreciate the incredible distances it has to fly each year: 9,300 miles from south to north every spring, and 9,300 miles from north to south every autumn. That annual journey of 18,600 miles is equivalent to three and a half round trips, by car, between Los Angeles and Washington, D.C.*

---

* A red knot banded in May 1987 was identified again on the Delaware Bay in May 2000. During the intervening thirteen years, this single bird flew approximately 242,350 miles, a distance greater than that between the earth and the moon (the average distance between these two celestial objects is 238,855 miles).

A flock of red knots in flight.

Red knots migrate in enormous flocks, considerably larger than those of most other shorebirds. Most migratory birds cover enormous distances without stopping, but red knots tend to segment their journeys into sections of about 1,500 miles. As a result, they have several specific "staging areas" along the Atlantic coast. They stop in the same places at approximately the same times year after year. Their favorite stopping-off points are familiar, and they can expect to find food at each location. On the downside, however, these sites make the bird susceptible to poaching, habitat change, endemic diseases, and toxins. For example, one research study proved that extensive hunting of red knots in the nineteenth century "no doubt contributed to the declining numbers of [birds]" during those years.

Each long-distance journey poses significant physiological challenges for the red knot, and their bodies make several adaptations in order to survive the trip. Immediately prior to each journey, the birds' flight muscle mass increases while their leg muscle mass decreases. Their stomach and gizzard masses decrease, while fat mass increases by more than 50 percent. Throughout their wintering range in South America,

KEY FACT

Red knot females lay four eggs that together total more than half her weight.

they feed primarily on small mussels and other mollusks, shell and all. However, having shrunken their gizzards, they eschew those hard foods on the journey and instead rely on the soft eggs of the horseshoe crab. Because of the superabundance of the eggs across Delaware Bay beaches, the birds save considerable energy in not having to hunt for food.

When red knots arrive at the Delaware Bay, they are exceedingly thin, almost to the point of emaciation. They need to eat constantly in order to increase their fat mass sufficiently to continue their journey. It is not unusual for them to gain up to 10 percent of their body weight each day and to double their body weight during their time along the bay. At least one researcher has estimated that each red knot must eat approximately 135,000 horseshoe crab eggs in a period of about two weeks in order to double its weight.

ANOTHER SHOREBIRD THAT VISITS THE DELAWARE BAY ANNUALLY IS the ruddy turnstone, a short-legged bird about eight to ten inches in length. It has a short, dark bill that is slightly upturned at the end and a harlequin pattern of black, white, and rust-red in alternating patterns on its back, along with a black patch on its chest. Its belly is white, and its legs are coral-red. In summer, the feathers along its back are a combination of white, rusty red, and black. To me, the ruddy turnstone looks like it has been playing in an artist's palette, carrying away a variety of colors here and there on its body.

The ruddy turnstone winters on coasts from California to New Jersey to Argentina, spending considerable time in a host of near-water habitats, such as mudflats, sandbars, sandy or muddy shores, beaches, and rocky coasts. It breeds primarily along coastal tundra from western Alaska east to Greenland, and it can also be found in selected Arctic regions of Europe and Asia. A good swimmer, it may spend hours bathing and preening in shallow water areas.

When searching for food, the ruddy turnstone flips over rocks to look for small animals, typically invertebrates. This unique rock-flipping action gives it its name. (Some folks call it the "seaweed bird" because it often feeds among the kelp at low tide.) In addition, it can dig into the sand in pursuit of tiny crustaceans. Its diet is a diverse and eclectic mix of small mollusks, crustaceans, grasshoppers, insects, larvae, maggots, worms, and, of course, the eggs of horseshoe crabs.

Male and female ruddy turnstones will pair off either before or after reaching their breeding grounds. They tend to build their nests in open, grassy areas near the water. After the female lays approximately four eggs in a grassy area, both parents will trade off incubating the eggs. Male

A ruddy turnstone (top) and a flock of sanderlings.

turnstones are extremely territorial; they patrol the border of the nesting site and will aggressively chase away any potential intruders. About twenty-two to twenty-four days after the eggs are laid, the chicks will hatch. Both parents care for the young, but the female will leave before the chicks are fully fledged while the male remains.

ANOTHER SHOREBIRD THAT FREQUENTS THE DELAWARE BAY IS THE small (at seven to eight inches in length), plump sanderling. In summer, its back, head, and neck are a bright rusty red with splatterings of black. It also sports a white belly with black legs and bill. In flight, it shows a strong white

Semipalmated sandpipers migrate from South America to the Arctic Circle.

wingbar. In the winter, however, the sanderling is very pale—almost white—apart from a dark patch on its shoulder. This is the source of its species name, *alba*, which is Latin for "white." Sanderlings are distinguished from other wading birds by the absence of a hind toe (birders note: you have to be really, *really* close to a sanderling to see that it doesn't have this appendage). Sanderlings are some of the smallest of all shorebirds, weighing from 1.4 to 3.5 ounces.*

Like the red knot, the sanderling is a circumpolar breeder, wintering primarily in the southern regions of South America, Africa, and Australia. Known as a highly gregarious bird, it will often form enormous flocks on sandy beaches or coastal mudflats. Its diet consists mainly of small crabs and other tiny invertebrates. It is also distinguished by a unique "bicycling" motion as it scampers across the beach, stopping frequently to pick up small food items. A flock of these birds moving across the beach looks very much like the peloton of the Tour de France as it winds its way around deep valleys and across vineyards during the annual three-week race.

After departing the feast on the Delaware Bay, the sanderling heads for its breeding grounds in the high Arctic region. There the female will lay a

---

* A sanderling weighing fifty grams (1.7 ounces, or the weight of ten nickels) can eat one horseshoe egg every five seconds for fourteen hours a day (that's 10,080 eggs a day).

clutch of three to four eggs in a ground scrape. While in these polar regions, its diet changes considerably; it eats everything from insects to various kinds of plant material.

THE LAST OF OUR SHOREBIRDS IS THE SEMIPALMATED SANDPIPER. (Palmation refers to the webbing between an animal's toes. A semipalmated bird has very short webbing. Once again, you would have to be *really* close to this bird to notice this.) The adult sandpiper ranges in length from five to seven inches, with moderately long black legs and a medium length bill that may droop slightly at the tip. Its body is gray-brown on top and white underneath with a streaked breast. One of the sandpiper's most distinctive habits is its ability to sleep on one leg with its bill tucked into its back.

The semipalmated sandpiper's nonbreeding winter range extends along the coastline of the northern half of South America, from the southern tip of Peru all the way around to southern Brazil. Its summer breeding range covers primarily aquatic territory from northwestern Alaska across northern Canada and up into the Arctic Circle.

Like many migratory birds, semipalmated sandpipers nest on the ground. The male makes several shallow scrapes on the ground, while the female patiently waits. She then carefully selects one of the scrapes, adding grass and other plant material to line their nest. The female will lay about four eggs in the nest, and the male assists with the incubation process. The female, like ruddy turnstone females, leaves the young with their father after just a few short days. Soon thereafter, the young begin feeding for themselves.

Semipalmated sandpipers migrate in flocks that can number in the hundreds of thousands. Flocks of these birds, flying in formation, are quite a sight as they sweep over their favored feeding locations along the Delaware Bay. These birds tend to congregate on mudflats, and they often forage for aquatic insects and small crustaceans when not dining on horseshoe crab eggs.

IN 2008, FILMMAKER ALLISON ARGO PRODUCED A PBS NATURE VIDEO entitled *Crash: A Tale of Two Species*[†] that examines the incredible synchronicity between the red knot and the horseshoe crab. Much of the film centers on how this fragile balance may be imperiled by a variety of events. These

---

† Argo, Allison. (2008) *Crash: A Tale of Two Species* (PBS Nature/Argo Films). Chicago, IL: Questar Entertainment.

may include a combination of man-made events (e.g. harvesting horseshoe crabs for fishing bait, using horseshoe crab blood for medical purposes) and natural events (hurricanes, oceanic storms, reduced food sources).

The film visits the red knots in Brazil, where they are preparing for a four-day, nonstop flight over vast oceanic expanses to the beaches of Delaware and New Jersey. At the same time, the horseshoe crab is answering a siren call several millennia old—a call that brings them up out of the bottom silt of the Delaware Bay to spawn. The film poses the ecological question of whether the horseshoe crabs will deposit sufficient eggs on the bay's shores to feed the long-distance travelers during their two-week feeding frenzy.

The film states that, because approximately three million horseshoe crabs are currently harvested for eel and conch bait each year, the number of eggs available as food for red knots has declined appreciably. A typical female crab will deposit about eighty thousand eggs in one season, and when those eighty thousand eggs are multiplied by three million fewer crabs, that means an approximate loss of 240 billion eggs. The film claims that the current decline in the red knot population has occurred simply because the fuel the birds need to power their journey to the Arctic is not available. One scientist chillingly asks, "Will the [horseshoe crab] population recover in time for the red knot? No one knows."

KEY FACT

A million horseshoe crab eggs together would weigh slightly more than a pound.

One of the final segments of the film follows a group of scientists traversing the Arctic in search of red knots. Everywhere they search, and everywhere they travel, the red knots are absent. It is as though the birds have disappeared entirely. The implication is that a lack of horseshoe crab eggs in and around the Delaware Bay has made it very difficult for the birds to make it all the way to their traditional nesting grounds. According to the filmmakers, the lack of eggs is due, in large measure, to a lack of horseshoe crabs, and the decline in the horseshoe crab population is caused principally by human intervention, including harvesting horseshoe crabs for bait and lax environmental regulation. One scientist makes a haunting statement that hangs in the air: "The fate of animals like the red knot are [*sic*] really in our hands."

I asked Dr. Carl Shuster, the leading horseshoe crab expert (and the subject of Chapter 12), for his take on this relationship. Shuster assured me that

Red knots crowd around horseshoe crabs.

there is a healthy population of horseshoe crabs—upward of eighteen million adult crabs in the Delaware Bay and several million more on the continental shelf in the vicinity of the entrance to the bay. Shuster said, "I think the biggest myth is…the fact that because the birds were [in decline], horseshoe crabs must be linked to that. Some of the local [news]papers were [saying] that the horseshoe crabs were in danger."

Shuster emphatically told me, "We know there are plenty of horseshoe crabs," but there may be a decline in the subpopulation of young adult females, which bear the eggs and are often the ones harvested for bait. That said, Shuster was also quick to point out that there is a constant and current environmental challenge for all horseshoe crabs. "The damage being done," he said, "is not on the shore, but out on the [continental] shelf." That damage is often the result of human actions (e.g. pollution, overfishing, indiscriminant trawling) that have the potential to impact horseshoe crab populations well into the future.

MORE THAN A MILLION SHOREBIRDS STOP TO GORGE THEMSELVES ON horseshoe crab eggs before continuing their northward migration. During their stopover, the four most abundant shorebird species will consume approximately 539 metric tons (1,188,279.4 pounds*) of horseshoe crab eggs. While this may seem like an awfully large number, it's partly because of the low metabolic efficiency of the birds. The birds eat the eggs, and the eggs pass through the birds' gastrointestinal tracts, but the cuticles of those eggs are resistant to both chemical and enzymatic digestion. As a result, very few of the eggs are broken down and available as nutrition for the hungry birds. But, birds being rather bird-brained, they continue to stuff their bellies with as many eggs as they can cram into their gullets, irrespective of their low nutritional value. Some scientists have calculated that at least 1.8 million female horseshoe crabs must spawn on the shores of the Delaware Bay to provide the seven billion eggs that the migrating birds consume each year.

There is no doubt that shorebird populations are under pressure. Numerous surveys have shown significant declines in their numbers. The sanderling population alone has decreased an alarming 80 percent over the course of the last several decades. Some of the suspected causes of the decline include use of pesticides in the winter grounds, loss of coastal wetlands along migration routes, competition with humans over prime coastline areas, and a possible decrease in available food. Only fat, healthy birds can survive the long distance migration to Arctic breeding grounds, and the short Arctic summer means they have time to raise only one small brood. This low rate of reproduction makes it challenging for any species of shorebirds to sustain a healthy population.

Biologists and birders are constantly tracking shorebird movements and population trends, which over time may help clarify the factors causing their numbers to decline. It remains to be seen whether the birds will be able to survive changing and challenging environmental conditions over which they have no control. The good news is that, despite the billions of eggs they consume each year, current evidence suggests that shorebird feeding has little or no impact on the overall horseshoe crab population.

IN 1963, ALFRED HITCHCOCK DIRECTED THE CLASSIC HORROR FILM *The Birds*. The story takes place in picturesque Bodega Bay, California, which, for reasons that are entirely mysterious, is suddenly subjected to a series of violent bird attacks over a period of several days.

---

* In case you were wondering, 1,188,279.4 pounds (of horseshoe crab eggs) is equivalent to the weight of 2,495,346 Big Macs from McDonald's, 4,659,917 orders of medium french fries from Burger King, or 3,046,869 small Frosties from Wendy's.

The plot centers on Melanie Daniels, a young socialite who meets lawyer Mitch Brenner in a San Francisco pet shop. Intrigued, she purchases a pair of lovebirds and makes the one-and-a-half hour drive up U.S. 101 to his house in Bodega Bay. Sneaking across the small harbor in a motorboat, she leaves the birds and a note at his house. As she is heading back across the bay, a seagull swoops down and attacks her.

Over the next few days, there are additional bird attacks. A gull hits the front door of a house Melanie is visiting; birds attack a birthday party; a friend is discovered dead in his bedroom. There's another attack at the local school, and at least one person proclaims that the attacks are a sign of the apocalypse.

A motorist is attacked while filling his car with gasoline. He is knocked unconscious, and the gasoline continues to pump out onto the street. Another man, unaware he is standing by the gasoline puddle, lights a cigarette and drops the match on the ground, resulting in an explosion and fire.

The climax of the movie occurs when Melanie, Mitch, and Mitch's family take refuge in the Brenners' house, boarding up the windows. The house is attacked by the birds, and they almost manage to break through the doors. In the evening, when everyone else is asleep, Melanie hears noises from the upper floor, and discovers that the birds have broken through the roof. They attack her violently, trapping her in the room until Mitch comes to her rescue. She is quickly patched up, but she must go to the local hospital.

In the final scene—one of the most compelling and frightening in all of moviedom—Mitch and Melanie slowly and cautiously exit the house as tens of thousands of still and silent birds shuffle around them on the ground. Climbing into the car, Mitch carefully navigates through this endless avian ocean. The birds are unmoving, ominously and patiently watchful as the car creeps along the winding road. There is an eerie stillness and sense of foreboding in the air. Will the humans escape, or will they encounter more terror down the road? The question is left unanswered as the credits roll.

Each time I see that film—even though I know exactly what is going to happen—I still take a deep breath and steel myself for the murderous onslaught of thousands of birds upon the hapless residents of a small northern California town. Even now, whenever I see large groups of birds,* I still feel a tiny ribbon of apprehension creeping up my spine.

That is, except when I see hundreds of thousands of shorebirds along the edges of the Delaware Bay. Their *raison d'être* is much more honest…and considerably less frightening.

---

* A group of storks is known as a "mustering," a group of hawks is called a "cast," a group of hummingbirds is known as a "charm," a group of woodpeckers is a "descent," a group of larks is known as an "exaltation," and a group of owls is called a "parliament." And, in a fitting piece of scientific nomenclature, a group of crows is known as a "murder." Interestingly, a *Nature* episode on PBS ("A Murder of Crows," 2009) discussed "new research indicat[ing] that crows are among the brightest animals in the world."

CHAPTER 9

Hatching Out and Moving On

Growing Up is Hard to Do

TYPE "GROWTH AND DEVELOPMENT" INTO GOOGLE, AND YOU will discover an entire subculture devoted to promoting information about the growth and development of those tiny humans referred to as children. If you are a parent, some of this information can be frightening, if not downright mind-boggling. After an hour or two, you begin to question your abilities as a parent. Here, from a single website,* are some topics guaranteed to keep you up late at night incessantly worrying:

- Breath-Holding Spells

- Is Your Child Too Busy?

- Your Child's Changing Voice

- Am I "Too Tough" When I Discipline My Kids?

- Positional Plagiocephaly

- Binge Eating Disorder

---

* http://kidshealth.org/parent/growth/index.html

- Food Allergies

- Should I Worry About the Way My Son Walks?

As parents, we are rightly concerned about how our children grow and develop; all parents are. Well, most all parents. Unfortunately, in the case of horseshoe crabs, the parents don't have anything to do with the growth and development of their offspring, which are sent out into the world with nothing but a few evolutionary rules and regulations. With a little bit of environmental luck, they'll be able to make it to adulthood, but the road there is fraught with all manner of ecological roadblocks. Most don't make it; but those that do follow a carefully scripted series of steps that lead from tiny egg to mature adult. Let's take a look.

IF YOU HAVE KIDS, YOU KNOW THAT THE CHANCES OF THEIR REACHING adulthood are pretty good. Most of the human babies born will reach adulthood. In short, human newborns eventually become human adults with a relatively high success rate. According to the World Health Organization (WHO), mortality in children under five years old in 2008 was estimated at sixty-five per one thousand live births, and worldwide about 94 percent of babies reach the age of five. WHO is careful to point out that there are considerable regional and national differences in infant mortality rates.

For horseshoe crabs, the survival rate isn't as good. Think about all the billions of eggs those females laid on the beaches of the Delaware Bay. Literally acres and acres of eggs. Football fields full of eggs! Yet, only a measly 0.06 percent of those eggs will survive to hatching. Many will be consumed by birds, many will perish because they were laid in an area inhospitable to their development (for example, an area lacking oxygen), and many will be swept away by waves or tides.

Let's look at it this way: for every ten thousand eggs that are laid, just six will actually hatch. And things don't get any better for newly hatched horseshoe crabs. Most marine creatures have it easy compared to what horseshoe crabs have to put up with in their formative years.

Horseshoe crabs start off as embryos in shell-less, greenish eggs, each of which measures about 0.059 inches in diameter (that's roughly the size of the tapioca pearls used in some Thai desserts). The green outer surface of the egg (the *chorion*) is characteristically sticky, which helps the eggs stick together to form a protective cluster. If we were to put that into more anthropomorphic language, we could say that the eggs on the outside of a cluster are protecting the eggs on the inside.

The stickiness of the eggs is also useful in helping ensure that they will become totally covered in sperm during the fertilization process. After the males deposit their sperm near the females' eggs, nature wants to be sure that the sperm and the eggs get together. Because the eggs are coated with a sticky substance, that "getting together" is virtually assured; almost every egg a horseshoe crab lays is successfully fertilized. Within a few days of fertilization, the chorion breaks away to reveal the translucent inner layers of the egg.

After fertilization, each egg consists of three primary elements: a central yolk, an embryo, and a thick outer membrane. In many ways, it resembles the chicken eggs with which you may be more familiar. The eggs develop quite rapidly early on. By the fourth day after fertilization, simple horseshoe crab appendages such the telson can be seen inside the eggs; by the eighth day, the legs and book gills are visible to the naked eye.

After hatching, horseshoe crab young are called trilobite larvae, because they resemble the ancient trilobites that used to crawl across the floors of prehistoric oceans. These larvae are natural swimmers. During this important developmental stage, the larvae remain buried in the sediment. They are beginning to resemble their parents in form and shape, but they are exceedingly small—small enough to swim in the tiny droplets of water trapped between individual particles of sand.* They often move to the surface of the sand at high tide, and then swim back down again at low tide. With each upward movement, some larvae are exposed, making them vulnerable to hungry birds, wandering crabs, or pounding waves. Often, the larvae will emerge from the sand during periods of high water, such as high tides or significant storms. This, of course, makes them even more vulnerable.

KEY FACT

The embryo molts four times inside the egg.

---

* Those readers familiar with the 1966 movie *Fantastic Voyage* will immediately see some parallels here. In that movie, a submarine is shrunken to microscopic size—along with a group of scientists, including Raquel Welch—and injected into the bloodstream of a diplomat who has been nearly assassinated. They must travel throughout his bloodstream in less than an hour to repair a dangerous blood clot while battling rampaging white blood cells, incorrigible bacteria, and other arterial demons.

Recently, researchers have discovered that some of the larvae, particularly in northern areas of the Atlantic seaboard, have the ability to overwinter in the sand. They can stay lodged in the sand for up to eight months, then they emerge during warmer weather, typically in the spring, and before the onslaught of all the migratory birds.

After eventually finding their way into open water, the larvae will typically remain close to shore for protection. They often mix in with shoreline plankton for six to eight days before settling to the bottom and molting to their first juvenile stage. Only about 2.5 percent of larvae survive to this stage. As we've seen, the odds were astronomical against the eggs making it, and now the odds are nearly as astronomical against the larvae making it. They're not even adults yet, but the world has already turned out to be a cold, cruel, and hard place.

The tiny crabs are now at the next stage of their overall development, known as the first *instar*,* or post-larval stage. At this time in their lives, the crabs measure approximately 0.19 inches across their prosomas, and they will look very similar to adults, except with longer spines and a much shorter telson. In contrast to the adults and the larvae, these juveniles live on tidal flats. They are typically most active in the two hours before the daytime low tide, staying buried in the sediment at other times. By the end of the first year, most juveniles will have reached the sixth instar and will measure about a half inch across their prosoma (in the Delaware Bay). Several studies have shown that only about thirty-three of every one million larvae that emerge from the beach survive to this stage.

KEY FACT

After molting, a horseshoe crab will increase its body size by about 25 percent.

As the juveniles grow, they eventually move away from the shoal water "nurseries" into deeper water. When they reach a prosomal width of about three-and-a-half inches, they begin moving offshore. At this stage, the ratio between males and females is about one to one. Some of these sexually immature horseshoe crabs continue moving into deeper and deeper water. Some large subadults have been dredged up from waters as much as eight hundred feet deep.

Noted horseshoe crab expert Carl Shuster has determined that it normally takes a horseshoe crab approximately nine to eleven years (or seventeen to eighteen instars) before it reaches sexual maturity. However, this may vary

---

* An instar is a developmental or growth stage of arthropods, such as horseshoe crabs, between each molt.

Only about thirty-three of every million larvae make it through their first year.

depending on where they are located, north to south. According to Shuster, females tend to be larger than males "because of either greater growth with each molt or more molts before maturity." Large size in females may be advantageous, because females must tow males during the spawning season, and also because a large body cavity can contain more eggs. However, surveys on spawning beaches and in trawls always find more males than females. This may be because females molt more frequently, and mortality increases during molting.

When horseshoe crabs become adults, they begin their annual spring migration to the spawning beaches. Thus, the horseshoe crabs you see on the beach are not all the horseshoe crabs in the Delaware Bay (or wherever you may be standing). Thousands—no millions—of others, in various stages of development, remain further out and further down in the water. You are just seeing the tip of the proverbial horseshoe crab iceberg.

ALTHOUGH NUMBERS ARE DIFFICULT TO ARRIVE AT, MOST HORSESHOE crabs have a maximum life expectancy of about twenty years. A rough estimate of a horseshoe crab's age can be determined by observing the number and density of hitchhiking plants and animals (bryophytes, worms, etc.) on the shells of these animals. The more plants and animals (particularly after the final molt), then the older the crab is. We'll discuss these fellow travelers a little bit later in this chapter.

For comparison purposes, you may want to match the maximum life expectancy of horseshoe crabs against a few select members of the animal kingdom, as illustrated in figure 9.1.

Trying to determine the age of a horseshoe crab involves a whole lot of guessing and a little bit of luck. Scientists assign adult horseshoe crabs to one of three very broad categories:

Young adults typically have a carapace that is lustrous with few, if any, scratches or free-riding plants or animals. Virgin males can be identified by the fact that they do not have the easily recognizable "boxing gloves" used to grasp females during spawning, while virgin females will have a pristine shell with no mating scars.

Middle-aged adults, from nine to fifteen years of age, will have carapaces in which the luster of youth is being worn away. Both males and females will exhibit a random collection of scratches and scars. Females will show mating scars on the back corners of their shells where the claspers of the males have attached during spawning. There are usually various types of marine hitchhikers on the carapace.

Old-aged adults tend to have carapaces that are almost completely blackened, with a great deal of erosion and a plethora of cracks, scars, and indentations. The shell is often thin and can be easily depressed. *Epibionts* (hitchhiking plants and animals) are almost always present and may have spread across the shell. An old-timer would be about twenty years old.

POP QUIZ: WHAT IS THE HUMAN BODY'S LARGEST ORGAN? MOST PEOPLE will say "lungs," "heart," or "stomach," but the correct answer is "skin." That's right, the largest organ in your body is your skin.* An adult male has

---

* Interestingly, there is considerable disagreement on the number of organs in the human body. Some medical texts state that there are 78 organs, while others state that there are 22 internal organs (+ 1 external organ [skin]). Other texts list 13 major organ systems in the human body. Suffice it to say, skin is the largest human organ with the liver (#2), the brain (#3), the lungs (#4), and the heart (#5) as the next largest organs (in descending order).

Figure 9.1. Maximum life spans of various animals

ANIMAL	MAXIMUM LIFE SPAN
Burrowing Mayfly (*Dolania Americana*)	5 minutes
Hessian Fly	48 hours
Mosquito	100 days
Bedbug	18 months
Hummingbird	12 years
Horseshoe crab	20 years
Snail	30 years
Cow	48 years
Alligator	75 years
Human	122 years
Koi	226 years
Black Coral	4,000+ years
Sponge	15,000 years

between twelve and twenty square feet of skin on his body, and that skin weighs between nine and fifteen pounds.

Your skin protects you from extremes of hot or cold. It's a barrier against the effects of wind and sun. It keeps all the water inside your body (your body is about 60 percent water). It controls your body's internal temperature. And it can fold, crease, bend, stretch, and expand wherever your body wants to fold, crease, bend, stretch, or expand.

Amazingly, a lot of your skin is dead. In fact, when you look at another person, what you see is dead skin. That's as true for sexy young fashion models as it is for wrinkled old men.

Your skin is actually composed of two distinct parts. The outer part, known as the *epidermis*, is made of several layers of dead skin cells. These dead cells form an overlapping coat of protection. Even your hair and nails are made of dead skin cells (and keratin—a protein). Interestingly, you shed millions of dead cells during the thousands of movements your body performs every day. You may shed up to five pounds of dead skin cells in the course of a year; if you live to be seventy years old, that's nearly 350 pounds of skin—which, in case you're interested, is the weight of the average gorilla. Much of the dust in your house is actually composed of dead skin cells. Your house is also filled with thousands of tiny insects called dust mites that subsist entirely on dead skin cells from humans. For some, it may be scary to think that no matter how much you clean, you can never get rid of all the dust mites. But if you did get rid of them all, you'd have piles of skin cells collecting in the corners of the kitchen, around the TV set, and under the living room sofa.

The part of the skin below the epidermis is known as the *dermis*. Here, skin is alive and growing. The cells here are continually dividing and replacing the dead cells above them. A single skin cell lives for about three weeks, during which time it moves from the dermis to the epidermis. By the time it reaches the outer layer, it is dead and has been pressed into a flattened shape. The dermis also is the part of the skin that contains all the blood vessels, sweat glands, nerve endings, and oil glands.

The thickness of your skin ranges from about a hundredth of an inch on your eyelids to about a fifth of an inch on your back. The skin on the soles of your feet, which are subject to the most wear and tear, is eight times as thick as it is on your eyelids. I'm sure most readers will not be surprised to learn that, in general, a man's skin is thicker than a woman's.

As we grow up, our skin expands and stretches. But generally speaking, the skin you were born with is the skin that stays with you throughout your life. Not so for many animals. Their skin doesn't expand as does ours, and so they routinely cast off a part of their bodies—often, but not always, an outer layer or covering—either at specific times of year or at specific points in their life cycle. This is known as molting (and also as sloughing, shedding, or ecdysis).

Molting doesn't always involve an animal's skin. It can also involve pelage (hair, fur, wool) or some other external layer: wings in some insects, feathers in birds, hair in mammals, skin in reptiles, and the entire exoskeleton in arthropods (see figure 9.2).

Figure 9.2. The different ways animals molt

ANIMAL	WHAT IT DOES
Birds	Almost all birds replace their feathers. Essentially, feathers are dead structures at maturity, and they gradually wear down and need to be replaced. Depending on the species, birds may molt once, twice, or three times during the year. For birds, molting is a comparatively slow process, and birds seldom shed all their feathers at once.
Dogs	Dogs shed their fur twice a year, in the spring and fall; or more often, depending on breed, living environment, and temperature. If you have to vacuum your living room couch almost daily to suck up all the dog hairs, you may argue that this shedding process is much more frequent than twice a year.
Reptiles	The most familiar example of molting in reptiles is a snake shedding its skin. This is done by rubbing its head against a hard object, such as a rock, causing the already stretched skin to split. The snake continues to rub itself on objects until it is eventually able to crawl out of its skin.
Amphibians	Frogs and salamanders molt regularly. And, intriguingly, they will consume their discarded skin. Sometimes the skin molts in pieces, and sometimes it comes off in one solid piece.
Arthropods	In arthropods, such as insects, arachnids, and crustaceans, molting is the shedding of the exoskeleton (often called its shell), typically to let the organism grow a little larger. This is necessary because the exoskeleton is rigid and cannot grow like skin. The new exoskeleton starts out soft, but hardens after the old exoskeleton has molted.

IF YOU'VE EVER WALKED A BEACH ALONG THE EASTERN SEASHORE OR the Florida coastline, you may have run across the empty shells of horseshoe crabs. These shells, or casts, indicate that there is a population of *Limulus* in the area. They also indicate that one or more horseshoe crabs may be in the process of molting their now too-small skin. This is a natural process both males and females go through many times during their lives. The American naturalist Samuel Lockwood (1819–1894) colorfully and succinctly explained that a molting horseshoe crab looks like "it is spewing itself from its own mouth."*

Like all arthropods, horseshoe crabs must molt in order to grow. When an individual horseshoe crab is ready to molt, a new, soft, folded exoskeleton begins to form beneath the old one. Burrowing into the sand to protect itself, it begins to take in water. The water causes the pleats in its new shell to expand and unfold, splitting open the front edge of the old shell. Once the forward edge of the old carapace has entirely split, the horseshoe crab can crawl out. This mode of molting—crawling forward out of the old shell, leaving it intact—is unique among arthropods.

The now soft horseshoe crab is highly permeable to water and swells up, increasing in size. At the same time, the exoskeleton begins absorbing minerals from the seawater. After a period of time, the carapace hardens and the horseshoe crab expels the excess water, leaving it room to grow into its new carapace. For young horseshoe crabs, the molting process may take as little as one hour to complete. For older ones, this procedure may take a day, or even longer, to complete.

KEY FACT

After molting, the horseshoe crab's new shell will harden in about twelve hours.

Horseshoe crabs molt numerous times as they grow from their larval stage, shedding their exoskeleton at least sixteen or seventeen times before reaching sexual maturity at nine to eleven years of age. The molting process occurs most often during the warm-water months, and it becomes more challenging and time consuming each time.

IF YOU LOOKED CLOSELY AT A HORSESHOE CRAB, YOU WOULD PROBABLY see that it resembles a walking hotel, providing portable lodging for a wide variety of critters.

A horseshoe crab's carapace is an ideal vehicle for plants and animals that enjoy a free ride, transportation to a variety of interesting locations, and shuttle

---

* Dr. Lockwood did not confine his studies to horseshoe crabs; in an article in a 1872 issue of *American Naturalist*, he describes a new parasite he discovered embedded in the adipose tissue on the entrails of the common eel. He spends a great deal of time discussing the unusual snout of this newly discovered critter.

A horseshoe crab that died of unknown causes in mid-molt.

service to a variety of underwater buffet dinners. Some of the freeloaders include barnacles, blue mussels, slipper shells, bryozoans, sponges, flatworms, diatoms, fungi, and bacteria. For most of these passengers, the horseshoe crab shell is readily available and easy to latch on to—similar, I suspect, to a family minivan transporting all the neighborhood kids to Little League.

For the most part, these hitchhikers have little or no effect on the day-to-day life of the horseshoe crab. However, there are some passengers who apparently don't know a good thing when they see one. Although the horseshoe crab's armored shell seems to be virtually indestructible, it suffers from daily wear and tear that can leave it with small cuts or scratches. These imperfections provide an opportunity for fungi and chitinase bacteria to gain a foothold. They grab hold of the abrasions, cuts, and scratches, and slowly begin to eat through the shell. Over time, this makes the horseshoe crab vulnerable to all sorts of additional microbes, some of which may prove to be fatal over time.

There are, however, various species of flatworm that don't ride on top of the horseshoe crab but, instead, glide around underneath it. While they're gliding, they're also eating scraps of food that the crab misses in its haphazard method of feeding. These flatworms often cement their eggs to the horseshoe crab's gills, causing small portions of the gill to become rigid and stiff. That stiffness in turn causes hairline cracks to appear in the gills, allowing deadly bacteria to invade the horseshoe crab's body.

WHEN HORSESHOE CRAB LARVAE HATCH, THEY DON'T NEED TO FEED. They depend on leftover yolk to nourish them while their digestive systems complete development. Their diet evolves in stages as they grow. Early in their life cycle, they feed on bits of organic matter in the sediments. As they continue the maturation process, they begin to consume tiny crustaceans and polychaetes, a class of annelid worms. As the youngsters begin assuming the form and anatomy of adults, they begin consuming almost anything they can capture.

Adults are opportunistic foragers; that is, they take advantage of a wide range of locally available prey. The food of horseshoe crabs falls into two major categories—marine worms and bivalve mollusks—and the mollusks they most frequently eat include razor clams, macoma clams, surf clams, blue mussels, wedge clams, fragile razor clams, soft-shelled clams, nut clams, and dwarf tellins. Bivalves comprise the vast majority of the ingested food during all seasons, making up 93 percent of the weight of their diet and 94 percent of their caloric intake. However, Mark Botton at Fordham University has identified fifty different groups of organisms from the stomach contents of adult horseshoe crabs, including mollusks, arthropods, polychaete worms, and vascular plants. Although horseshoe crabs do not efficiently assimilate vascular plant material and organic matter, these foods may be important in providing components to build chitin.

ALTHOUGH THERE IS STILL SOME RESEARCH TO BE DONE, HORSESHOE crabs almost certainly use chemical cues to detect prey. First, a horseshoe crab will dig into the muddy bottom of the ocean or bay in search of clams and worms. Under the broad protective dome of the prosoma, the legs probe into the sediment, producing a slurry from which they can more easily pluck their prey. The six pairs of book gills on the opisthosoma may indirectly contribute to food gathering; these appendages probably move pulses of water beneath the carapace to loosen the substrate, making it easier for the claws to grab prey.

The horseshoe crab may also locate prey using chemical receptors on their claws and on their gnathobases (the bristly areas near the bases of the walking legs). As they use their legs and gills to stir up sediment and water, they are able to "sniff" chemicals in the water, eventually capturing the prey with their legs. Collectively, the chemosensory signals from three million receptors on the chelae (their pincer-like claws) and one million receptors on the gnathobases provide a major sensory input to the *Limulus* brain. Like children at a baseball park, horseshoe crabs can detect all sorts of available food items in the vicinity. Most researchers think vision may be less important to a horseshoe crab during feeding than chemical and tactile cues.

Many people incorrectly believe that horseshoe crabs eat while they are walking. I can only imagine that this myth began when people realized that they use their feet to eat as well as to move. However, the biomechanics of walking and feeding are quite distinct, even though the same appendages are involved. It's important to keep in mind that the swinging motions of the bases of the legs during locomotion are at right angles to the "biting" movements used in feeding. Horseshoe crabs do not tear or shred the food they eat; rather, the gnathobases macerate* it while it is moved toward the mouth with the legs.

THERE'S A VERY SLIM CHANCE OF A LITTLE GREEN EGG MAKING ITS way to a twenty-year-old adult. It's astounding to me, and achingly sad, that so many potential eggs never make it. But a slim chance is just enough. All of the environmental odds seem to be working against the horseshoe crab, yet it has survived longer than 99.9 percent of all the animals that have ever lived on this planet. Is it because of the millions, billions, or trillions of eggs deposited and fertilized each year? Is it because the horseshoe crab has figured out the clues necessary for long-term environmental survival? Or is it because the fates, the odds, or the forces of nature have thrown the evolutionary dice in favor of this prehistoric beast? While I may not know the answers to all those questions, I am constantly in awe of the horseshoe crab's evolutionary persistence.

When it comes to horseshoe crabs and their ability to survive, never bet against them.

---

* In biology, *macerate* refers to the mechanical breakdown of ingested food. In cooking, however, it means to make soft by soaking in a liquid—soaking bread in a bowl of milk, for example.

Sand, surf, sun, and horseshoe crabs in Florida.

CHAPTER 10

Where the Boys Are

Spring Break in Florida

N 1960, AN AMERICAN FILM ABOUT FOUR MIDWESTERN COLLEGE coeds who spend spring break in Fort Lauderdale, Florida, burst into movie theaters all across the country. *Where the Boys Are* was one of the first films to examine adolescent sexuality and the evolving morals of college students. The title song was sung by teen pop sensation Connie Francis, who was also one of the movie's stars (in her first acting role).

The film opens with an overhead shot of a mass of boats moored in Fort Lauderdale, along with the iconic palm trees, golden-sand beaches, and blue skies of Florida. A deep baritone voice sets up the storyline for the film:

> For fifty weeks of the year, Fort Lauderdale, Florida, is a small corner of trop-
> ical heaven basking contently in the warm sun. During the other two weeks,
> as colleges all over the country disgorge their students for Easter vacation, a
> change comes over the students. Students swarm to these peaceful shores in
> droves—twenty thousand strong. They turn night into day...and the small
> corner of heaven into a sizeable chunk of bedlam. The boys come to soak up
> the sun and a few cartons of beer. The girls come, very simply, because this
> is...*where the boys are*! [A crescendo of soaring orchestral music follows.]

As the film opens, we look inside a typical college classroom as Merritt An-
drews (played by Dolores Hart, who later became a nun), the assertive leader

of the quartet, shares her feelings about premarital sex: she's all for it. Her views influence the seemingly insecure Melanie Tolman (Yvette Mimieux) to lose her virginity shortly after the group arrives in Fort Lauderdale. Tuggle Carpenter (Paula Prentiss), who wants to be a "baby-making machine," is looking for a man (any man) to fulfill her sexual wishes. Angie (Francis), a naïve romantic, rounds out the group.

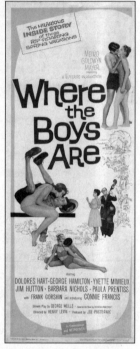

Yours truly was only thirteen years old in 1960, so this was all pretty heady stuff for me.

After Merritt begins seeing the debonaire Ryder Smith (George Hamilton), she comes to the conclusion that sex can wait for a while. Melanie quickly learns that she was being used by a boy whom she was sure loved her. Tuggle falls head over heels for the eccentric TV Thompson (Jim Hutton). Her infatuation takes a beating, however, when TV turns his attention to an older woman, a "mermaid" dancer (Barbara Nichols) at a local bar. Angie takes up with jazz musician Basil (Frank Gorshin, a.k.a. "The Riddler" from the *Batman* TV series) and his over-the-top glasses.

These escapades sober the four friends. Their previous freewheeling beliefs have been challenged, and they realize those ideals carry certain consequences, and that they need to be much more responsible and mature. The film ends with two lovers on the beach with the sun streaming over the waters of the Atlantic Ocean and through the palm trees.

As I thought about that film and the hordes of college students who still descend on Florida beaches annually, I couldn't help but think of the parallels between them and horseshoe crabs in Florida (figure 10.1).

Although the American Horseshoe Crab is most abundant in and around the Delaware Bay, it is found throughout the Atlantic seaboard, from Maine down past Virginia and South Carolina, around the Florida Keys, up the western coast, and along the panhandle. A small population of crabs also frequents the tip of the Yucatán peninsula.

In order to get a sense of *Limulus*'s range, I decided to sacrifice a spring break and make a trek to Florida. It would mean leaving the snow-covered tundra of Pennsylvania for the warm sunshine of Florida—a supreme sacrifice, but one I was willing to make in the name of scientific research. And so,

Figure 10.1. Boys versus *Limulus* in Florida

	WHERE THE BOYS ARE	WHERE THE HORSESHOE CRABS ARE
1. Hordes of sexually mature females arrive on Florida beaches.	√	√
2. Even larger hordes of sexually starved males congregate around the females.	√	√
3. Many males vie for the attention of a single female.	√	√
4. Every male is in competition with every other male.	√	√
5. The beaches are crowded and often noisy.	√	√
6. The antics on the beach are monitored by interested observers (police officers and/or biologists).	√	√
7. While on the beach, many of the participants are found on their backs.	√	√
8. Much of the action takes place in the waves and on the beach.	√	√
9. They live happily ever after.	?	?

I booked my ticket for Tampa; packed my bags, tape recorder, and author's notebooks; and, like a migratory shorebird on a mission, flew south.

I FLEW INTO TAMPA, SPARRED WITH A SUBSTANDARD CAR RENTAL company that didn't even have any local road maps (can you imagine?), and somehow found my way to northbound Route 19/98. I drove two hours through Florida's tourist-saturated West Coast (where "visitors can see West Indian manatees every day of the year") to the quaint, picturesque, and very civilized town of Cedar Key.*

---

* At least one promotional site advertises this bucolic town with the following: "See what Key West was like 40 years ago."

Cedar Key, Florida.

Just before coasting into Cedar Key, at the end of State Route 24, I took a quick left after the bridge and parked behind the Kirkpatrick Research Lab, where I had an interview scheduled with Tiffany Black. Black's title is Biological Scientist in the Crustaceans Department of the Florida Fish and Wildlife Research Institute. She is also the coordinator for the statewide, volunteer-based horseshoe crab spawning beach survey. I wanted to visit her to get some perspectives on population shifts in the Sunshine State's horseshoe crab population.

With a sparkle in her eyes and the enthusiasm of a child opening presents on Christmas day, Black informed me that the Florida horseshoe crab monitoring project is only a small part of her job. "I work with stone crab monitoring for 95 percent of my job and horseshoe crabs for the other 5 percent," she said. "Our lab is mandated by the Atlantic States Marine Fisheries Commission to submit a compliance report, because Florida falls within the horseshoe crab's range, and we do have a small fishery here. We do have a pretty good abundance of horseshoe crabs. Not anything like the mass spawning up in New Jersey and Delaware, but you can see hundreds at one time. A big spawning event here would be one or two thousand animals."

I was curious about the specifics of the monitoring effort, and asked her to clarify that effort across the state. "Yes, we do a statewide spawning beach survey that's all volunteer based," she said. "It's more of a presence/absence survey rather than a real abundance thing. Again, it's part of our inter-jurisdictional fisheries grant, although there's no money associated with it. We advertise this program through the media, and we also have a horseshoe crab hotline where people can call to report a sighting. We also have a survey on our website people can fill out. We're just trying to ascertain where horseshoe crabs are in Florida and trying to get a general idea of abundance, although, being a volunteer effort like this, it's difficult to be exceedingly accurate."

Black told me that she has sometimes received reports of a thousand animals from some volunteers, but that this information can never be verified, because she is seldom supplied with photos or real-time records of the sightings. Nevertheless, since she often gets multiple reports from the same areas year after year, she can determine that the horseshoe crabs are coming back to the same areas year after year. The reports come predominantly from the West Coast of the state, because that is where the main office is located. Reports from the East Coast of Florida are fewer in number, and arrive with less regularity, she said.

I asked what Black does with all the data collected from around the state. "All the data comes to me," she said, "and I ensure that it is entered into a database program, which documents where the animals were, time of day, ratio of males to females, number of juveniles, whether the animals were mating, etc."

It became clear to me that the monitoring of horseshoe crab populations in Florida is, at best, a challenge. It's difficult to trust the numbers, what with so much of the effort dependent upon volunteer help, and those volunteers potentially having different perspectives on how sightings should be reported. Add to that the fact that Florida has two different coasts, each with varying populations of horseshoe crabs, and the monitoring effort becomes a logistical nightmare.

Nevertheless, I asked Black to tell me a little about the monitoring effort as it applies specifically to Cedar Key. With her usual enthusiasm, she replied, "It doesn't seem like there has been a whole lot of fluctuation over the last several years." She took over the project in 2009. "Anecdotally, the residents say that you used to see thousands and thousands of them...you couldn't even walk without stepping on them," she said. "Now, you might find four hundred or more horseshoe crabs at any particular location...that's still a pretty high number."

"I have a good picture of Seahorse Key the way it used to be," Black said. She pulled out the photo of Seahorse Key, a small spit of land about two miles from Cedar Key. Pointing to the photo, she said, "That's a lot of animals there. I've never seen that large an abundance. I think that this was probably a common sighting about twenty years ago."

Black told me that Cedar Key is part of the Lower Suwannee and Cedar Keys National Wildlife Refuges. As a result, there's federal protection for the horseshoe crabs, and so neither locals nor tourists typically interfere with the spawning. "It may also have an impact on the stabilization of horseshoe crab populations around the state," she said. "That said, many of the locals around Cedar Key frequently testify that in the seventies and eighties there were considerably more crabs on the beaches than there are now."

I was eager to learn how the locals have embraced the notion of preserving these unique marine specimens. Once again, Black's eyes lit up. "They really do embrace the spawning survey," she said. "I get reports from all kinds of people regularly. Of course, a lot of 'snowbirds,' but local people, too. They're interested in the fact that the beach survey is going on. So, I have an exceedingly good response from our citizenry here. They come down, they go to the library, they see my poster, and they call it in. It makes them proud to have assisted in some way and makes them feel a part of the community."

Black's passion for public involvement in surveying horseshoe crabs was palpable, and her enthusiasm contagious. She told me, "I do like the idea that a public survey of these animals can give us so much information. I think that it engages the public in making a difference, and in ways they might never have looked at before. This survey is very positive, because it engages the public with something they may have not noticed before."

AFTER DEPARTING BLACK'S OFFICE, I SLOWLY COASTED INTO CEDAR Key, a tiny city, population 790, on a group of islands fifty miles southwest of Gainesville and three miles out into the Gulf of Mexico. The surrounding islands make up the Cedar Key National Wildlife Refuge. This is a town with plenty of charm to go around. There are no fast-food franchises; no hustle and bustle; and no noisy arcades, whirling amusement rides, or cheap souvenir stores. Most of the businesses are mom-and-pop operations housed in well-worn storefronts. Victorian buildings, traditional Cracker homes, long piers stretching out into the bay, outstanding seafood restaurants (try the broiled Florida grouper), and a slower pace of life are the norm. This is old-time Florida, a town that knows how to cater to snowbirds and other tourists without having to go over the top.

As I discovered later, Cedar Key is one of the oldest ports in Florida, and a town with a unique and memorable history. Cedar Key is named for the

Eastern Red Cedar (*Juniperus virginiana*), which once grew abundantly in the area. Harvesting red cedars, especially for pencil manufacturing, was very important to the development of northern Florida in the late 1800s and early 1900s. In 1849, German entrepreneur J. Eberhard Faber (you may recognize the name) arrived in the United States to hunt for splinter-free wood for pencils. He found abundant red cedar in Florida's Gulf Hammock/ Waccasassa Bay area between the Suwannee and Withlacoochee Rivers. He bought land and timber, floated logs to the Keys, and shipped logs to the family factory in Germany. In 1858, Faber built a slat mill at Atsena Otie Key and began shipping slats instead of logs. In 1862, he built the Faber Pencil Factory on New York's East River, near the current site of the United Nations, and supplied it with slats from his Atsena Otie mill. This practice was facilitated by the 1861 completion of David Yulee's Florida Railroad, which connected the Keys with Fernandina Beach on the east coast of Florida. Shortly thereafter, the Eagle Pencil Company followed Faber's lead, building its New York factory in 1868 and supplying it with red cedar slats from its own mill. The Eagle mill was built in 1876 on the site of the current Faraway Inn, which happened to serve as my overnight accommodations. The industry flourished around Cedar Key until the local resources were depleted and the slat mills were destroyed by a hurricane in 1896.

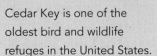

KEY FACT

Cedar Key is one of the oldest bird and wildlife refuges in the United States.

I checked into the Faraway Inn, a collection of funky cottages and rustic buildings painted in pastel colors and spread out over half a block of shaded flower gardens. Indeed, the scent of gardenias filled the air with memories of tropical rainforests and botanical gardens. This was definitely not a plastic and chrome Holiday Inn—and thank goodness for that! I quickly shed my traveling clothes, jumped into a pair of shorts and a T-shirt, and headed for the beach on the eastern rim of the island. High tide was scheduled for 4:15 p.m.

I pulled my rental car into a small parking lot fronting "Lil Shark Park" on the southeastern edge of Cedar Key. Slogging my way through the thick sand, I came upon a short beach, where two horseshoe crabs were in amplexus. The first thing I noticed was that these horseshoe crabs were considerably smaller than those I was accustomed to seeing on the beaches of the Delaware Bay. I also noted that their shells were much lighter in color than those of their northern cousins—a mystery I would solve sometime later in my investigations. The female had quite a collection of organisms—both flora and fauna—growing across her carapace; northern horseshoe crabs seemed to have fewer of these hitchhikers.

As with all horseshoe crabs, they were totally unconcerned about my observing them. "Blasé" was what I recorded in my notebook.

I watched as a single male crawled up out of the water. He paused for a few moments, perhaps realizing there were no immediate females in the area, and headed back out into the bay. Just as soon as he had dipped beneath the waves, he turned around and headed back toward shore (a change of mind, perhaps). He was apparently scouting the territory, and I began to slowly move with him as he tracked a path parallel to the shoreline. I wasn't sure whether he sensed a receptive female in the area, but he was moving with purpose and conviction. After about five minutes, unable to locate an appropriate mate, he finally turned into the waves and retreated into the Gulf.

I reached the end of the beach, where a concrete and stone jetty jutted out into the bay, forming an "L" with the shoreline. Clustered inside the angle of the "L" was a conglomeration of about fifty horseshoe crabs. Again, I noticed their smaller size and the fact that their shells were much lighter than I'm used to. There were about fifteen or twenty seagulls hopping in and out of the mass of horseshoe crabs, squawking and scratching and making their usual disturbance as they searched for eggs.

These horseshoe crabs seemed fairly laid back. There were only three or four females, each with a single clasping male. The females weren't really digging into the sand, and there were no satellite males. The remainder seemed to be resting. There wasn't much spawning going on, even though the tide was high and it was the middle of the season. The seagulls were making a lot of noise, but moving very little as they waited around for eggs to be deposited. Most of the gulls were dancing a sloppy "do-se-do" with the horseshoe crabs. One crow was trying his best to secure a handout, to no avail.

As I was standing on this tiny stretch of beach, I heard an old fisherman behind me. He was perched inside a small wooden structure on the jetty renting out all sorts of watercraft—canoes, kayaks, paddleboards—and dishing out free advice and information. He was clad in a pale pink shirt, green pants, and a salt-and-pepper beard that made him look like the figure on a package of Gorton's Fish Sticks. He was talking to a passing tourist, sharing facts and information about the horseshoe crabs. It was obvious he really knew his stuff. He was up to date on the horseshoe crab's anatomy, habitat, spawning cycles, and gender identification. He even passed out self-printed sheets that provided relevant information and listed related horseshoe crab websites.

A beach party of Florida *Limuli*.

To get a perspective on the size of the horseshoe crabs in front of me, I bent over and laid my right hand over a very compliant male resting on the sand. I continued my rudimentary measuring with other crabs, and noted that most were about the length of my hand—eight inches—and almost all were about an inch wider than my hand—five inches. A few of the females seemed to be a little larger, roughly ten inches by eight inches. I was amazed by the diminutive size of Florida horseshoe crabs.

As I was carrying out these measurements, a short, stocky man in his early thirties approached me and asked, "What the hell are those?" "Aha,"

I said to myself, "a chance to revert to my role as a college professor and do a little lecturing." And so I proceeded to give him a three-minute introduction to the horseshoe crab's evolutionary history, the basics of their anatomy, their approximate ages, and how they spawn. He told me, "I'm from Chicago, and we don't have those things in Lake Michigan."* I provided a few more details about this amazing creature ("Did you know it has ten eyes?"), and a look of absolute amazement spread across his face.

By now, I had a feeling that there must be some sort of sign on my back saying, "Ask this guy about the strange creatures on the beach," because after the Chicago man left, another man, a visitor from Norway, approached and asked me, "What are those things?" He, too, was amazed by the horseshoe crabs, and when I told him that their fossils have been discovered on the European continent, he stared at me with his mouth agape. Soon, four young boys stopped, equally fascinated by the actions of the horseshoe crabs on the beach. One of them asked, "Hey, mister, what would happen if I stepped on one of these?" He got a short explanation, but it wasn't exactly what he expected.

After about half an hour of explanations, descriptions, and narration for other beachgoers, I was finally left alone. Not only had people returned to their condos and rental units, the horseshoe crabs had slowly retreated back into the warm waters of the bay. I was exhausted from the long day, and so I made my way over to a seafood restaurant for a bottle of Corona and their sumptuous seafood special.

My alarm went off at 5:00 a.m. the next morning, and I leapt out of bed (well, okay, more like stumbled). High tide was scheduled for 6:12, and I wanted to see how many horseshoe crabs would make their way up the beach this crisp and breezy morning. After a quick shower and a granola bar, I crawled into my car and made my way back to Lil Shark Beach.

There was very little light, but I noticed a few isolated *Limulus* on the beach. I found one by itself and three others in a tight group nearby. The rough surf was causing a couple of problems for the guys, but they were persistent, if nothing else. It was completely dark, except for some ambient light from the condos and apartments to my left and the pier off to my right. The waves, about six inches in height, were breaking hard, and these creatures were struggling mightily to hold on to the sand.

---

* I was tempted to tell him that a 340-million-year-old ancestor of modern-day *Limulus* (*Paleolimulus longispinus*) has been discovered at Bear Gulch Creek, Montana, and that a Carboniferous (359-299 million years ago) specimen (*Paleolimulus avitus*) was discovered near Mazon Creek, Illinois. However, I decided I'd better not overextend my professorial welcome.

I flipped open my portable chair and placed it on the beach at the high-tide mark, just as a contingent of five horseshoe crabs crept out of the water and along the shoreline. There were two just off to my left and three just slightly off to my right. In short order, we were joined by two more males making their way slowly out of the rough surf. It didn't seem as though the conditions were ideal for spawning, but perhaps these were early morning scouts trying to get the lay of the land.

A cool breeze blew in from the bay, and the temperature was in the low seventies. The moon was waning (the full moon had been about five days earlier), and there was not a cloud in the sky. Like diamonds on black velvet, the stars were still twinkling, but on the beach, it was just me and the horseshoe crabs.

KEY FACT

Florida has 2,276 miles of tidal shoreline.

I counted six horseshoe crabs in front of me, fairly well spaced out. A few rested about seven feet to my left, and a couple more two feet to my right. Ten feet off to my right, a new guy was scurrying out of the surf. As quickly as he could, he crawled up above the high-tide mark, then turned around and crawled back down, then turned again and crawled back up. It seemed as though he couldn't make up his mind. He finally turned around once more, slowly crawled back into the waves, and headed outward.

Just off to my right, two more exited the surf and crawled onto the beach, and fifteen feet further off to my right, a single one came out of the surf. The two on my left moved back into the surf, as did two single ones to my right. At this point, there were eleven horseshoe crabs on the beach.

The waves were pounding the eleven stalwarts, who were just holding on to the sand as best they could. The moment of high tide arrived, and the faint glow of sunrise appeared on the horizon. The sky started to lighten just a little as day began to break. I watched the seaside drama for another thirty minutes, and then it was time to leave, at least for me.

I packed my bags and pushed them into the backseat of the rental car. Just before leaving Cedar Key, I walked over to the beach just off the western end of my hotel. As I stood there looking up and down the shoreline, I noticed an older (human) couple fifty yards up the beach to my right. As they walked along, they came upon a solitary horseshoe crab resting on the beach. They stopped to look at it and ponder what it was (it was apparent, even from my distance, that they were confused as to what it might be). Eventually, they continued on their way. Deciding to visit the horseshoe crab myself, I made my way down the beach. I immediately noticed that this solitary female had flipped over, so I bent down and gently righted her. Apparently, she had come up during the high tide three hours earlier. I watched as she gained purchase on the wet sand and very slowly began a methodical journey into the safety of the Gulf of Mexico. In less than two minutes, she had made her way into the darkening water and disappeared into the depths.

I HEADED UP THE COAST, ALONG RURAL AND QUITE DESERTED ROUTE 19/98. Traffic was sparse, the road was flat, and I zoomed between the wide stands of trees that lined both sides of the road like silent sentinels. It was as though the road had been cut through a dense and tangled forest; there were no dwellings, no strip malls, and few signs of human life. I later learned that this part of the state was one of the last to be settled, because the land was inhospitable for farming and there was little, if any, access to the gulf. This was a rugged landscape dotted with a few struggling towns and a superabundance of vegetation. You would not want to break down along this road.

I was headed eastward on U.S. Highway 98 to the tiny town of Panacea,* snuggled against the densely forested shoreline of Dickerson Bay. I had scheduled an interview with Anne Rudloe, one of Florida's leading experts on horseshoe crabs.

Dr. Rudloe grew up in coastal Virginia on the shores of the Chesapeake Bay, and she "was always running away to the ocean." In high school, she had an inspirational teacher who encouraged her to consider a career in biology. "At the time... This was in the 1960s, and women weren't really known for field biology, especially not marine science," she said. But Rudloe was hooked. After college, she "started applying to graduate school and knew I wanted to go to Florida, because I was tired of the mid-Atlantic winters, and at the time I had this idea that Florida was the hot place for marine science and oceanography." So she ended up at Florida State University as an oceanography master's degree student. After obtaining her degree in oceanography in 1972, she entered the university's doctoral program. One day, in a conversation with her advisor, Bill Herrnkind, and her future husband, Jack,

---

* In the early 1890s, Panacea was a resort town crowded with pastel hotels, restorative baths, and long wooden boardwalks. Tourists flocked here to soak in the abundant mineral springs. Interestingly, Panacea (Greek for "healing all") was actually the town's second name. The original name, Smith Springs, didn't quite have the marketing punch the locals were looking for in the late nineteenth century.

The Gulf Specimen Marine Lab in Panacea.

the topic turned to horseshoe crabs. Herrnkind said, "Oh, horseshoe crabs. We don't know anything about horseshoes crabs. They are really nice."

As Rudloe recalled, "It turned out to be a really good choice for a dissertation project, because the logistics were easy. I was proposing all kinds of logistically difficult problems that I didn't know how logistically difficult they were, how important that was. But we have a lot of horseshoe crabs in this area, so they were readily accessible. I was studying crabs on the beach, adult breeding beaches, and juveniles in tidal zones and nesting behavior. It turned out to be an animal that there wasn't much known about it at the time, so I got a lot of information very inexpensively, which was good, because I didn't have any money. That's how I got interested in it. When I finally defended my dissertation, somebody on the committee said, 'You didn't have to do this much work for a dissertation.'" She obtained her Ph.D. in biology in 1978 and started a career as an adjunct professor in biological sciences at Florida State—a position she has held ever since.

Rudloe and her husband also run the Gulf Specimen Marine Lab† in Panacea, a multibuilding enclave that's part nonprofit biological supply company, part research lab, part open-air schoolhouse, and all about the indigenous

---

† The Gulf Specimen Marine Lab (http://www.gulfspecimen.org/) supplies scientists, schools, and colleges (more than 1,300 clients) with sea horses, starfish, and crabs for academic research and teaching. York College, where I teach, orders all its sea urchins for biological dissection from the lab.

marine species of this corner of Florida. Nearly four hundred school groups and eighteen thousand visitors trek to this out-of-the-way attraction forty-five minutes southwest of Tallahassee each year. If you want to interact with sea creatures, stand shock-eyed over enclosures of oversized sharks, and observe tanks bristling with horseshoe crabs, spiny sea urchins, and dozens of creatures with scientific names longer than this sentence, this is the place.

When I arrived at the aquarium, I saw a phalanx of yellow school buses parked in front of the blue and white building, which is tucked into a forest of tightly woven slash pines and lush vegetation. An army of yelling, screaming kids filled the tropical atmosphere as I exited my car and made my way into the building. The friendly folks tending the store and ticket office directed me down the street to Rudloe's home, a stilt house converted from a World War II barracks that she and her husband had originally bought for a mere $500. The structure was cradled against the bay, with a 300-foot-long dock extending into the water and the resplendent shimmer of Florida sunshine bouncing off the glassy surface.

Inside, the house was unpretentious and plain, with comfortable furniture and large open windows allowing the soft afternoon breeze to dance through every room. A cacophony of birds and other wildlife pierced the afternoon. The view of a primeval forest of trees, dense Florida horticulture, and the bluest of skies reminded me of being on the top level of the Swiss Family Robinson tree house—except the Rudloe tree house is prowled by McDonald ("He eats everything and anything"), their very friendly and very large Maine Coon cat. McDonald jumped into my lap as soon as I sat down in a well-cushioned oversized chair—a chair on which he was apparently planning to take his afternoon nap.

Down-to-earth, straightforward, and casually dressed in a pink blouse and tan pants with no shoes, Rudloe was about as passionate about horseshoe crabs as anyone can get. After discussing her education and background, I asked her why these critters, and particularly the Florida population, are important.

"I think there's more concern now with conservation issues," she said, "and people are beginning to monitor them a little bit, but we constantly hear, 'When I was a kid in Pensacola, we saw them all over the beach, and now they are not there.' There isn't a kind of systematic work being done to see if they are declining, but I know they are extremely sensitive to red tides.* So, if you are in an area like south Florida where they have red tides

---

* A red tide is an overgrowth of microscopic marine algae. This overgrowth creates blooms

all the time, the horseshoe crabs are probably getting hammered. We had a red tide here in the late nineties, and it took ten years for the populations to recover. So if you have a red tide every two or three years, you are going to lose them. Whether that has anything to do with people making that comment so often, or whether it's just that when you get older, you just don't spend as much time on the beach and don't see them—it's not really clear."

She talked about this particular part of Florida, where there is still a lot of undeveloped coastline along the Gulf Coast. She made a clear distinction between this nearly pristine environment and the rampant industrial pollution in the Northeast. "The populations here are probably better off than they would be in more urban areas on the East Coast. Given that we have as much undeveloped coastline as we do on the Gulf Coast, that might eventually be a real stronghold for them," she said.

I wanted to know why the average person on the street should know or should care about Florida's horseshoe crabs. She told me, "It's one of the few really spectacular natural migrations that's readily available to see in reality, rather than on TV. The fact that they are medically important is enormous. Most people have no idea that there is any connection at all between our health and some animal out in the ocean. If you are at all interested in science, the fact that they are living fossils is very impressive. It makes us look at time in a different way."

When I asked about the most fascinating aspect of horseshoe crabs, she smiled and said, "Probably the way they use their environment to protect themselves. The nests are at the highest high tide, and the timing of the migration onto the beach [is] with the high tide. I don't think anyone has a clue yet about how the crabs determine that, and what the cues are. But that precise timing of the breeding puts the eggs in the safest possible place. The juveniles are active at low tide, which protects them from predators, because the hot sun doesn't have much that can harm them. They can come out at low tide and do their thing in relative safety. As they get bigger and move off shore, their sizes protect them from most predators, except sea turtles and sharks. I think that probably has something to do with why they have persisted for so long. They have escaped from most predators."

That Rudloe is passionate about these creatures is a given. But she was also quick to point out that there are volumes of information we still need to learn. "We need to learn what they're doing when they're not on breeding

---

that make the ocean appear red or brown. Red tides often release toxins that can kill large quantities of fish and other marine organisms.

beaches," she said. "They're like sea turtles; everybody studies them to death on breeding beaches. What are they doing out there the first week of March in thirty feet of water? How are they mobilizing, what's going on? How important are they in eighty feet of water? We don't know a thing about them, except for their tidal [behavior]. That's kind of typical of marine animals that have no great commercial value. We know so little about them."

She continued, "Yet, we talk about the idea that we are supposed to manage this planet ecologically. We are just continuing to trash it; we don't have the information we need. I'd rather think that biology in the last fifty years or so, in its rush to do molecular biology and genetics, has really dropped the ball on old-fashioned natural history." Ever the biologist, she lamented all the species for which we know so little. She pointed out that if we did have that information, we might be able to make better environmental decisions—not just short-term ones, but those that will stand the test of time.

"What would you most like to tell the world about horseshoe crabs?" I asked. Her answer was as crisp and precise as a politician's. "If you really want to see an awesome natural spectacle, this is an easy one to see," she said. "All you have to do is go during high tide, and go to a low-energy sandy beach in an area that is not too polluted, and you can see [the horseshoe crabs spawning]. It impresses people when they see it. When I was working on horseshoe crabs, people would see me fooling around with a horseshoe crab, and they would always come up and they would have three questions: what is it; can you eat it; well, what good is it? I always give them the standard speech about the [horseshoe crab] blood, and people would be happy. The human tendency to evaluate the value of everything on this planet by 'what good is it to humans' is a major part of what's causing the problems we have today."

KEY FACT

Florida horseshoe crabs are frequently cream-colored.

After our conversation, Rudloe took me back to the lab and gave me a one-on-one tour of the facilities. The Gulf Specimen Marine Lab contains roughly 8,500 square feet of interior exhibition space, with enough aquaria to hold 30,000 gallons of seawater. About two hundred species of marine animals are housed here, including sea turtles, myriad varieties of fish, sharks, seahorses, spiny lobsters, eels, and other assorted fauna. Again, Rudloe's passion for the sea shined through as she escorted me from room to room and tank to tank explaining the history of the place.

Rudloe may be proudest of the aquarium's role in educating the youth of Florida, many of whom have never touched, much less seen a marine organism outside of Discovery Channel or Animal Planet programs on TV. The screams and shouts of the youngsters earlier in the day testified to the fact that this is very much a hands-on place. Kids don't just see the creatures behind protective and sturdy glass barriers as they would in your everyday aquarium. Here, Rudloe and the kids roll up their sleeves and plunge their arms in right up to their shoulders to touch, feel, and go face-to-face with some of the most unique creatures of the sea. It's an experience they will not soon forget.

After snapping countless photos and taking voluminous notes, I slid back into my car and made my way back to U.S. Highway 98 to head south. As I journeyed along through the rustic countryside, I couldn't help thinking about Rudloe's parting words to me...prophetic words with particular importance to Florida residents and tourists.

"Go see them, and get in touch with the natural world that's beyond the pavement, and see what impact it has on your life," she said. "Make the effort. We are getting more and more disconnected [from the natural world]. The attendance of national parks is declining significantly. The baby boomers use them, but the next generations coming up are not. Go to a little aquarium where you can hold something—whatever it takes to see that there is something there beyond the human world. Learn to appreciate it."

I CONTINUED ON TO BALD POINT STATE PARK, ONE OF THE PLACES Rudloe recommended for sighting spawning horseshoe crabs. After a few miles, I made a left onto a side road and traveled through a very flat and sandy expanse of real estate. There were a few houses along this nearly empty road, but they were separated from each other by sand dunes and hillocks of tufted grass. After driving for several miles, I entered the park, donated the requisite four-dollar entrance fee to the Florida State Park System, and pulled into the parking area. I grabbed my beach shoes, portable chair, and camera, and I set out across the beach for the shoreline.

As soon as I walked out onto the wide and expansive beach, I could see dozens of horseshoe crabs sprinkled up and down the shoreline. Approaching the water, I came upon a grouping containing a single female with five satellite males clustered around her. Another group of four or five was off to my left, and about three feet away there was a large female with a single male attached. The clusters, for the most part, were small, a counterpoint to the masses of conjoined horseshoe crabs more typical in northeastern waters.

A conglomeration of horseshoe crabs at Bald Point State Park.

But just like the northerners, these clusters were scattered up and down the beach in an array of bulbous mounds flanked by flocks of chattering birds.

The birds were dipping and dancing in and out of the water. Many were skittering along the waterline, dipping their bills into the moist sand and plucking out tasty morsels. For the most part, the birds ignored the horseshoe crabs, zigging and zagging in and around the spawning beasts. I could identify sandpipers, black-headed gulls, and a half-dozen other birds skipping and hopping up and down the beach. The surf was breaking at four to five inches, and high tide wasn't due for about another half-hour or so, but there was quite a bit of activity going on.

I picked a spot on the beach directly in front of seven quite busy horseshoe crabs. I saw one on my left, a female and two satellite males about two feet to my right, another female coming up the beach, and one more female almost completely buried in the sand with a single male trying to get close enough to cast his seed across clusters of unseen eggs. The waves, six to eight inches in height, were relentlessly pushing and shoving paired horseshoe crabs in several different directions at once. It's one of Mother Nature's constant struggles: the power of the ocean against the powers of reproduction.

The wave action brought another male over and swept him into the mix on my right-hand side. He was tumbling about, the wave knocking him over momentarily, but after about ten seconds he was able to right himself, and he then became a satellite male to the female just slightly to my left. There were now three males interested in this single female.

Another female tumbled by from right to left, the water pushing her over and over as she attempted to right herself. She tried to get purchase on the shore, but she was not very successful. Two new satellite males who had suddenly appeared out of the waves approached the female to my right.

This female was soon approached by yet one more male who had been washed up by the waves. She was beginning to come up out of the sand, apparently done with her spawning, but at least two of the males were persistent in their clasping. The female slowly turned and began plowing her way back down into the bay, pushing an awful lot of sand in front of her. One male gave up, but the smaller male was clasping onto her with a vengeance. Another washed up, and he, too, wanted to get in on the action.

It was now about fifteen minutes before high tide. Two females, each with two males clasping them tightly, were directly in front of me. Closer to the wave action was a solitary female with no males nearby. As is always the case with a group orgy, the dynamics changed rapidly. The males would get swept down by the waves and find themselves tumbling past a ready female, or they would get lucky and get close enough to a female to grab on to her.

High tide arrived at 5:28 p.m. There were still strings of horseshoe crabs all the way up the beach to my right and long lines of horseshoe crabs all the way down the beach to my left, with trios or pairs every four to five feet. It was a spawning extravaganza as far as the eye could see in either direction. It was time for me to leave and search for my own food sources, but I knew my attentions would not be missed by any of the creatures that now laid claim to this beach.

THE NEXT MORNING STARTED EARLY AGAIN, AS I ROSE AT 5:30 A.M. IN order to catch the high tide at 7:58. I headed to nearby Mashes Sands State Beach, which, I had been told by both Black and Rudloe, is a prime area for spawning horseshoe crabs.

The morning was foggy, and the lights in the motel parking lot cast an eerie glow. Dense fog hung over the roadway as I made my way southward to Mashes Sands. I was the only person on the road, and as my headlights tried to pierce the mist, I somehow felt as though I was in some bad science fiction movie with a mysterious figure ready to lurch out of the woods at my car. I turned up the volume on a Van Morrison CD, and the frightening images quickly vanished.

Mashes Sands is a beautiful expanse of hillocks and dunes. This morning, a fiery sun was rising over the Gulf of Mexico. As I set out on the beach,

I met an old man and his dog. I asked him if he had seen any horseshoe crabs on his travels, and he told me there was not a one to be found on the beach this morning.

I walked for nearly a mile down the beach, my only company congregations of shorebirds and a few itinerant crows. The birds danced beside the lapping waves, occasionally weaving in and out of the sea grass that poked its way up out of sandy hillocks. They were looking for tiny morsels of food for their morning meal. There was not a single horseshoe crab in sight. Finally, I saw a solitary sandpiper and an equally solitary egret along a spit of sea grass. They eyed me warily as I snapped their photograph. They were patiently waiting for their food to come in on the gentle waves that rolled in from the gulf.

High tide arrived at 7:58. A raucous crow perched on a sign ("Warning: no lifeguard on duty"), birds skittered up and down the beach, the sun rose over the gulf...but the crabs were absent. Perhaps they had all gone home for spring break. Perhaps tides and time had signaled the end of another season, the end of another orgy.

LATER THAT EVENING, I RETURNED TO MASHES SAND BEACH FOR ONE last viewing. High tide was scheduled for 6:07 p.m., and I was hoping to catch a final glimpse of the arthropod tourists from the gulf. As in the morning, the beach seemed lonely and empty. I decided to head off to my left, where a long expanse of sand dunes, small hillocks, sea grasses, rippling waves, handfuls of birds, and the lines and curves that characterized this remote environment lay before me. Soon after I set out, I saw a familiar shape beside a small patch of sea grass. Approaching, I noticed it was a stranded horseshoe crab, an upside-down male waving his telson plaintively in the air. I picked him up and gently turned him over. He waited a few moments, as if contemplating the deserted beach one last time. I was immediately reminded of the final scene in *Where the Boys Are*, where the human characters, too, are reluctant to leave their little slice of paradise. They, like so many visitors, pause on the sand one last time, consolidating the memories and cherishing the view.

Then, the horseshoe crab slowly...ever so slowly...scuttled into the water. Once in the surf, it slid across the bottom and out into deeper water. I watched as it slithered through the ever-deepening muck of the gulf and out of sight. But, just as college students migrate to Florida shores each spring, it too would return.

CHAPTER 11

"To Protect This Remarkable Mariner"

How an Intrepid Band of Citizens is Defending Horseshoe Crabs

B
Y NOW, YOU ARE AWARE OF MY YOUTHFUL INFATUATION WITH alien creatures, reanimated prehistoric critters, and bad-tempered monsters. But I also had another predilection during my formative years: I was a hero-worshiper. I loved reading about brave men who could vanquish evil, combat dastardly villains, and confront crime wherever it might occur. I devoured Marvel comic books, consumed Hardy Boys mysteries, and embraced the exploits of Superman and Batman. Many of my youthful champions were TV characters: the Cisco Kid,* Hopalong Cassidy,† Davy Crockett ("King of the Wild Frontier"),‡ and, of course, the Lone Ranger.

Every Sunday evening at 7:30, the Lone Ranger would ride out of the ABC television network and into our living room. Each week, I got to ride with the masked stranger as he defeated enemies, rooted out evil, and made the West a better place to live. Each week was a new adventure, a new episode about the cleansing power of good over evil.

---

* *The Cisco Kid* (1950-1956) is notable for being the first television series filmed in color.

† *Hopalong Cassidy* was the first network Western series (June 1949).

‡ The actor who played Davy Crockett—Fess Parker—later went on to run an award-winning winery and vineyard in Los Olivos, California. As a child, I had an official Davy Crockett coonskin hat, which I wore everywhere. Just imagine what that hat would be worth today on eBay.

Of course, nothing is more emblematic of that now-classic show than the opening musical theme and narration:

[Opening theme music: "William Tell Overture"]
Announcer: The Lone Ranger.
Background Voice: Hiyo, Silver.
Announcer: A fiery horse with the speed of light, a cloud of dust, and a hearty "Hiyo, Silver." The Lone Ranger!
Background Voice: Hiyo, Silver...away!
Announcer [extremely serious now]: With his faithful Indian companion, Tonto, the daring and resourceful masked rider of the plains led the fight for law and order in the early West. Return with us now to those thrilling days of yesteryear. [Almost shouting.] *The Lone Ranger rides again.*
[Theme music continues.]*

Many years ago, noted anthropologist Margaret Mead opined, "Never doubt that a small group of thoughtful, committed citizens can change the world. Indeed, it is the only thing that ever has." That statement serves as a template for dedicated groups of individuals who wish to make a difference—who, much like the Lone Ranger and Tonto, enjoy a moral challenge. In many ways, it is also the mission of the Ecological Research & Development Group (ERDG).

As you have discovered, horseshoe crabs go through life trying only to survive, spawn, and continue the species. While our focus in this book has been on the American horseshoe crab, the three species that live in Asia have the same ultimate goal in life. It's a focus that has been maintained for several million years, but it is sometimes at odds with the desires of human beings.

For one thing, humans like you and I have a tendency to want to play, live, and work near the seashore—the very places horseshoe crabs need to procreate. Because numerous horseshoe crabs die from stranding on beaches during the spawning season each year, their carcasses create an odorous and untidy shoreline, often in areas where the value of luxury homes, sprawling condominiums, and high-priced resorts depends on a pristine environment. As a result, these prehistoric beasts are often reviled and vilified. Many people think of horseshoe crabs as something to get rid of rather than an

---

* This one minute and thirteen second bit of narration and theme music has been preserved by The Lone Ranger Fan Club (http://www.lonerangerfanclub.com). Unfortunately, the club does not offer members classic premiums such as the official Lone Ranger Six-Shooter Ring or the official Lone Ranger Deputy Badge. Darn!

important element of the seashore ecosystem worthy of preservation. Far too many people see the negatives in horseshoe crabs rather than the positives.

But this situation also presents a unique opportunity, because it is here, in the areas where humans and crabs comingle, that a new conservation framework is being established; not one of rules and regulations, but one built on the basis of ownership.

Founded in 1995, the Ecological Research & Development Group (ERDG), the world's leading environmental group dedicated to the preservation of horseshoe crabs, has a philosophy unlike other considerably larger and more visible environmental entities. ERDG believes that building an engaged community is the best way to approach wildlife conservation, and that a community, if given the chance, will achieve more than a (typical) "conservation through regulation" approach. The philosophical anchor of ERDG is the belief that an engaged community is more aware of changes in the environment; is best positioned to educate neighbors and visitors; and is more likely to assist stranded or injured animals, help with scientific analysis, shape public opinion, and report infractions of regulations.

For example, many environmental initiatives consist of laws, rules, and regulations that take time to draft, time to review, time to implement, and even more time to achieve significant results. But those rules and regulations often fail to regulate human behavior—particularly when people think the legislation conflicts with economic growth or their individual livelihoods. In fact, the regulatory process, because it is "top down" rather than "bottom up," frequently alienates the very communities that should be assisting in the stewardship of the natural resource.

ERDG thinks differently. It tries to save horseshoe crabs by giving communities a sense of ownership in the task of preserving this species. Communities can "buy into" the process, instead of having the process forced on them. When people feel that ownership, the group achieves a self-sustaining and long-lasting energy. Ultimately, horseshoe crabs are given a new lease on life.

LITTLE CREEK IS A VERY, VERY SMALL TOWN IN SOUTHERN DELAWARE.[†]
I went there to visit with Glenn Gauvry, tireless promoter of horseshoe crabs everywhere and president of ERDG. Gauvry's house is one of those classic

---

† According to the U.S. Census Bureau estimate of July 2009, "Little Creek has an elevation of 10 feet; a population of 218; a land area of 0.14 sq. miles; a water area of 0 sq. miles; and a population density of 1,568.35 people per sq. mile."

two-story wooden houses often found in small towns in Delaware. Built in 1790 (it's on the National Register of Historic Places), the house is a mere stone's throw from the Little Creek Wildlife Area. It's an equally short distance from Cattail Gut, Taylor's Gut, and Old Woman's Gut ("gut" is a local term for a small creek). The front room of this piece of colonial American history is also the headquarters of ERDG.

Gauvry looks like he just stepped off the set of a 1960s TV western (he would be one of the good guys). A practicing Buddhist,* Gauvry greeted me clad in a traditional Japanese kimono and graciously offered me a warm cup of tea. We both recalled that we had met several years earlier on Broadkill Beach on a chilly May evening (see the Introduction). We spent the next two hours in a conversation that was comfortable as well as informative.

Gauvry became an environmentalist in a roundabout way. Initially trained as an air traffic controller by the Air Force, he eventually got his BFA in woodworking and design. In the late 1980s, while running a woodworking factory, he started to become more environmentally concerned. He started to think about the effect harvesting certain woods was having on the rainforest, and the impact some finishes were having on the environment.

"So it was just kind of a conservation, environmental awareness that…I don't know…I guess it had always been part of my mind but had never really been in the forefront," he said. Gauvry started looking for opportunities to do something about it, and ended up, through a series of events, meeting a group in Delaware that was well-known for traveling around the world rehabilitating native wildlife impacted by oil spills.

He began to do volunteer work with them. After a couple of years, he shut down his woodworking business and moved entirely over to wildlife rehabilitation, specializing in oil-spill response. In 1996, he worked on the enormous oil spill from the Sea Empress off the coast of Wales. "There were several thousand animals all oiled, waiting to be cleaned, and you could only deal with so many per day; if you're lucky, fifty," he said. "At the end of the day, you're still looking at a thousand, and you knew that many were going to die because you could not get to them in time. It was right around that

---

* In early 2011, Gauvry received a certificate that in part states, "…who has in many past lifetimes learned Buddhism and engaged in cultivation….The Commission of Holy Virtuous Ones From Around the World Respectfully Invited by International Buddhism Sangha Association to Seek and Recognize, has recognized you as such a reincarnated one, with the qualifications of a *rinpoche* who transmits *dharma*, and has given you the *dharma* name Sangjie Tieba." The term *rinpoche* literally means "jewel among men."

ERDG is the leading organization devoted to protecting horseshoe crabs.

time where I just really started to burn out from years and years of being on the mop-up end of environmental problems and watching countless numbers of animals die from human activities. And I decided that I longed to be more proactive, kind of get on the front end of this thing." We were less than ten minutes into our conversation, and I could already sense his passion and commitment.

It was then that Gauvry decided to start ERDG. "Initially, the focus was to work anywhere, actually, to prevent or mitigate the damage to native wildlife populations from human activity," he said. "So anywhere there was a rub between humans and the native wildlife population, we could insert ourselves. And that was the original mission. I followed a voice and wasn't necessarily driven by education. The education had to be acquired to do what the voice required of me. But the voice was what was pushing me along, not the education."

Gauvry is the driving force that keeps ERDG focused and on task. It was clear from early in our conversation that he has the responsibility to solicit funds, promote initiatives, and corral several different—often competing—interests.

"One of my primary responsibilities is to be the moral compass," he explained. "ERDG probably could be much larger and be doing much better financially, if we were willing to bend the rules in ways that I see a lot of environmental groups do in order to generate financial support."

Gauvry noticed the furrows on my brow. "Why," I was thinking to myself, "wouldn't an environmental group want to do everything in its power to generate as much money as possible?"

His response to my furrows was refreshing. "When I first started this group," he said, "I was rather surprised at how cutthroat the environmental and the nonprofit organizations are. Everybody thinks that we're calm and happy and peaceful with one another. But everybody's competing for the same pool of dollars, whether it be a grant, favors for the foundation, or the public for public support. A lot of times, the public will get something that says, 'If we don't have your support now, this will be lost forever'…and there'll be sometimes these really tear-jerky type of ads, you know, the…"

I interjected, "…sea turtle with tears."

With a slight grin on his face, he continued, "Well, no, the dog that has just been rescued from a pit, you know, fighting…that sort of thing. And then there'll be some music in the background, and that will pull at your heartstrings, and 'we need your help right this minute.' I can't do that. I've just never been able to play that game." Gauvry pointed out that the moral compass is his focus on the mission of the organization,* not on efforts to

---

* "Our mission is to seek solutions that prevent or mitigate damage to native wildlife populations and habitats due to human activities. ERDG accomplishes this goal through scientific research and development, environmental planning and management, and public education. ERDG works to inspire and assist individuals, communities, and organizations to solve problems, change behaviors, and promote sound decisions in order to achieve sustainable ecosystems. ERDG believes environmental stewardship can thrive within a

solicit money from the pockets of citizens or the coffers of giant corporations. "I think that my primary function is having the vision of where we need to be going and to see around that corner, and to have the moral compass to not lose sight of why we do what we do, and why we feel that what we do is important," he said.

Running an environmental group can sap the energy of even the most dedicated conservationist. Gauvry knew that he and his burgeoning group couldn't tackle the issues in isolation; they needed the strength of numbers if they were to have any significant effect on what was, at that time, perceived to be an endangered population. To do this they conceived of a sanctuary program, initially called Backyard Stewardship. They realized that most of the residents of the Delaware shoreline didn't like horseshoe crabs, and they knew it would be crazy to even suggest to those residents that they should start liking them.

Gauvry told me how every year the shoreline would be hammered by winter storms, and every spring, the residents would petition the state to come in and dredge those beaches. But there was little commerce along those beaches to justify the expense of replenishing the shoreline. Gauvry and his merry band of environmentalists told the community that if they could demonstrate to the state that they had an interest larger than themselves, larger than the value of their real estate, they would have a better argument when they talked to the state about why they should

KEY FACT

Adult horseshoe crabs can go for months without eating.

get replenishment dollars. Gauvry proposed that they become a horseshoe crab sanctuary. Amazingly, 95 percent of the community members signed on to the first sanctuary, because it was a way for them to get sand in their backyards.

That same environmental vision drives the organization today. For example, once a community decides to become a sanctuary, ERDG gives them an interpretive sign about horseshoe crabs and the community's commitment to protect and conserve them. Each community is also required to prepare a written statement as to why it chose to become a sanctuary. Groups form, committees organize, and the citizens begin to coalesce. Eventually, there's some local media coverage, and the group gets some traction. Citizens start

growing economy through healthy partnerships between industry, government, environmental groups, and communities." (www.horseshoecrab.org)

to become proud of something they accomplished, something they banded together to preserve.

With just the slightest twinkle in his eye, Gauvry told me, "It's a paradigm shift, and then they're with their friend from Philadelphia, and they're walking down the beach, and instead of walking down the beach with total indifference to the stranded horseshoe crabs, they stop and flip them over. Then their friend says, 'Well, why did you do that?' and they start to tell them the story about horseshoe crabs. Now they're educators, and what we found was that over time they started to become a community concerned about the resource and the words that they put on the sign. But in the beginning, it was self-serving. And I find that with lots of people out there, and I'm okay with that. I'm going to get you one way or the other, if I can, to get involved, and then hopefully I'm going to be able to work that crack into something a little bit wider, and then that's kind of the way we started and the way we continue to do business."

ERDG is the only organization that has been successful in convincing residential landowners to designate their private beaches as horseshoe crab sanctuaries. In addition to its first sanctuary at Broadkill Beach, ERDG has also enrolled the communities of Kitts Hummock, Pickering Beach, Slaughter Beach, and Prime Hook National Wildlife Refuge (Fowler Beach) in Delaware, and it is continuing its work in establishing additional horseshoe crab conservation areas in communities up and down the Atlantic coast. To date, more than twelve miles of prime horseshoe crab spawning habitat has been protected through this program. Ultimately, ERDG's goal is to protect the horseshoe crab spawning habitat throughout its spawning range worldwide. While that goal is ambitious, Gauvry and the other members of ERDG know that the future survival of the world's four horseshoe crab species ultimately depends on the preservation of its spawning habitat...and the involvement of dedicated citizens.

"But why horseshoe crabs?" I asked. "Of all the animal species you could have picked to protect, why horseshoe crabs?"

His response was certain and rock solid. "Nobody really was taking an advocacy role for the horseshoe crab, and that was what really stepped us up," he said. "These animals needed an advocate. Nobody was doing it. Here we are at the world's epicenter of horseshoe crabs, and there's no advocate. That just shocked me, the day I realized that. Of all the environmental groups, we're at the epicenter of a species that's in decline, and nobody was stepping up to be their voice."

I asked, "Does every animal need an advocate?"

Gauvry paused for a moment, the wheels turning in his head. "That depends," he responded. "You can get into all kinds of issues trying to answer that question. On one hand, you could say that species do decline. Species do go extinct. That's just the way it is. That's the way it has always been. This isn't any different. And you could say, well, this particular species, for example, has been around for 445 million years through five great extinctions. It has handled what has been thrown at it quite well. All of a sudden, we're throwing at it changes at a rate that's too rapid for it to move through. Should we care? What would it matter if horseshoe crabs weren't around?

"When you start to go that way, you could say, well, maybe they need an advocate," he continued. "Maybe they need some help to balance and give them a little bit of a fair, level playing field. However, some species don't need that, so they don't necessarily need an advocate. There are people that step up because they like a particular critter and start a foundation or an organization around it to have what it looks like this particular critter needs, but the critter could find it without humans ever being involved. In fact, it would probably prefer it. But I think, if the critter is having a hard time because of an artificially imposed obstacle like us, particularly along coastlines and habitats, it needs some help."

In 1998, ERDG launched its Just flip 'em! Program to bring attention to the high mortality* horseshoe crabs incur from being stranded upside-down during spawning, and to encourage, through a simple act of compassion, an appreciation for this remarkable creature. The program seemed almost too simple…too obvious…for an animal rights group to propose. "Why devote time and effort to a project with no economic benefits?" I asked.

"We started the Just flip 'em! Program many years ago, and that one has caught on…and it has caught on up and down the coast," he said. "But what you've got is, you've got people who used to bury crabs in holes. Here in Delaware, they'd get backhoes and just bury them under. Now they're flipping them over, and the first thing that they start to realize is the thousands that are dying on the beach, smelling up their beach and drawing flies and making recreational activity somewhat unpleasant, the vast majority would have gone back in the water if they had just been flipped over. That's the first thing we started hearing from these communities—it's like, 'Geez, we have a lot less horseshoe crabs to die on the beach.'"

---

* Studies have shown that as much as 10 percent of the spawning horseshoe crab population die each year from being stranded upside down during spawning.

Gauvry recounted how he used to sit in on the council meetings at Slaughter Beach, one of the large spawning beaches in Delaware. A couple of years ago, one of the issues at the meeting was whether they would get the tractor fixed that year, because they only used the tractor to go down on the beach and pull this big wagon to collect dead horseshoe crabs. "But the community decided that, as a result of flipping over horseshoe crabs, there were so few crabs dying on the beach they could live with that, and they didn't need to spend their little bit of budget money on the tractor. So that's a program that I really like," he said.

ERDG sponsors a variety of environmental initiatives that encourage elementary and high school students to become stewards for these ancient creatures. Outreach efforts to young people include the Horseshoe Crabs & the Arts Competition and the Horseshoe Crab Conservation and the Arts In-School Program. The Arts Competition is for poems, stories, and images by students from prekindergarten through twelfth grade. ERDG's ultimate goal is to engage students around the world and encourage them to express their appreciation for this remarkable creature through their art. In the Arts In-School Program, a visiting instructor conducts classes that both introduce students to the wonders of horseshoe crabs and teach the students to make handmade paper.

Gauvry explained these two related projects to me: "Years ago, we started the Young Voices program. Originally, it started off to be a drawing contest, and we were mainly focused on—and we still are—focused on your expression: how do you feel? You can talk about the science if you want, but it better be right. I'm not so interested in the kids regurgitating what they've read. I really want to know how they feel. And so we encourage teachers to tap into that. Our In-School Program with our people is geared more toward that expression, and so these kids started this rolling, and then we would get these poems, and then we were starting to get a few too many. It was like, all right, poems…it's drawing and poems. And then we started to get stories, so then it was, okay, drawings and stories. We've gotten some origami and some sculptures."

Each year, ERDG receives between five hundred and seven hundred entries from around the world, of which about thirty-five to forty are selected

KEY FACT

At night, a horseshoe crab's photoreceptors in its compound eyes become up to a million times more sensitive to light.

for the ERDG website. Entries have come from as far away as Mexico, Japan, Singapore, and Taiwan. The winners have also been displayed in selected galleries around the world, from the Perkins Center for the Arts in New Jersey and the Cheltenham Art Center in Philadelphia to a traveling exhibit that recently toured Japan.

By this point in our conversation, Gauvry was bubbling over with excitement. "So that's a program, a program I like a lot," he said. "There's a poem that I'd like to share with you. Can I read you something?"

"Absolutely," I replied, caught up in his enthusiasm.

"Now, in Japan, they don't have many horseshoe crabs. Their population of horseshoe crabs is maybe a few thousand spawning pairs for the whole country," he continued. "But there's a connection through mythology in Japan between the crabs and the samurai. In fact, if you look at the Japanese horseshoe crabs, they almost look like samurai helmets. This one particular girl, Ashley Tomasello from Lambertville, New Jersey, was knowledgeable about Japanese mythology and the use of horseshoe crabs in the biomedical industry. She was in ninth grade when we selected her poem [in 2003] called 'The Samurai,' and I'll read it for you:

The Samurai
Once the great shores,
were guarded and protected,
by warriors fierce and strong.
Adorned, these were
by mantles of fine armor,
with helmets set upon their brow.

No more are these shores watched,
by those unflagging sentinels.
Their bodies have returned,
to the sand,
from whence they came.
Their people now fall to shadow,
with no guardian remaining.

But in the moonlight,
upon the sand,
comes to shore,
the embodiment of their spirit.

Waves billow, and on them ride,

those helmets that once adorned the brow,

of warriors of old.

The souls are in these creatures,

of those fierce and strong.

And in each drop of blood they give,

their people go on.*

Gauvry noticed the awestruck expression on my face. "Isn't that cool?" he asked. "And the blood she's talking about is LAL. I read this to a group of biologists in Huntsville, Alabama, where NASA was doing research on LAL in space, and they were absolutely spellbound. I've yet to get a crowd, when they hear this, they just go, 'Whoa!' These kids do stuff like this. And they move us. That's that spark we were talking about earlier, the voice that leads you."

One of ERDG's most innovative initiatives has been the Alternative Gear and Supplemental Bait project. As described in Chapter 4, a number of years ago waterman Frank Eicherly came up with an innovation—a bait bag—that drastically cut back on the number of crabs he was using for bait. According to Gauvry, "He was cutting back his bait by 50 percent. We [ERDG] got involved in a study with [the] Virginia [Institute of Marine Science] to validate those claims—which were correct. So based on that, we produced the bait bags and manufactured them, then made some modifications.... We distributed them free of cost to watermen up and down the Atlantic coast. The Atlantic States Marine Fisheries Commission now attributes that device and that effort on our part as being one of the single largest conservation measures affecting horseshoe crab populations..., and a lot of the watermen have gone on to modify these devices to make them more efficient. Some of them are only using one-eighth. This has also allowed them to live with the regulations."

Late afternoon sunlight was reflecting off the walls of Gauvry's cozy living room. By this point in the conversation, I couldn't help but think of Margaret Mead's quote and how a small organization such as ERDG so beautifully epitomizes the power of that statement. But I was also curious about an equally pressing issue.

"Why should someone in Kansas or Montana or New Mexico care, or think about, or be concerned with horseshoe crabs?" I asked.

---

* Tomasello, Ashley. "The Samurai." Lambertville, NJ: South Hunterdon Regional School (Ninth Grade). 2003.

Glenn Gauvry says, "Horseshoe crabs are a metaphor for a much larger issue."

Gauvry paused for a moment and then responded, "You know, I can make the whole biomedical connection. I can connect every man, woman, and child and domestic animal in the world—if you use medical services—to the horseshoe crab. So [if] you don't want to see testing go back to the millions of rabbits that we used to use, then you should be concerned, because I don't see in the near future you're going to stop having your kids vaccinated and your animals vaccinated, or you're going to stop using saline solution. You're not going to have knee replacements and hip replacements and all the other things that we are required to test for the presence of endotoxins, and we use the horseshoe crab's blood in the test."

I wanted to press him a little more and asked, "So, is one of the goals of ERDG to change the public's perception?"

Gauvry smiled and said, "Yes. That's the moral compass. I find that horseshoe crabs are a metaphor for a much larger issue. It's the lack of compassion in the world for things we don't understand, and things that don't at first blush appeal to us, and as we grow [into] a society with an even shorter attention span. I think that we don't give ourselves enough time to ask ourselves why, if it's not warm and fuzzy and doesn't make a nice sound, we move on. The horseshoe crab requires us to slow down a little bit and really start to question things. Humans should examine things that might not necessarily look all that friendly or all that inviting, find that if they pry and probe a little bit they can actually find a reason to care. Then they could do that with anything. They can do it with their next-door neighbor who doesn't share their views. They could do it with someone who is grossly disfigured as a result of an accident. They could do it with just about anything. You know, it's peeling back that aesthetic or that, you know, that image, that illusion that we carry of what's good and what's not good. So to me, why should someone in Kansas care? They should, because it's a model to look at, to probe your own mind, to search your own heart a little deeper."

"So ERDG is a model?" I ask.

"I like to think we are," he responded with a genuine smile.

Shadows began to slip around the window curtains when I asked Gauvry for his final thoughts on horseshoe crabs and the work ERDG does on their behalf. He pondered the query for a few moments and replied, "Horseshoe crabs will not survive your indifference. I would say indifference, ignorance, and intolerance are really three words I would use. But ignorance and indifference is what really plagues [them]…indifference is really the biggest obstacle that they have."

As I drove out of Little Creek, I couldn't help but think that we could easily replace the term "horseshoe crabs" in Gauvry's quote above with names such as "California condors," "Hawaiian monk seals," "polar bears," or dozens of other endangered species, and its import would not be lost. Suffice it to say, ERDG knows that indifference, perhaps more than financial resources, four-color brochures, or extensive membership lists, is the ultimate stumbling block for any environmental effort. It is also the crucial determinant for the group's future success…and the preservation of an ancient species.

THE LONE RANGER WAS A CLASSIC OF EARLY TELEVISION. HARDLY A week went by that my friends and I didn't discuss the latest episode about "the masked man and his faithful Indian companion." When I compare *The Lone Ranger* with some of the shows currently on TV, it seems like a message from another world. Did you know that the Lone Ranger

- never kissed a girl;

- never shot to kill, only to disarm;

- never drank, cussed, or smoked;

- never accepted reward money;

- never showed his face to anyone but Tonto;

- always respected the rights and beliefs of others; and

- always upheld a moral code?

This moral code underscored each radio and television episode. In fact, the writers of the show were required to include elements of it in every episode. While, as a young lad, I was not aware of the specifics of the code, it seemed as though every show and every plot revolved around one or more of its values in some particular way.

Here are three (of nine) elements of that code, as listed on the Lone Ranger Fan Club website (www.lonerangerfanclub.com):

> "I believe:
> - That…everyone has within himself the power to make this a better world.
> - In being prepared…to fight when necessary for that which is right.
> - That sooner or later…we must settle with the world and make payment for what we have taken."*

As I reflected on my interview with Gauvry, I couldn't help but think that if the Ecological Research & Development Group had a written code, it would in all likelihood be very similar to the code of the Lone Ranger.

Hiyo, Silver…away!

---

* "The Lone Ranger's Creed: The Moral Code Upheld by the Masked Man." Copyright Random House. Used with permission.

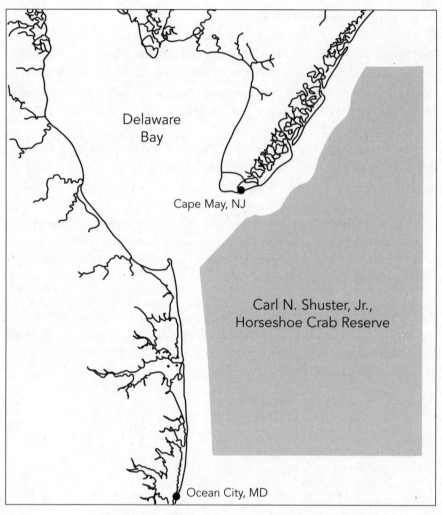

Delaware
Bay

Cape May, NJ

Carl N. Shuster, Jr.,
Horseshoe Crab Reserve

Ocean City, MD

Boundaries of the Carl N. Shuster, Jr., Horseshoe Crab Reserve.

A Friend in Need is a Friend Indeed

One Man and His Lifelong Passion for *Limulus*

VERY FEW OF US WILL EVER HAVE A MUNICIPAL COURTHOUSE, college building, bridge, freeway, or battleship named in our honor. Those rewards are reserved for the very distinguished, the very famous, or the very political. Former Mississippi Senator Trent Lott has a middle school, an airport, an academic building, and dozens of other sites throughout his home state festooned with his name. More than thirty buildings, a bridge, and a telescope in West Virginia all bear the name of the late Senator Robert Byrd. A dozen presidents have had submarines named after them, ten presidents have had aircraft carriers named after them, and three presidents (Abraham Lincoln, George Washington, and Theodore Roosevelt) have had both.

Hordes of tourists regularly visit our nation's capital just to snap photos of the Lincoln Memorial and the Washington Monument. While some politicians get their names on buildings and shopping malls while alive, some of our most celebrated Americans have had to wait in line. The Lincoln Memorial wasn't constructed until more than fifty years after Lincoln's death, while the submarine USS Abraham Lincoln (SSBN-602) was commissioned on March 11, 1961, and the aircraft carrier USS Abraham Lincoln (CVN-72) was commissioned on November 11, 1989, one hundred and twenty-four years after his assassination. The Washington Monument was completed eighty-nine years after our first president passed away, and the Jefferson Memorial wasn't completed until

1943, one hundred and seventeen years after the third president's death.

University buildings named for generous donors, soaring steel bridges named after doddering politicians, and national monuments named for presidents are all part of our cultural landscape. However, in 2001 the National Marine Fisheries Service did something most unusual: it established the Carl N. Shuster, Jr., Horseshoe Crab Reserve in federal waters off the mouth of the Delaware Bay estuary. The reserve's southern boundary lies just north of Ocean City, Maryland, and the northern boundary is just south of Atlantic City, New Jersey. No commercial harvesting of horseshoe crabs is allowed within the sanctuary's waters. To the best of my knowledge, Shuster is the only individual in this country who has had some 31,069,566,054,489.6 gallons* of the Atlantic Ocean named in his honor.

The sanctuary is named for the distinguished Carl N. Shuster, Jr., the world's leading authority on the American horseshoe crab and an adjunct professor of marine science at the College of William and Mary (a quick glance at the bibliography at the end of this book will reveal his influence). In May 2000, Shuster recommended to the Atlantic States Marine Fisheries Commission (ASMFC) that a sanctuary on the continental shelf off Delaware Bay be established to protect both spawning female horseshoe crabs and immature juveniles. Shuster has long been concerned about the current and future danger of commercial overharvesting of horseshoe crabs in this region. A draft environmental impact statement was prepared, circulated, and approved, and the reserve was officially established on March 7, 2001.

I'LL ADMIT, I'M NOT A BIG FAN OF WASHINGTON, D.C., TRAFFIC. TRYING to find one's way through the maze of highways, freeways, routes, bypasses, arterial routes, main routes, offramps, onramps, and the usual traffic congestion in and around our nation's capital is frequently a lesson in frustration.

On this particular sojourn, I was on my way to Arlington, Virginia, a quaint suburban neighborhood just across the river from D.C., to interview

---

* My colleague, the always approachable mathematician Jim Troutman, had to hold my hand for these calculations: The sanctuary is 1,500 square nautical miles (1,986.44 square miles) in size, with an average depth of 75 feet. Multiply 1,986.44 by 75, then multiply that number (148,983) by 5,820 feet, and then by 5,820 feet again. This gives us the total number of square feet of water in the sanctuary. Multiply that result by 7.4805 (the number of gallons of liquid in one square foot), and the answer is 31 trillion-plus gallons of ocean water…give or take a few gallons.

Shuster. I knew that if I was to have a complete book on the life and times of horseshoe crabs, it would have to include a chapter on the man whose passion for this creature has elevated it to the top ranks of scientific consciousness. Admittedly, during my research, I often found it difficult to determine who is more significant: Shuster or the horseshoe crabs he has studied for more than sixty years.

After fighting through the late morning traffic (and, at least, one missing exit sign), I pulled up to his quaint modern colonial home a few minutes before our scheduled appointment. The brick house occupies a corner lot in a well-kept, tree-lined neighborhood. Fringes of snow hugged the curbs, and colorful leaves ebbed in and out of the neatly trimmed yards. Clouds scuttled across the sky, allowing short bursts of mid-January sunlight to fall across the landscape.

Shuster greeted me enthusiastically and ushered me into the house. After quick introductions, he escorted me into his den, which houses a museum-like assembly of every conceivable horseshoe crab knickknack, souvenir, and artifact ever manufactured. He showed me quilts, photographs, candles, posters, toys, commemorative plates, and dozens of mementos, each with a picture, impression, or carving of one or more horseshoe crabs. If anything in the world has been made bearing the likeness of a horseshoe crab on it, it is more than likely that Shuster has it somewhere in his house.

We eventually retired to the tidy kitchen, where I turned on my tape recorder and sat enthralled for the next two hours as he passionately and powerfully[†] responded to my questions.

Shuster's fascination with horseshoe crabs began in the late 1940s. His academic adviser gave him a bottle of *Limulus* eggs and larvae, which led to a thesis study on the development of the juvenile horseshoe crab's digestive tract. Then, in May 1949, he accompanied his mentor, Professor Thurlow C. Nelson, to Cape May, New Jersey, on a weekend trip to observe horseshoe crab spawning. When they walked onto the beach just before dawn, the area was shrouded in a heavy mist, and no wind was blowing. There was only the sound of the gentle lapping of the water on the beach, accompanied by a constant "click clack." As Shuster recalls the scene today, it was like stepping out of the present into prehistory. As they approached the water's edge, they saw what appeared to be groups of rounded stones. But the stones were moving; they were, in fact, nesting horseshoe crabs. The click-clacking came from

---

† At the time of my interview, Shuster was ninety-one years old. I wish I had the same level of energy and passion at my tender age of sixty-four.

their bodies bumping against one another. Shuster noticed many things that weekend, including "the impact that changes in the amplitude of the waves striking the beach had on the size of mating groups, the mating scars on the females, and the incessant feeding by migratory shorebirds on the *Limulus* eggs that were strewn over the beach."

Shuster quickly discovered he had a knack for studying horseshoe crabs. He has always contended that he was able to observe things his professor hadn't considered and that hadn't been studied. Through observation, he told me, he "learned that rough waves during a storm swept unattached males away from spawning females. I found a clear advantage for males attaching to females." After that, he said, "I had the opportunity to break lots of new ground—almost uninterrupted for twenty-five years—because it wasn't a very interesting topic at the time." He's since discovered that interest in horseshoe crabs has spiraled because of new land development patterns and interest in issues such as climate change.

Since those early years, Shuster has observed spawning activity hundreds of times at locations from Alabama to Maine and throughout Japan. With pride, he told me that his "interests in horseshoe crabs have included their natural history and ecology, morphology [the study of the form and structure of organisms], morphometrics [an analysis of the size and shape of organisms, which is particularly useful in analyzing their fossil record], functional anatomy, evolution of mating, serological relationships [the comparative study of blood serum and other bodily fluids], the fossilized species, and the conservation and fisheries management of the species."

It's important to note that Shuster's approach to the study of horseshoe crabs is less experimental than most. As he put it, "My approach is that of a naturalist. I spend a lot of time observing, a lot of time looking at behavior. I want to know why an animal does what it does and how it does it."

Most scientists will tell you that naturalistic observations come with a certain perspective as a research tool. For example, observing animal behaviors in a natural context (along a seashore, for example), without any human manipulation or interference, makes the behaviors exhibited by an animal more credible, because they are occurring in an authentic environment. By comparison, an artificial environment—say, a twenty-gallon aquarium tank inside a college biology laboratory—may produce behaviors that are not normally exhibited by that same animal.

Shuster related how, back in the early 1950s, he noticed that one of the adult male horseshoe crabs he was studying at Woods Hole, Massachusetts, had a piece of old claw attached to its clasper. Horseshoe crabs normally

Dr. Shuster displays the object of his fascination.

molt every year, but at about the tenth year the forward part of the male crab metamorphoses from a claw to become a fist-shaped clasper. As you will recall from our study of reproductive habits (Chapter 7), the male uses these claspers to grasp a female during mating. Normally, the old claw drops off as soon as the male mates with a female, but Shuster noticed that this particular male still had a piece of immovable pedipalp attached to his clasper. Most of us would have regarded this extra piece of claw simply as an interesting curiosity, if we noticed it at all. But this observation niggled at the back of Shuster's brain. What could this tell him about the horseshoe crab's life?

And so, he began to measure horseshoe crabs, both live ones and dead ones. By measuring them, he felt he could nail down an answer to a question that had stumped experts for years. In the span of three days, he measured 115 female and 288 male horseshoe crabs. He separated the males into three individual groups: adult virgin males who had atrophied parts attached to their pedipalps, middle-age males he had found crawling on the bottom, and old males with worn shells he had found lying dead on the beach. His measurements showed that the average width of the virgin males' shells was approximately 166 millimeters, the average width of the middle-aged males' was 167 mm., and the average width of the old males' was 168 mm.

Suddenly it dawned on him. The old crabs were ten years older than the virgin crabs, but they were still approximately the same size. This could only mean one thing: males stop growing and shedding their shells after they reach sexual maturity. It also suggested that females, who are sometimes up to twice as large as males, keep growing and keep shedding their shells.

One of Shuster's colleagues pointed out that that didn't make sense. Logically, he said, males of many animal species keep growing so as to compete with other males. But Shuster told his friend that male horseshoe crabs don't need size to compete, they just cluster around the females and release their sperm. In fact, a smaller male might even have an advantage, because he could crowd in closer to a female to inseminate her eggs.

Shuster's friend then asked why the females would keep growing. Shuster hypothesized that the bigger the female, the more eggs she can produce and the easier for her to tug attached mates around.

Additional observations suggested to Shuster that "males do not molt: the obvious carapace deterioration over time, the internal chitinous rods [trabeculae] that reinforce the adult carapace, and the age of the organisms living on the crabs' shells [epibionts]" prove it. "Unless the internal rods are dissolved during a premolt phase," he noted, "an adult male could not emerge from its old shell because its flesh would be enmeshed in the interstices of the trabeculae." Sexually mature males are essentially trapped in their own bodies, unable to molt or to grow any further. Shuster's conclusions led other researchers to calculate that the life expectancy of horseshoe crabs in the Delaware Bay may be as much as seventeen to twenty years.

His observations and clever conclusions about horseshoe crabs led to a doctoral dissertation from New York University ("On morphometric and serological relationships within the *Limulidae*, with particular reference to *Limulus polyphemus*"). It also provided him with confirmation for his naturalistic point of view, in which observations generate questions and questions generate discovery. It was a satisfying stamp of approval that would direct his research for the next half-century and more.

Shuster likes to explain that children, like the earliest human inhabitants of this planet, are *natural* naturalists; they ask questions, and they look for the answers to those questions by observing the world around them. In education, we often refer to this as an inquiry-based approach to learning. Providing youngsters with opportunities to pose questions about their world, question basic assumptions, or actively seek solutions to various mysteries places value on the power of the human mind. Inquiry-based science education, for example, offers students opportunities to make sense out of their world by encouraging them to take responsibility for their own learning. As Shuster would no doubt agree, science is often *learned* more than it is *taught*.

I was curious about the history and future of horseshoe crabs, particularly in the Delaware Bay. Shuster proceeded to tell me that he has "seen or experienced such a wealth of information on the abundance of horseshoe crabs in the Delaware Bay area that I could write a book on the subject." It is a subject that has attracted much attention, he said, but few people have either an intimate knowledge or correct interpretation of the subject. Besides studying horseshoe crabs firsthand since 1949, he has delved into the long history of their harvests in the dark bowels of the U.S. Department of the Interior library.

KEY FACT

The horseshoe crab's curved shell allows it to plow through undersea muck and mud in search of buried food.

Shuster discovered that the fisheries harvest data revealed a trend of lessening harvests starting in the 1930s, with a halving of the take each decade until the fishery ended in the 1960s. According to Shuster, this information does not provide an estimate of the total adult population of horseshoe crabs, nor the reasons for the collapse of the fishery. A declining population, the introduction of chemical fertilizers, and public health considerations were probably all factors in the decline. Except for a small eel bait harvest, and use of the horseshoe crabs locally for fertilizer, the fishery was virtually nonexistent by the 1960s. Then, in the 1970s, the conch-bait fishery began.

"Up to that point," he said, "no one had studied the impact this growing fishery had on the opportunities for the crab population to begin to increase after the King Crab fishery ended. However, it appears that the conch-bait fishery was working on a large crab population in the Delaware Bay. Any substantial increase due to migrations from outside the normal range of the Delaware Bay crab can be ruled out from tagging results and genetic data.

"Then, in 1992," he continued, "the crab population crashed to about 50 percent of its 1990 and 1991 populations. [It] leveled off until into the 2000s, when, due to the ASMFC horseshoe crab management plan, initiated in 1999 and amended in subsequent years, the numbers of crabs during the spawning season markedly increased. By 2010, on certain beaches such as Pickering Beach in Delaware, the spawners covered some 100 meters of the beach in a swath that was usually two tiers deep and sometimes three, and up to four meters wide and then disappearing bayward into the water.

"When you look at the harvest rates and the condition of their population back in the year 1950, horseshoe crabs were being taken at low rates," he said, explaining why harvesting for fertilizer died out in the sixties. "One [reason] was the horseshoe crab numbers were lesser than in the previous fifty years, but so were the old fishermen that were collecting them. There [were] only about one or two men in that decade that were still collecting the crabs, and the only outfit that produced the crab meal was producing fertilizer in neat little packages for home use," he said.

Shuster told me that right after World War II, housing projects started encroaching on these areas and soon people were complaining about the stink. So, for public relations and the fact that newer fertilizers were being developed, several fertilizer manufacturers decided to quit using horseshoe crab meal. They started to use the offal from blue crab plants, which they ground up and added as a supplement to their fertilizer.

KEY FACT

Horseshoe crabs were once known as horsefoot crabs because their shell resembles a horse's hoof.

"Into the seventies, there wasn't that much going on," Shuster said, "until about the mid-seventies, [when] all of a sudden the bait industry providing bait for conch—or whelk, actually—started building up, and so, while the horseshoe crabs were slowly regaining numbers, they were being harvested at the same time, so…its numbers leveled off.

"But by the nineties," he continued, "the increasing bait industry had caught up with them, and for one reason or another, there was practically an overnight shift from great numbers down to 50 percent of the crab population." Shuster explained that this lower number remained constant through the rest of the nineties. He was quick to point out that none of this was ever a very accurate count, just a ballpark figure good enough to track trends.

Then, with characteristic zeal and a bit of indignation, he added, "But there are those idiots who claim that unless we have a statistical analysis, it can't be verified, so they can't rely on such observations…. When you read about the horseshoe crab population being first heavily harvested in the nineties, don't believe it. It started back in the seventies, and I've got a picture of the fishery vessel *Elizabeth C* with a deck-load of horseshoe crabs, probably numbering a few thousand, on deck off of Cape May in 1978. Fisheries biologists knew the crabs were being collected, and the *Elizabeth C* was only one of a fleet of trawlers collecting horseshoe crabs back in the late seventies. Trawling was escalating, and it was in the eighties that things really picked up to a great extent, particularly on the shores of Delaware Bay."

By this point in our discussion, it was evident that a conversation with Shuster is a history lesson, a science lecture, a plea for common sense, and a validation of the value of naturalistic observation. His fervor was palpable. Like a conductor leading a symphony, this was a maestro in his element.

I asked Shuster what kept him involved with these critters for more than half a century. "It's not only about the crabs," he stated emphatically, "because I've got plenty of other things that I have to get done and should be doing. It's the fact that I was blessed with arriving on the scene when there was no one else really looking at the natural history and the beginnings of the ecological studies of horseshoe crabs. I don't claim that I was the only one, but I was the major one doing that type of work, and since that time there have been many others. In essence, probably they have been the stimulus keeping me interested, more than the horseshoe crab, because they've come to me—either in meetings or otherwise—wanting to know how to move on these sorts of things. What's kept me going on this is the fact that they seem to feel I have a form of wisdom relating to the horseshoe crabs, so people keep coming to me."

I decided to enter dangerous territory and ask Shuster to tell me what he would like to tell the politicians—the people who pass the laws, rules, and regulations about horseshoe crabs. He was merciless:

"Where the Environmental Protection Agency went wrong in its program emphasis was when [they] decided that lawyers should run the EPA instead of scientists," Shuster said. "That is the basic problem with EPA. Politics runs it, science does not, and it's been screwed up ever since. Leave it to the scientists, even though we know that scientists sometimes screw up."

Shuster was emphatic that where environmental matters are concerned, it would be prudent, if not practical, to depend more on facts provided by scientists. "I'm one of the old school people more interested in conservation," he said, "and basically I believe that conservation is a wise use of resources. It isn't necessarily a politically correct thing today. In a nutshell, we should rely more on science, common sense, and sound judgment, and try to take a more balanced view, and be practical about it."

Shuster and I then spent a few moments talking about Green Eggs & Sand, the innovative program for middle school and high school educators you will encounter in the following chapter. He is an ardent fan of the GE&S project and one of its staunchest supporters.

Shuster is passionate about the role of education in helping people, particularly young people, know what the truth is and how they should act on that truth. Too many people rely on the popular press for their information, he said, and teachers should help students see all the perspectives of a situation—the good, the bad, and most definitely the ugly—before making up their minds. Without solid scientific information, rational decisions are virtually impossible to make, he said, and he would like to see a science curriculum based on naturalistic observation and critical thinking.

I wanted to know what he considers his proudest accomplishment in his study of horseshoe crabs. "Probably my relationship to others," he said, with a gleam in his eye. "I have been a source of information, based upon my observations during fieldwork and my literature searches. I have always shared what I know with anybody. That's part of the story. I've had great associations with many people."

KEY FACT

Horseshoe crabs feed mostly at night, although they will eat during the day if food is plentiful.

Shuster proudly pointed out that he has probably the largest library of reference material on the horseshoe crab of anyone in the United States. But, he was equally quick to point out that there is a lot more that we don't know about this creature. At one time, he was the only person in the country studying these creatures, he said, and since then he has amassed a library full of information, research, and data that he will quickly share with others, and that is both reliable and sound. Almost every single research paper or peer-reviewed article on horseshoe crabs includes references to Shuster's work.

Our time together was drawing to a close, so I quickly peppered him with a few final questions:

Why should the man on the street know or care about horseshoe crabs today?
Shuster: Why care? That such a seemingly primitive creature has a significant natural role in the ecology of local areas and is important to man—in research, LAL, bait, beach erosion, predation, environmental tourism, etc.

What excites you most about these creatures?
Shuster: Most exciting: the relationship between their anatomy and their innate mechanical abilities. They appear to be able to cope with every environmental condition, except being able to back up. The evolution of their body

plan and their behavior when beaches are seemingly saturated with spawners are also exciting.

Why is the Delaware Bay so critical to horseshoe crabs?
Shuster: This bay, within a geological time frame, is a very suitable habitat, due mainly to its geographical position within the middle of the range of the species, its hydroclimate, extensive sandy beach incubators of its eggs, shallow water nurseries of its young, and continental shelf preserves of prey. But like any other geologic feature, it will change in time, and another area will probably take its place.

What would you like to tell the world about horseshoe crabs?
Shuster: They may have had more said about them and contributed as much or more to human health and welfare than other species, but they are best viewed as one of the good windows/insights into the world about us.

What is the population status of the American horseshoe crab? Are they endangered?
Shuster: Not within foreseeable time at Delaware Bay, but undoubtedly in some future geologic process. At sites of lesser populations, there is always potential endangerment. Although populations may suffer, others survive; hence, overall the species probably would not be endangered. Of course, we wonder which, among the populations that were wiped out, might have been the only ones to survive into the future.

Finally, I asked him what we still need to learn about these creatures. Without hesitation, he responded, "In some respects, we never can learn too much about anything. For example, one great opportunity at Delaware Bay would be for four retirees to rent a cottage on the beach of one of the spawning areas and record in detail all sorts of information from mid-April through mid-June. Among the questions to answer are, A, can a beach be saturated with spawners such that many cannot spawn? B, what do these not-able-to-spawn crabs do, come back on less favorable tides? And, C, does a saturated beach produce more eggs available to the migratory shorebirds?"

After a pleasant conversation with his wife, Helen, I stepped out of the house and onto the walkway, at which point Shuster hit me with a final thought—a thought that consumed me as I fought the outbound traffic on the Friday afternoon drive back home. "You will find that I do not get very excited about natural events and objects," he said. "They have occurred, are occurring, and will occur in the future. What is exciting is when you figure out some aspect of this yourself. I am reminded of this by the great excitement expressed by the late Dr. Robert Barlow when he told of how he had realized that his graduate students were reviving themselves after late-night experiments by eating candy bars. He determined that that might be the same or a similar phenomenon to what was seen in the response of horseshoe crabs to darkness. That's what was important; he had discovered an important biological process."

A FEW MONTHS AFTER THIS INTERVIEW, I CAME ACROSS ANOTHER Shuster story that underscores his passion for horseshoe crabs. It took place at his home in Arlington one night as he was preparing some materials for publication. Startled by a noise coming from one of the large plastic trays in which he was temporarily keeping horseshoe crabs, he found an adult male trying to scramble up a corner of the tray. When he bent down and looked straight at the front of the animal, he was struck by how fierce it looked with its legs outstretched and waving. This uncommon view of the crab reminded him of reconstructions of ancient sea scorpions he had seen at the Smithsonian Institution's Museum of Natural History. Their legs were spread out beyond the edges of the carapace—giving them an imposing, and perhaps fearsome, appearance. This led him to wonder why horseshoe crabs have persisted, while the often-gigantic sea scorpions and the more numerous, complex, and ornate trilobites became extinct.

Carefully putting the pieces together, Shuster decided that it was the horseshoe crab's ability to live through changing environmental conditions that ensured its survival. Perhaps the evolution of a superior protective cover—the domed carapace—was what provided the key step in its long-term survival, he thought. The vaulted underside not only protects the crab's appendages from enemies, it also provides a sort of caisson under which the appendages can operate within their own environment, whether feeding, walking, burrowing, or laying eggs. Shuster surmised that the horseshoe crab's vault distinguished it from the relatively flat-bottomed sea scorpion and trilobite and may have contributed to its evolutionary success. As in most of his work, Shuster's hypothesis was formulated as a result of his naturalistic observations and careful interpretation of the facts.

SINCE MY INITIAL INTERVIEW WITH SHUSTER, I HAVE HAD THE opportunity to observe him in action in numerous situations, working with

Carl Shuster and Jane Brockmann chat at Green Eggs & Sand.

both teachers and children. He is a master educator, encouraging his students to ask questions and providing just the right amount of scientific detail.

He is a strong advocate for teaching natural history in public schools through direct observation. He often talks about early man, and how primitive people relied on their powers of observation to survive and to learn more about the world around them. In almost every encounter with students, he says that his approach to science in general and horseshoe crabs specifically is naturalistic. "I spend a lot of time observing," he says. "I like to look at an animal's behavior. Why does it do what it does? When does it do it? These are not, as you might expect, easy questions to answer. But they are answerable nonetheless when we watch what animals do in their natural environment."

I observed one workshop session where he was explaining the carapace of a horseshoe crab to a rapt audience of middle school students. He deftly brought it to their level, defining chitin as "similar to your fingernails, the horn of a cow, or the outer covering of a cicada." You could almost see the light bulbs glow over the students' heads as he presented them with an analogy that would make sense...and would be remembered.

Yet, if there is one trait that distinguishes Shuster, it is his lifelong recognition that information is never static. He will say, "I'm willing to accept another point of view, particularly if it is better than mine." He freely admits he doesn't know it all, and he embraces the research of others as a way to increase his own knowledge, as well as the knowledge of those who will make the decisions that will determine the survival of the species. This is science as it should be—evolutionary, changing, expanding.

A FEW MONTHS BEFORE MY INTERVIEW WITH SHUSTER, I INTERVIEWED Jane Brockmann (whom you met in Chapter 7), another horseshoe crab expert. She told me that Shuster has a marvelous way "of bringing people together." She said, "One of the real assets of Green Eggs & Sand [Chapter 13] is that Carl Shuster has participated from the outset, so the science is very sound. Carl always speaks his mind; he doesn't always agree with what the rest of us think, and that's fine. It means that there is [always an] openness about what we can say."

If there is a giant in the field of horseshoe crab research, it's Carl Shuster. According to the late Bob Barlow (whom you met in Chapter 6), "Carl Shuster is a national resource. No one person in the world knows more about horseshoe crabs than Carl Shuster." Glenn Gauvry (Chapter 11) told me this about Shuster: "The depth and breadth of Carl's knowledge of the world's four horseshoe crab species is unequaled, but it is the character of the man that I love the most."

Thirty-one trillion gallons of Atlantic Ocean seawater may be small homage to one of the horseshoe crab's most fervent observers.

CHAPTER 13

Back to School

Green Eggs & Sand

NEW JERSEY FREQUENTLY GETS A BAD RAP.
When I was growing up in southern California, my friends and I thought New Jersey was simply one enormous metropolitan area—an overpopulated expanse buried under asphalt, teeming with mobsters, crisscrossed by cars, and littered with decrepit factories spewing mushroom-shaped clouds of pollution. New Jersey was old, tired, and broken-down, like a distant relative nobody wants to visit. We believed New Jersey was New York's blighted backyard, filled with corrupt cops, dishonest politicians, and insolent citizens who'd just as soon give you the finger as help you across the street.

Now that I live next door to the Garden State, I've definitely changed my tune. The erroneous perceptions I had of New Jersey as a kid have changed now that I see it with a clearer set of lenses.* According to the New Jersey Division of Travel and Tourism, the state has 130 miles of sun-drenched beaches, a rich and rewarding arts scene, a vast array of cultural venues, dozens of family-friendly amusement parks, an abundance of historical sites and museums, and everything from picturesque lighthouses to championship golf courses.

---

* I should mention that my wife, Phyllis, was born and raised in New Jersey. Thus, there are many things to love about the indigenous population of the Garden State.

New Jersey is also brimming with horseshoe crabs,* which is why I was headed there on a chilly, gray Friday afternoon in May. I had registered for a session of the Green Eggs & Sand workshop at the Wetlands Institute in Stone Harbor, near the southern tip of the state and close to the tourist destinations of Cape May and Wildwood. Green Eggs & Sand (also known as GE&S) is an intensive three-day series of workshops, lectures, presentations, and hands-on activities designed to help middle school and high school educators integrate horseshoe crabs into their science programs. GE&S also features a set of curriculum modules that explores the Atlantic Coast horseshoe crab/shorebird nexus and the issues surrounding their management.

Green Eggs & Sand workshops differ from traditional teacher workshops, in that the focus is more on promoting understanding of the issues and science surrounding horseshoe crabs than on demonstrating the curriculum itself. Consequently, much of the agenda involves listening to presenters—including leading horseshoe crab and shorebird biologists, fisheries managers, commercial fishermen, and biomedical experts—share their knowledge, insights, and perspectives. Activities from the curriculum are sprinkled between these sessions, both to serve as breaks from the presentations and to provide a taste of the curricular content. A field trip to observe spawning horseshoe crabs at a nearby beach, featuring hands-on interpretation by experts on horseshoe crab biology and ecology, is also an integral part of the experience.

The workshops are typically timed to coincide with the horseshoe crab spawning peak at the full and new moons in late spring. Attending teachers eat, sleep, and breathe horseshoe crabs from Friday night to Sunday afternoon. Because of growing interest in horseshoe crabs since the program was inaugurated in 2000, GE&S workshops have been held up and down the East Coast. They've been attended by educators from nineteen states and two

---

* New Jersey is also brimming with legislation. Consider the following regulations, rules, statutes, and laws that the citizens of New Jersey have previously endured, or must currently obey:
  - In New Jersey, it is illegal to wear a bulletproof vest while committing a murder.
  - It is against the law in New Jersey for a man to knit during fishing season.
  - In New Jersey, it's illegal to slurp soup.
  - New Jersey has a law forbidding people to "frown" at a police officer.
  - There is no horse racing allowed on the New Jersey Turnpike.
  - In Trenton, you may not throw a bad pickle in the street. And, pickles are not to be consumed on Sundays.
  - Unless you have a doctor's note, it's illegal to buy ice cream after 6:00 p.m. in Newark.

foreign countries, as well as marine biologists, aquarium workers, park rangers, and interpretive center personnel. Also included are folks from outside the traditional education field, such as writers, artists, media people, scientists, fisheries managers, and others interested in learning more about these enigmatic creatures. The cast of characters who populate a GE&S workshop is always interesting, and the connections that result are an added bonus.

I DEPARTED MY SOUTH-CENTRAL PENNSYLVANIA HOMESTEAD AND steeled myself for a driving experience similar to the running of the bulls in Pamplona, Spain. I traversed the Pennsylvania Turnpike (a $10.70 toll) eastward, the New Jersey Turnpike ($2.35) southwest, the Atlantic City Expressway ($3.00) southeast, and the Garden State Parkway ($1.00) south toward the southern tip of New Jersey. Four-and-a-half hours and several Eagles and Eric Clapton CDs later, I arrived at the Ponderosa Campground just outside the little town of Cape May Court House and checked into the rustic yet functional cabin that would be my home for the weekend.

I met my roommate, Walter, who has been teaching for forty-three years, the last dozen or so at an alternative school for juveniles with emotional, social, and behavioral challenges. He had a jovial disposition and a hearty laugh, and he was deeply committed to his students. He told me he wanted to provide them with unique experiences that are unavailable in science textbooks and that would give them opportunities to connect with the world of nature and solve problems that have immediate application to their lives. Walter was here to not only challenge his students, but to challenge himself as a teacher. He asked me, "If I can't grow, then how can I help my students grow?"

At 6:00 p.m., Walter and I drove to the Wetlands Institute in Stone Harbor for dinner with the thirty or so other GE&S participants and a series of introductory workshops. After a dinner of warm pizza, sodas, and baskets of chocolate chip cookies, we engaged in an icebreaker activity designed to build group solidarity for the coming weekend.

After getting to know each other, we were introduced to the life and times of the horseshoe crab by Gary Kreamer, coordinator of the Delaware Division of Fish and Wildlife's Aquatic Resources Education Center and one of the originators of the GE&S program. In the spring of 1999, Kreamer and Mike Oates, a local videographer who had long been documenting horseshoe crabs in the Delaware Bay, worked together to create a video of eighth graders getting hands-on experience on Bowers Beach—banding shorebirds, interviewing a waterman, and interacting with scientists. An ambitious idea was born: "Why not create an entire curriculum around horseshoe crabs?" they thought.

The more they talked, the more Kreamer and Oates saw horseshoe crabs as a subject that could teach students everything from statistics to critical reading while focusing on the local environment. They decided to enlist the involvement of educator colleagues from Maryland and New Jersey, and together they recruited a handful of master teachers from each of the three states, along with key people from the horseshoe crab and shorebird research and management communities, to take part in the first Green Eggs & Sand workshop, held during the spawning season in 2000. The scientists made presentations to the teachers, and the teachers participated in that year's spawning survey and gathered ideas for a new science curriculum.

According to Kreamer, "At the end of the workshop, all the teachers agreed that a curriculum built along these issues was worth doing, that the workshop was extremely valuable, and that, whatever we did, the workshop experience should be part of it." Most of the teachers in that first gathering signed on to write lesson plans for the evolving curriculum. Early on, it was decided that the project would be divided into four critical segments: one for horseshoe crabs, one for shorebirds, one on human connections, and a final one (tying together threads from the other three) on resource management. Over the course of that first year, the groups worked on the design, implementation, and coordination of the curriculum. They also planned another workshop for 2001 and signed up new teachers from a wider geographical area.

"We started Green Eggs & Sand because there was nothing really there to teach about this in the schools," Kreamer told me. "We basically had teachers in our schools teaching ecology through the study of the Australian kangaroo rat or prairie dogs or tropical rainforests—all things worthy of studying ecology. But in our own backyard, we had this amazing phenomenon of the crabs and the birds, and there really wasn't stuff in the schools."

SEVERAL MONTHS BEFORE THE GE&S WORKSHOP IN NEW JERSEY, I traveled down to Smyrna, Delaware, to interview Kreamer at the Aquatic Resources Education Center's Mallard Lodge, a rustic, well-weathered building located amidst a vast stretch of wetlands along Route 9. Kreamer and I sat in a conference room surrounded by posters, models, educational paraphernalia, learning modules, photos, and all manner of things aquatic. This is where teachers gather periodically throughout the year to attend workshops and get up to date on the latest research.

A Green Eggs & Sand workshop in action.

I asked Kreamer to sum up the Green Eggs & Sand program in twenty-five words or less. He replied, "That's a hard one to answer, but it's certainly to provide an awareness of the phenomenon at the first level. You know, the crab and bird connection: the significance of each animal; how it has come to be so important to humans; and for the different bait, biomedical, and ecotourism values. Really, where we hope to get the participants is to give them an awareness—at a deeper level of understanding—of the animal, and the challenge and the controversy of managing a resource like this. It has multiple uses, many different stakeholders, and lots of scientific data."

As I was listening and recording the conversation, I was also writing down words like "passionate," "thoughtful," "animated," and "absolutely engaged."* A conversation with Kreamer is like two old friends chatting at a bar on a Friday night.

At this point in the conversation, Kreamer brought out a small tub of newly hatched horseshoe crabs, which scuttled across the bottom of the pan looking like tiny aliens. "These guys hook you in," he said. "Whenever we go and do events… You can have the fanciest looking exhibit in the whole

---

* In a subsequent interview with one of Kreamer's colleagues, I was told that he is "passionate about all he does. He has an intense love of nature and an intense love for horseshoe crabs. He is always trying to give people an appreciation for, and an understanding of, one of nature's most amazing creatures."

world, but if you have something that introduces the public to these little guys…it's amazing how strongly that grabs the people and gets them interested in learning more."

"It sucks them right in?" I asked.

"Yeah," he said. "The kids certainly [are], and this really connects them at any age. Most people have no idea. They seem to have this idea that horseshoe crabs are these big ugly things that come up on the bay beaches and are left behind to die and stink up the place. That's what they see, and they have no idea it takes them so long to get to that age, so seeing them in little hatchlings that will take at least another eight to ten years to become the adults they see on the beaches gives them a whole other outlook."

As is often the case in a comfortable conversation, the topics shifted back and forth. Kreamer and I talked about adaptive resource management ("How many horseshoe crabs does it take spawning in the Delaware Bay to produce the superabundance of eggs that support adequate population levels of red knots?"), shifts in horseshoe crab populations over the last several years ("You'll see a lot in the media that horseshoe crabs are declining. They're not!"), restricted horseshoe crab harvesting for eel fishermen ("It's been especially hard on eel fishermen in Delaware, where a small male-only horseshoe crab harvest is now in place, since eel fishermen require female horseshoe crabs for bait. I mean, these guys have to go out of state to get their bait."), to conservation issues ("I have to say, I have felt like the fishermen have moved more to the environment than the environmentalists.").

> **KEY FACT**
>
> Horseshoe crab eggs are the primary source of fat for about twenty species of migratory shorebirds.

Eventually the conversation moved back to the topic of Green Eggs & Sand, and I asked Kreamer if he would categorize GE&S as a conservation initiative. He told me, in no uncertain terms, that it's not a conservation but rather an educational initiative. "We certainly have a conservation benefit that has come out of it," he said. "I always look at the impacts that, to me, make the most difference. For example, when I find out that a teacher who came to Green Eggs and went back to school and got her kids going out on a volunteer survey, or maybe someone got involved in efforts to influence conservation, then that's cool. Or, some of their kids want to do [extended] projects, and some have even carried out biomedical research projects. So it's those kinds of offshoots, those kinds of anecdotal accounts that translate into some action, some involvement, or engagement. But if nothing else, I think if they come and they listen, they come away with a much expanded view of the fact that there are these different stakeholders, these different livelihoods, economic impacts, ecological impacts, of benefits to us, and that management of these resources is a challenging thing, and it relies on informed citizens. GE&S is an opportunity to be informed citizens...to participate. People can go to public meetings. They can write letters. They can get involved on any level. Those are the kinds of things that are happening with this that will have a conservation impact. But, by and large, GE&S is about education."

I asked Kreamer to tell me what he sees as the future for this educational initiative. His eyebrows rose, and his enthusiasm ratcheted up one more level. He told me that a lot of environmental issues ride a wave, and often it's a pretty brief wave. Those waves sometimes rise, and sometimes fall off to something else. He cited tropical rainforests and acid rain as good examples of those rising and falling waves. GE&S hasn't ramped down since he's been involved, he said, but at some point it will. He was quick to assert, however, that the story of these animals and their connection to the birds is always going to be engaging.

"The interest in the workshop will be there," Kreamer said. "But I think as an environmental issue, particularly as crabs continue to increase in this area, [they] will be replaced by something else. The birds are another story. We certainly hope that they will bounce back in time, too, but it's too early to tell right now."

Kreamer shared how he and others are continuing to work to make GE&S better. At the time of our interview, the curriculum designers were working on a complete revision of the program and updating of the curriculum. Concerned about the program's exclusive emphasis on the Delaware Bay, they were attempting to make the workshop more regional and design a curriculum that could be used up and down the Atlantic seaboard. They added several new lessons, made improvements to existing lessons, and revamped the visual design. Eventually, materials would be in place that would give students more opportunities to see how horseshoe crabs impact not only the region, but also their specific lives.

It was early afternoon in the late fall, and the sun was slowly lowering itself behind the salt marsh that rings the education center. The temperature was beginning to dip, but Kreamer's intensity never wavered. He was as passionate about this program as you would be if your son hit a home run in the Little League city championship.

Workshop participants search for eggs.

I asked him for anecdotes about graduates of the Green Eggs & Sand program: what have they done, what have their students done, and how has the program transformed their lives? "There was a high school student from Delaware, Abigail Bradley, who did a science fair project about the biomedical use of horseshoe crabs," he said. "In fact, she did some experiments we eventually adapted for use in the curriculum. These experiments allowed teachers to use the LAL material from pharmaceutical companies. Biomedical companies donated thousands of LAL vials to the workshop. Abigail eventually went on to the University of Delaware and ended up being a marine biology graduate student as a result of that interest."

Kreamer then told me that the same girl, now a young woman, eventually petitioned to have the horseshoe crab named as the state marine animal of Delaware. The governor announced that her petition was successful while one of the GE&S workshops was taking place. Bradley was invited to the press conference, and afterward had an opportunity to attend the GE&S workshop, meet notables such as Carl Shuster, and accept the congratulations of all the educators in attendance.

Kreamer also told me the story of how participants at one workshop took up a collection for waterman Frank Eicherly, whom you met in Chapter 3. They gathered several hundred dollars, with one of the participants, who came all the way from Maine, sending him a check for $500. The money was used to make repairs to his boat, a restored oyster schooner and the oldest working boat on the East Coast. He bought a new mast and sail so that he could work without using his motor.

Kreamer was quick to say, "You can't stereotype these fishermen. A lot of people want to, but I've found that they're very independent, interesting people. Frank, for example, has learned to play guitar and sing, and will bring his guitar and sing sea chanteys and other kind of folk songs about working on the water at various GE&S events."

I had an inkling of how the program got its name. (Let's see: horseshoe crabs lay eggs that are green, and they lay those eggs in the sand. So, let's call the program Green Eggs & Sand. Brilliant!) While that seems perfectly logical now, it wasn't the original name for this education initiative. The original name (Tri-State Horseshoe Crab/Shorebird Education Project) was subsequently changed to make the initiative more familiar and more comfortable to educators. However, Kreamer told me that the new name also lends itself to some misinterpretations by noneducators:

Kreamer: Before we came up with Green Eggs & Sand, the name we called ourselves was Tri-State Horseshoe Crab/Shorebird Education Project, which was descriptive but very boring. There were many names we were thinking about. "Orgy of Sex and Gluttony on the Beach" was one of them. Now that would really grab the middle schoolers' and high schoolers' attention!
Me: Might be hard to get some funding for that one.
Kreamer: We almost lost funding for Green Eggs & Sand because of our name.
Me: Oh, a little too close?
Kreamer: We had money several years ago to do some important video work on Green Eggs & Sand, and the funding agency thought we were doing some Dr. Seuss type thing. The agency actually had a $48,000 contract for all the key radio/video work. We had it all signed and sealed by our people. But the state was in a budget crisis, so everything was getting higher levels of scrutiny, and someone thought [our project] was fluff. So we had to fight really hard, and fortunately our director was able to make the case for retaining funding for the project. But it's funny how it almost got undone because of the name perception.

Later that afternoon, as I swung my car back onto Route 9, I realized that I'd been seduced. That Kreamer has a love affair with horseshoe crabs is a given; so too is it a given that he will transmit that love affair to anyone fortunate enough to step into his philosophical circle, whether that be a GE&S workshop, a casual interview in Smyrna, or a Friday evening session down at the local pool hall.

AT THE GE&S WORKSHOP IN NEW JERSEY ON THAT FIRST NIGHT, THE group engaged in a Horseshoe Crab Molt Lab exercise in which we had to identify features of the anatomy and physiology of various horseshoe crabs. This was a hands-on exercise in observational skills, classification, sexing, and measuring. At each of eight stations, we were asked to examine a dead horseshoe crab and respond to a series of questions.

I was paired with Tracee Panetti, who has been teaching high school science for ten years. Although she had lived near the shore, she was not very familiar with horseshoe crabs. Panetti told me she saw the GE&S workshop as a unique way of getting her students interested in large environmental issues as well as local concerns. She wanted to introduce her students to the ways in which horseshoe crabs are part of their everyday lives. Excited about the prospect, she took voluminous notes as we visited the eight stations of the exercise.

Panetti told me she wanted to have her students compare the invertebrate horseshoe crabs to vertebrate shorebirds, and then learn about the interaction between the two. She was amazed by all the interactions, and she told me emphatically that the materials she was gathering at the workshop would help her and her students make these comparisons and connections.

"I think they're going to be fascinated," Panetti said. "What we are doing tonight is showing a lot about how these animals developed. [Students] will be able to learn about creatures they may have heard about, but not paid much attention to. They'll begin to see how important biology is, becoming aware of how biology can influence decisions politically and environmentally."

I recalled what Gary Kreamer had told me about the redesign of the GE&S curriculum, and I asked Panetti about the value of the workshop for students in other parts of the country. "It makes us aware of how we have to protect our resources," she answered. "How the resources are protected one year, and then six years or ten years later the resources are entirely different. And that we have to be aware of our environment. I think all of those things are really important. [We can] talk about global warming, water temperatures, changing oceans, how all those environmental factors influence where horseshoe crabs spawn, what beaches they spawn on, the temperature of the water, and how that affects spawning. Or the eggs aren't here when the shorebirds come, or the shorebirds aren't laying their eggs when the mosquitoes hatch: what are the effects on the populations across two whole continents? That time is critical."

I asked Panetti how this program might improve the teaching of science. She said that one of the things she was learning here was that we need to think of life "like a *Jeopardy* game: the answers are there, we just have to think of the questions." She wanted to have her students ask more high-level thinking questions and eventually to have the means, motivation, and resources to pursue answers to those questions. *Why is this like this, and how can we comprehend it?* It was obvious to me that she was fervent about getting kids actively engaged in science. For her, as for many of the teachers in the workshop, science is not simply dishing out data and memorizing facts. It's providing opportunities for students to ask the necessary questions and to pursue, on their own, the answers.

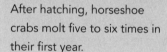

KEY FACT

After hatching, horseshoe crabs molt five to six times in their first year.

"This workshop is a unique combination of scientific research and the knowledge from the scientists that are out in the field, combined with valuable tools that are immediately ready for the classroom," Panetti told me. "As a teacher, I get knowledge of a whole new area that I didn't know before, [and] I now have materials to help me bring this into my classroom."

THE NEXT MORNING WE WERE TRANSPORTED TO THE CAPE MAY County Mosquito Control building for the day's activities. Over a simple breakfast of coffee and cornflakes, I chatted with Janet Mead, a seventh-grade teacher at Williamstown (New Jersey) Middle School.

"I want my students to know how horseshoe crabs are related to their daily lives," she said, "that there are medicines derived from these creatures that affect their lives. I want them to get a sense of pride knowing something that no one else knows. I also want my students to be scientifically literate. When reading something in the popular press, I want them to be able to relate it to something else. I want them to make connections, to open their eyes to something else."

Mead pointed out that it is always a challenge—particularly with a large class—to get students involved in hands-on activities, or to even get them out of the school building and into the real world where science takes place. "Real science is not book learning…it's doing science. We're fortunate at our school—we have a walking path, a pond, a worm bin, and a butterfly garden—so students can get some firsthand experiences," she said.

Mead told me that, like so many other teachers, she feels the need to connect her students to something that matters. She was concerned with the overemphasis on standardized tests that reward memorization at the expense of authentic learning. The GE&S program, she said, is "a way for [teachers] to promote [thinking] skills in a real-world, problem-solving way." For Mead, it's a matter of making connections; children need to see the relationships that exist between ecology, conservation, cells, and a dozen other elements to be scientifically literate citizens. "This is a program we can offer kids that moves beyond classroom learning into an application of that learning in the real world. I'm excited about those possibilities," she said.

OVER THE COURSE OF THE DAY, WE WERE PRESENTED WITH CRITICAL information that formed the foundation for the GE&S program. Experts such as Jane Brockmann of the University of Florida, Bill Pitts from the New Jersey Department of Fish and Wildlife, Stacy Epperson from the Maryland Department of Natural Resources, Jennifer Holmes from St. Jones Reserve, and Dr. Ron Berzofsky from Wako Chemicals regaled us with essential information behind the GE&S program, as well as the basic components and activities of the curriculum.

If you inadvertently picked up the GE&S curriculum, you might think it was just like every other school science textbook: detailed information, colorful photographs, charts, graphs, and predictable experiments. And, just like every other textbook that you've had in your life, your initial reaction would be to put it right back down. (Having written some college textbooks, I have a pretty good idea of what you'd be feeling.)

But the GE&S program is different; it is more of an invitation to learning than a data dump. The teachers who put this program together tried to assemble a package that was not only educationally sound, but would also capitalize on the natural curiosity of students. It relies on an inquiry-based approach to learning, encouraging students to ask their own questions and providing them with the means and materials to pursue the answers.

The curriculum was designed around four sequential learning modules, each including an introductory video followed by a series of interactive exercises that deepen student understanding of the concepts and issues. It

Green Eggs & Sand participants practice administering an LAL test.

contains a collection of multidisciplinary activities designed for flexibility. Knowing that the program would be used in a wide variety of educational settings, the developers targeted the lessons to national curriculum standards for science, math, social studies, and language arts.

The first of the four modules focuses on horseshoe crab biology and ecology. Its lesson plans offer students insights into the biology and natural history of horseshoe crabs, including activities on anatomy, spawning requirements, ecology, and life cycles. One of the most illuminating hands-on activities in this module is the opportunity for students to raise juvenile crabs throughout the year—feeding them, collecting water-quality data, and recording observations. In essence, students become surrogate parents for an entire year.

Students then move into the second of the four modules, this one dealing with the shorebird connection. Here, students are offered activities that engage them in exploring and broadening their understanding of shorebirds, including lessons on identification, feeding behavior, adaptations, and energetics.* Several stimulating lessons on shorebird biology, natural history, and interactions with horseshoe crabs are provided for both middle school and high school students.

The third module in the program, covering human connections, features a plethora of activities on the historical uses of horseshoe crabs and their unique and varied biomedical applications. In one of the most fascinating activities of the program, students are provided with vials of LAL donated by a biomedical company and can test for endotoxins in a variety of substances and materials, such as drinking water, saliva, medical tools, etc.

The final module of the program brings everything together and gives students a perspective on the overall significance of horseshoe crabs. Throughout this module, video clips tell the story of the development of the Horseshoe Crab Fishery Management Plan. Correlated activities help students understand the complexities of managing a resource with multiple uses; develop an appreciation for the varying points of view of the stakeholders involved; recognize the importance of having sound scientific data when making decisions; and develop an understanding of how science, media, and politics can be used and misused in the process.

A major strength of the GE&S curriculum is that it does not instruct students to adhere to a single side of the story. There is no right or wrong here; rather, students are provided with the relevant data and are given multiple opportunities to weigh that data and make up their own minds. Appreciating the differing viewpoints of all stakeholders is key to helping students understand the importance of gathering rigorous scientific data before making decisions. The emphasis on the decision-making process distinguishes this program from more traditional curricula.

ONE OF THE MOST CAPTIVATING SPEAKERS ON THE SECOND DAY OF the GE&S workshop was Walter Chew (a.k.a. "Chewie"), a retired waterman who has been involved with the program for many years, who displayed a fisherman's knowledge of the sea, a capacity for recalling anecdotes, and a keen awareness of the ecological concerns surrounding horseshoe crabs.

Chewie said, "Watermen are driven by survival: not only the survival of

---

* Energetics is defined as "the study of energy under transformation." In nonscientific terms, it is how energy flows from one place to another.

their own families in a tough business, but also the survival of the very species upon which their livelihoods are dependent." He told us fishermen are currently in transition from being "hunter-gatherers" to being "harvesters." To support this thesis, he provided us with a chart demonstrating that fishing in the Delaware Bay from 1776 to 1977 was much like the Wild West. Anybody who could drop a line, drag a net, or bait a trap could take whatever he wanted, whenever he wanted. Then, from 1977 to 2010, state and federal governments stepped in and began to determine who had access to the waters, when they could access those waters, and how much they could take from those waters.

In 2011, the concept of "catch shares" was introduced, in which state and federal governments assist both fishermen and the fish they catch to "renew, rebuild, and recover." I later learned that there are three basic principles that underscore the catch-share concept. These include a catch limit determined through scientific analysis; individuals, groups, or communities being granted a "privilege" to harvest a certain portion of the catch; and fishermen being held accountable for fishing only their designated percentage. As a population of fish in the area grows, the number each designee can catch goes up automatically while their percentage of the total catch stays the same. Catch shares, which have been designated for several different varieties of marine life (including horseshoe crabs), are intended to provide fishermen with a personal stake in sustainability. Follow-up studies have shown that catch shares have had an impact in reversing the collapse of the world's fisheries and preserving fishing jobs. Chewie referred to catch shares as a form of semi-capitalism.

KEY FACT

Catch shares have revived several decimated fisheries, including those for Alaskan halibut and Gulf red snapper.

AFTER A HEARTY MEAL OF BAKED CHICKEN, SALAD, ZITI, MIXED vegetables, and peach pie, we all strapped on our boots and waders, piled into several vans, and headed over to Kimball's Beach, a narrow stretch of shoreline bordering the Delaware Bay. Once there, we were divided into three groups, and three *Limulus* experts provided us with some hands-on learning experiences.

Jane Brockmann led us in a lesson on the spawning behavior of horseshoe crabs. We watched as she pulled a pair in the midst of amplexus from the

Students prepare for class on the shore of the Delaware Bay.

water to show us their undersides. Holding the joined crabs in both hands, Brockmann described the various anatomical processes these crabs were engaged in. Her subjects were less than eager about this seaside show-and-tell, and they were doing everything in their power to escape her clutches. But Brockmann was persistent, and we were treated to an experience that was more authentic, and certainly much more exciting, than anything found in the pages of a textbook.

We moved to an area just off the beach, where Heidi Hanlon of the New Jersey Fish and Wildlife Service gave us a lesson on horseshoe crab tagging procedures. She demonstrated the fastening of the tags on another very reluctant horseshoe crab as it was trying its best to wriggle out of her hands. Hanlon drilled a small hole into the trailing edge of the horseshoe crab's shell and quickly inserted a tag with a Christmas tree-shaped pin into the hole. She used a standard Black and Decker rechargeable drill with a specialized drill bit outfitted with a rubber stopper to avoid drilling through both sides of the carapace.

Each tag had a number to identify the horseshoe crab and a telephone number that anyone finding it can use to report vital data. In some cases, people who report a tagged horseshoe crab will receive information on the project and specific horseshoe crab data. The tags also provide scientists with valuable information about the horseshoe crab's migratory pattern over several years, where and when it spawns, what side or sides of the bay it tends to inhabit, and the distances it travels from year to year. It also helps them track population counts in order to determine fluctuations in numbers.

At our third station, Carl Shuster was plopped into a beach chair, and we gathered around him in a semicircle at the edge of the incoming tide. With a very large male in his hands, he proceeded to tell us about the horseshoe crab's unique shell shape. "For most of them, you can draw an outline, a perfect circle that would encompass most of the prosoma," he said. "These creatures are architecturally strong. They can do all of their life functions— breathe, eat, spawn, locomotion…anything you can think of—underneath the shell, completely protected.

"Scientists seem to think that the ancestral type of horseshoe crabs is trilobites," he continued. "The trilobites superficially look a lot like horseshoe crabs." In high gear, Shuster reminded us of the longevity of horseshoe crabs and the fact that their unique architecture may have been an important factor in their evolutionary success.

Shuster spent time on a description of various anatomical features, using the (very reluctant) male as a living laboratory. From head to tail, we were regaled with stories about the function of selected body parts, with particular emphasis on the claspers. Shuster took time to clearly differentiate the differences between the American horseshoe crab and the three Asiatic species. Unlike the American horseshoe crab, he said, "all the Asiatic species have single male/female mating, and if there are multiple males, they are in tandem like a railroad train. Asiatic crabs have two pairs of claspers. The first pair, instead of being strong like in the American species, is weaker. The second pair of claspers are bigger and stronger."

We were eager students, but no less eager than our instructor. He said, "To me, that's pretty fascinating stuff. If there's anything a creature can do, this thing can do it. The only thing it can't do is back up. Its only option is to move forward. It's the only thing I've found that they really can't do. You have to realize that what you see today will never happen again. That's how complex this crazy thing is. The environment is just as important as the animal."

We were now on information overload. Exhausted, we headed back to the campground for a well-deserved night's sleep.

THE NEXT MORNING, SOME OF US WERE UP AT 4:30 A.M. IT RAINED hard all night, and the clouds overhead were still dark with moisture and the promise of another rainstorm. Although most of the camp was still asleep, many GE&S participants crawled out of their cabins and into a caravan of cars for the short ride to nearby Reed's Beach to see a mass spawning.

We rubbed our eyes, sipped from carafes of coffee, and shared anecdotes while bouncing along the back roads of rural New Jersey. One young woman told the story of a memorable day at Higbee Beach, a well-known birding spot in the Cape May area. She had gone there to view some of the local shorebirds, and while walking along the beach she began to notice that nobody was wearing any clothes (unbeknownst to her, Higbee Beach was, at that time, a nude beach). She thought, *what the heck*, and continued down the beach, watching for birds. The day was hot, she was sweaty, and so she finally decided, *when in Rome….* She doffed all her clothes at the far end of the beach and leaped into the water to cool down. While splashing in the surf, a naked man walked down the beach and sat down next to her clothes. The young woman, now embarrassed, stayed in the water as long as she could while her skin pruned.

As the naked man did not leave and she had become completely chilled, she finally decided to exit the water and retrieve her clothes. They exchanged a few pleasantries ("Hi, you new here?" "Yeah, I guess." "Would you be interested in playing a game of volleyball?" "No, not really. Thanks anyway."), and she retreated behind a dune and quickly re-robed. She never found the birds she had come for, but she definitely found some interesting wildlife along the beaches of the Garden State.

At Reed's Beach, we discovered an army of seagulls squawking like over-hormoned magpies. The gulls, like us, were awaiting the arrival of the horseshoe crabs and all their eggs. Although it was mid-May, the beach was a cold and windy expanse of sand covered with black and white bodies. Gulls were dancing along the edge of the waves, fighting for territory or guarding the tiny plots they had secured. Birds were also bobbing just beyond the wave line, as long strands of seaweed ebbed and flowed across the surface. To their dismay and ours, there was not a single horseshoe crab on this vast and lonely beach.

Part of the beach was cordoned off by long lines of yellow rope. Behind this artificial and presumably temporary barrier, a prominent sign warned people not to harrass the shorebirds (see photo at right).

We waited patiently for the horseshoe crabs to surface, but this was not to be their day. The surf was rough, the morning was rougher, and the conditions were less than ideal for spawning. Consequently, the horseshoe crabs remained in the protective waters of Delaware Bay. Perhaps their yearly pilgrimage over the centuries had imbued them with a bit of wisdom—a bit of wisdom that was clearly missing from the dozen of us shivering on the shore.

We returned to our cabins, grabbed our gear, and headed back to the Wetlands Institute. After coffee and bagels, we were guided through a rapid series of brief workshops on horseshoe crab management, shorebirds, environmental concerns, and shoreline configurations in the Delaware Bay.

This sign at Reed's Beach warns people that harrassing shorebirds is illegal.

Our minds swimming in data, we gathered up vast collections of maps, diagrams, posters, CDs, LAL vials, brochures, horseshoe crab molts, and other classroom materials. Business cards were exchanged, e-mails traded, and goodbyes said.

The sun began to slice its way through the slate-gray overcast as we all headed home. It was evident that classrooms of students, along with the horseshoe crabs they would study, would be the ultimate beneficiaries of the GE&S weekend.

"Cute" is probably not the first word you think of.

CHAPTER 14

"'Cause they're ugly!"
Are Horseshoe Crabs Worth It?

I SUPPOSE THAT IF ANY ANIMAL IN THE WORLD SHOULD HAVE AN inferiority complex, it might as well be the horseshoe crab. You would think that a creature that has been around so much longer than we have would get some respect. Alas, such is not the case.

Part of the reason many people might have a somewhat negative attitude toward *Limulus* is its looks. "Cute" is probably not the first word you think of in any face-to-face encounter with a horseshoe crab. Cute is a word normally assigned to soft, furry creatures such as koala bears and kittens that can be turned into stuffed animals or posted frolicking comically on YouTube. These are not the domains of horseshoe crabs.

Jane Brockmann tells a story about a time when she was on a beach in Delaware. As she was sitting there observing horseshoe crabs, she noticed a man and a woman walking down the beach. The tide was coming in, and a pair of horseshoe crabs in amplexus began to crawl up out of the water. The man walked over and looked at the spawning pair. He then picked up a nearby wooden board and slammed the animals as hard as he could...not once, but two or three times. Brockmann was so surprised and so incensed that she shot up and cried, "Why'd you do that?" He turned to her, a defiant look on his face, and replied, "'cause they're ugly."

Throughout the research for this book, there was one question I would pose to almost every scientist, marine biologist, environmentalist, horseshoe crab enthusiast, or researcher: "Why should the average person care about horseshoe crabs?" I was particularly curious as to why folks in Minnesota, New Mexico, or Oregon should have any interest in this enigmatic creature when there are none around those parts of the country. In almost every instance, the answer came back the same: "Because they are so much a part of our lives!"

Well after Brockmann's encounter on the beach, she reminded me that "every single person has benefited from horseshoe crabs, and that is primarily because of the medical tests. Drugs that go into the human body are tested to make sure they are not contaminated with bacteria. The LAL test has become the standard for all injectables. Hip replacements, heart valves, and anything else that goes into the human body has been tested against horseshoe crab blood," she said.

"From a personal point of view," Brockmann continued, "the answer to your question would be that they're just such fascinating creatures and so unusual. I always think to myself, when I've been in the field for a little while, it's like studying a Martian. They don't share a common ancestor with any other group for four hundred and fifty million years." For Brockmann, there's nothing else like them on this planet. "And yet, all of us studying their biochemistry, or their blood, or their visual systems are finding fundamental principles that apply to all kinds of species on the planet," she said. We all use lateral inhibition in helping us identify visual patterns—a critical principle first discovered in studies of horseshoe crabs. "So, although [horseshoe crabs] are Martians, in the sense that they don't share a common ancestor with anybody else, all life has these basic [and surprising] similarities. My personal view is that they're so absolutely fascinating, and they get even more intriguing as you learn more about them.

"I think," Brockmann said, "that it's very important to emphasize that this funny-looking creature that you don't think is worth much—this stupid, 'ugly' animal—is actually important to the ecosystem, to science, and to me." As a scientist, Brockmann was concerned about the ignorance surrounding these animals. She worried that there are so many individuals who hold the belief that these animals are of no consequence. "This animal *is* of consequence, and so are a lot of other animals," she said.

Carl Shuster made the point that the horseshoe crab's heart has been well studied, including the relationship between activation of the heart by nerve impulses and intramuscular activity, and that some of these processes come into play in human anatomy as well. Also, "much of what we know in the visual sciences has been aided by what has been studied in the horseshoe crab optical system," he said. "If you want to know something about the world around you and what influences it, and you want to pick an animal that's had greater influence than any other on human health and human life, the horseshoe crab maybe is it."

Glenn Gauvry of ERDG was equally emphatic. "I can connect every man, woman, child, and domestic animal in the world to the horseshoe crab," he said. He noted that humans are not going to stop having kids or animals vaccinated, and that those same humans are not going to stop having knee replacements or hip replacements. By the same token, medical personnel and pharmaceutical companies are not going to stop testing for the presence of endotoxins. "All of that is directly related to horseshoe crabs, whether those crabs were harvested from the Atlantic Ocean, or whether the products made from those crabs were eventually used in Nevada, Louisiana, or Wisconsin," he said.

KEY FACT

Enzymes from horseshoe crab blood are used by astronauts at the International Space Station to test surfaces for unwanted bacteria and fungi.

Gauvry made the point that the pharmaceutical industry is growing, on average, about 5 to 10 percent per year. As a result, he said, "There are more products, more devices, and more procedures, all of which need or require the use of LAL to ensure the safety of the general population. If we're interested in our health and our neighbor's health and our children's health and our animal's health, we need to be concerned about this animal, because it's giving of itself to help us.

"The horseshoe crab gives its blood to the biomedical industry, it gives its eyes to research, it gives its eggs to the shorebirds, and it gives its body to the fishermen," he continued. "It gives all these things, and as a result of all these gifts that it gives, it's just barely breaking that line with a certain minority of people who choose to pay attention, barely!"

IN THE 1960S AND 1970S, I WAS A JAMES BOND FAN. HE WAS A TRUE action hero, vanquishing the wicked, bedding the beautiful, and preserving the free world with his wiles, strength, and cunning. With each new book and film, I would envision him sneaking around world capitals and ornate castles to quash evil plans for taking over the world while disposing of nefarious individuals with European accents and very hungry sharks as pets.

About six weeks before the manuscript for this book was due to my editor,

I was offered the opportunity to view a place rarely seen by the public. I had been invited to the Eastern Shore of Maryland to tour the horseshoe crab bleeding facility of Lonza in the small college town of Salisbury. I jumped at the chance! However, before I made the trip, I was advised that I could not take any photographs, nor could I record any of the conversations I was to have with the plant manager; I could only take handwritten notes. This was top-secret, proprietary information, and naturally I began imagining myself as Bond. I was about to enter a secret facility where very secret people talked in low whispers, wore starched white lab coats, carried clipboards and walkie-talkies, and ate cellophane-wrapped sandwiches in sterile lunchrooms.

On top of all the secrecy, I was required to wear a blue hairnet, a white lab coat, baby blue booties, a sterile dust mask, and special goggles over my glasses. I wanted to try my Sean Connery impression, but the thick pad of gauze over my mouth muffled my voice, making me sound more like Cookie Monster on Sesame Street. I would have to leave the fight against the forces of evil and the worldwide plague of tyranny in Mr. Bond's capable hands.

Shortly after I arrived, I met the charismatic and personable facility manager, Denise Wolf. The facility is located in the eastern part of Maryland, a few miles south of the Delaware border and a stone's throw from the Atlantic Ocean. This geographical placement is designed to enhance the survival rate of the horseshoe crabs that are trucked in and out on a daily basis. (Salisbury is also the headquarters of Perdue Farms, and thus a leading center of American chicken farming.)

Denise informed me that all the horseshoe crabs bled at Lonza come from off the continental shelf, primarily to the east of Maryland and Virginia. None come from the Delaware Bay. She made it absolutely clear that all the horseshoe crabs used at the facility eventually go back into the ocean, unlike some horseshoe crabs processed by other biomedical companies that are sold for bait. *

---

* The harvesting of horseshoe crabs for biomedical use requires a special permit. Prior to 2001, biomedical companies were required to return all horseshoe crabs to the same location from which they were collected. Current regulations allow biomedical companies to sell their bled horseshoe crabs to the bait industry, although most bled horseshoe crabs are still returned to the ocean. Monthly reports to the Atlantic States Marine Fisheries Commission are required on harvest numbers and mortality percentage up to the point of release (including mortality occurring during harvest, shipping, handling, and bleeding). Additional regulations enacted in 1998 require biomedical companies to evaluate the post-release mortality of horseshoe crabs.

After informing me of some ground rules about what I could and could not do while inside the facility, Denise led me on a tour. I soon discovered that carrying on a conversation through the gauze of our masks and over the constant hum of machines (that I am not permitted to describe) would be a challenge.

As we entered the main bleeding room, I could see a long row of horseshoe crabs, each wedged between two white planks at about my eye level. Approximately twenty to thirty horseshoe crabs were each being bled into a 500-milliliter sterile bottle. Each of the horseshoe crabs is sprayed with a disinfectant prior to being bled, and after spraying, a worker comes by and uses a cotton swab to further disinfect each one's arthrodial membrane. Sterile conditions are maintained throughout the bleeding process at all times—more to protect the product than the donor, I was told.

Each horseshoe crab is stuck with a very sharp needle attached to a plastic syringe-like device. The needle pierces the hinge between the prosoma and opisithosoma and is inserted about a quarter of an inch deep. Shortly after the needle punctures the cardiac sinus of each horseshoe crab, its blue blood begins draining into a bottle placed beneath it. Workers must be careful to pierce the arthrodial membrane and the cardiac sinus. If the gut were punctured, its material would contaminate the bottle with bacteria. However, these technicians are pros, and their practiced hands, after hundreds or thousands of heart punctures, seldom make a mistake.

I watched the blood, which is almost turquoise in color, descend into each of the bottles. Some were barely dripping, while others were flowing at a fairly constant rate. Once the flow slowed to a drip, the needle was pulled out. A few of the horseshoe crabs decided not to cooperate; they weren't bleeding at all. After each horseshoe crab had been bled, I watched as one of the workers worked her way down the line and, using a portable electric drill, punctured the left-hand flange on the rear of its prosoma.† Because it was 2011, the hole was drilled into the left side of the carapace; 2012 is an even year, so the hole would be drilled into the right side of each bled horseshoe crab. During each harvesting season, fishermen look for these holes; if a hole is present, they can tell if the horseshoe crab has been bled in the current year or in a previous year.

---

† Each time a horseshoe crab is bled, it sacrifices approximately one-third of its blood. Once returned to the ocean, it will quickly replenish its blood supply, but it takes a few months for its cell count to fully recover. Current regulations allow for only one bleeding per horseshoe crab per year (thus, the drill holes).

Each of the 500 ml bottles used to collect the turquoise-blue blood also contains an anticoagulant to prevent clotting. Immediately after the cadre of horseshoe crabs had been bled, they were removed from the holding devices, put into oversized bins, and wheeled out of the bleeding room. Then a few workers cleaned the stainless-steel tables with disinfectant. A new set of horseshoe crabs was rolled in, wedged between the boards, and the operation was repeated.

I watched closely as a technician named Sheila (I'm allowed to use what is apparently her real name) went through the entire process. Sheila has been bleeding crabs here for thirteen years, and she has a good eye for the process. She was business-like, methodical, and knew her craft well. She went through the procedures efficiently as well as with apparent respect for the creatures she was handling. To her, these were not inanimate objects, but rather life-saving organisms temporarily entrusted to her care.

After departing the bleeding room, we took off our coats, masks, and booties, and then dressed up again in similar gear prior to entering the processing room. The bottles from the bleeding room had been passed through an airlock and into this section of the facility, where they were put into a centrifuge designed to separate the blood cells from the serum, or hemolymph. After centrifuging, the cells were left on the bottom of each container, and the blue hemolymph solution was poured off. One of the workers then resuspended the blood cells and washed them in liquid media. After the washing process, they went into the centrifuge again. Once centrifuged, the cells can then be lysed (broken down).

KEY FACT

The needle used to drain blood from horseshoe crabs is a 20-gauge needle—the same size a vet might use to inoculate a horse.

One absolute throughout the processing of LAL is constant attention to sterility and disinfection. Denise informed me that the biggest part of their day is devoted to disinfecting everything: machines, gloves, working surfaces, bottles, horseshoe crabs. Everything is cleaned on a regular basis. Even gloved hands are sprayed with disinfectant.

We left the processing room and passed through the holding room in the front of the building. The horseshoe crabs bled today were stacked in large bins awaiting transportation back to the ocean later in the afternoon. This was also a receiving area for arriving horseshoe crabs, which are brought in big blue tubs every day. Incoming horseshoe crabs are rinsed thoroughly with well water to get loose debris off, and every effort is taken to not injure them.

We passed back into the bleeding area, and as we observed the blood collection process again, this time from the other side of the room, I asked Denise about the ratio of male to female horseshoe crabs during the bleeding process. "The number of males and females is reported to the Maryland Department of Natural Resources, with the [goal] being roughly a fifty-fifty ratio of males to females for the entire season," she said. The Maryland Department of Natural Resources monitors the number of trawls, how long each trawl can be, how many horseshoe crabs are caught by each fisherman, how many males and females he brings in, and how many are rejected for being too small. Every aspect of the operation is controlled and monitored.

JUST BEFORE PULLING OUT OF THE TINY PARKING LOT, I PAUSED TO consider what I had just seen. I jotted notes and recorded some thoughts on my previously prohibited tape recorder. Upon my return home, I would need to wrap up the book and tie up any loose ends.

I pondered.

Unquestionably, the facilities I toured were clean and pristine, the workers were efficient and dedicated, and the hum of activity was constant and purposeful. The facility was part of a larger enterprise that was working to produce a product that one day may help me or you survive a medical procedure. But it wasn't the facility that impressed me, it was the small creatures aligned in long rows with people sticking sharp needles into their backsides that impressed me most.

The horseshoe crabs didn't ask to be here. The day before, they had been peacefully crawling over the sand and silt scattered across the bottom of the Atlantic Ocean. Then, from out of nowhere, a big scoop or net came along and snatched them away. Human beings piled them into large blue tubs, put them on a truck, and hauled them about thirty miles to a nondescript white building in a small town in Maryland.

There they were sorted into categories and placed into other bins. They were wheeled into a long, chilly room where a pair of human hands lifted them, bent their bodies in two, and wedged them between two wooden boards. Their backsides were swabbed with disinfectant, and then a very sharp object pierced their body and punctured their heart. They were forced to sit there for five to ten minutes while some of their body's vital fluids drained into a large glass bottle placed beneath them.

Then they were pulled from the racks, deposited back into portable tubs, and rolled into a back room. They waited there a while, and then they were loaded into trucks, transported back to the ocean, and placed back into the Atlantic Ocean. All without complaint; all without resistance.

I guess in some small way I had developed a kinship with these creatures; we were brothers of a sort. They were a part of my life—as they had always been—but now I was armed with personal information about the critical role they played in my life, in the lives of my wife and children, in the lives of my friends and neighbors, and, most likely, in your life, too. Biologists have a term for this in the animal world: it's called a symbiotic relationship. Symbiosis is defined as "a close and often long-term interaction between different biological species." Symbiotic relationships include those associations in which one organism lives on another (mistletoe, which grows on the branches of trees, is a good example) or where one partner lives inside the other (like all the bacteria that live in your intestinal tract).

Do horseshoe crabs and humans have a symbiotic relationship? Do we have "a close and often long-term interaction"? Is one of us dependent on the other for our survival? If so, which one?

It's easy to see all the benefits you and I and a couple of billion humans have obtained from horseshoe crabs. But there was still a persistent question tickling the back of my brain, one I couldn't quite answer as I swung out of Salisbury and traced my way home along Route 50. Is what we offer the horseshoe crab in terms of protection and preservation in any way comparable to what it offers us in terms of biological or medical benefits?

I'll have to keep you posted on that one.

Orgy on Gandy's Beach

THE BOY WAS SIX YEARS OLD, AND ALTHOUGH HE LIVED FEWER than twenty miles from the beach, he had never been to the shore… until one special spring day. Armed with a new plastic bucket and shovel, he was eager to get to the waterline and discover a brand new world. As soon as his mother had pulled into a parking space, he leaped from the car and dashed to the beach, chattering like a squirrel on amphetamines. This was new territory for him, and he was going to explore every inch.

It was early May, and the beach near Fortesque, New Jersey, on the Delaware Bay, was pulsing with hordes of horseshoe crabs. They were strewn across the high tide mark, and scores of males and females in amplexus were frolicking across long stretches of gently sloping sand. The young boy dashed to the beach and stopped, transfixed by the unexpected sight before him. It wasn't long before his mother, who was busy retrieving chairs, a cooler, beach towels, and assorted toys from the car, heard him shout, "Mom, Mom, come quick, and bring your camera. I think they're fertilizing!"

EACH SPRING, MY WIFE AND I TAKE A TRIP TO THE TINY ENCLAVE OF Gandy's Beach, New Jersey, to spend a couple of days with our friends Nancy and Jack. Their beach house is on the Delaware Bay (a mere stone's throw from Fortesque), with a well-weathered deck jutting over the beach just above a long wooden bulkhead. Mornings with a cup of coffee, the sounds of shorebirds, the lapping of waves in the bay, and the absolute lack of civilization are the closest thing to nirvana I ever encounter. In the evenings, we sit with ice tinkling in our glasses, a shimmering sunset on the western horizon, and a gentle offshore breeze, and we discuss stupid politicians, old friends, and the novels we are currently reading.

We have been friends with Nancy (to whom this book is dedicated) for nearly four decades, and it was on a visit to her house many years ago that I was first introduced to horseshoe crabs. I still remember walking the beach with her on a cloudy May evening, turning over flipped horseshoe crabs and listening to the scuffle of shells against each other in the quiet of the evening. Birds danced along the wave line, and echoes of moonlight drifted across the deserted beach. It was like walking through a surrealistic painting.

This year's visit to Gandy's Beach took place in mid-June. The season was late, but a confluence of appointments, professional engagements, and some medical realignments on my sixty-four-year-old knees precluded an earlier visit. After a three-and-a-half-hour drive, we arrived on a shimmering Friday afternoon with lazy clumps of clouds hanging in the western sky. Seagulls punctuated the air with shrill cries and squawks. I climbed the steps to the deck, deposited my suitcase in the house, and walked (limped) over to the railing. There was not a horseshoe crab in sight. Gandy's Beach had been subjected to a fierce spring storm several weeks before, and all I could see was a broad shore littered with broken shells, cascades of small pebbles, and strands of dark green seaweed. It seemed as though all the *Limulus* had packed up and left town.

The next morning, the four of us traveled the short distance to the island of Fortesque for a late morning breakfast at Higbee's Luncheonette. This diner and the nearby marina are run by the genial Betty Higbee and her husband, Clarence. Betty has penned an engaging book about the life and times of Fortesque, filled with nostalgic photos and memories of long-ago lighthouses, violent summer storms, and turn-of-the-century boardwalks flanking tourist hotels and the occasional speakeasy.

Shortly after arriving, we met Marion and George, longtime friends of Nancy and Jack. Marion, a bubbling, vivacious font of local knowledge, told us the story that leads this chapter, and she regaled us with tales from the not-so-distant past about this little town far off the beaten track. Her husband, George, a local radio announcer, punctuated her stories with wry asides.

A plate of eggs over easy, home fries, thick slices of buttered toast, a slab of ham, and a tall cup of coffee meant I could skip lunch and subsist for the

A lonely visitor to Gandy's Beach returns to the sea.

rest of the day on this meal. Two hours and many stories later, we wended our way back to the house with talk of a long nap before reconnoitering on the deck for afternoon cocktails.

High tide returned later in the day, and so Jack and I set out for the public beach area of this little strip of land that hugs the southern shore of the Garden State. I wanted desperately to see the objects of my affection one last time before I wrapped up the writing of this book and shipped it off to my editor. I walked around one house perched over the water and through the stand of telephone-pole pilings holding it above the waves. And there they were: a veritable orgy of comingling creatures was strewn across the sienna-tinged sand. Threesomes, foursomes, fivesomes, and whateversomes were engaged in that ancient ritual which has driven them from the sea for centuries—nay, for millennia. Shafts of sunlight filtered through the pilings, drawing long parallel lines across the sand and through their shells.

As ever, I stood transfixed by the spectacle before me. These were creatures of an ancient time; organisms that had survived and thrived and endured for longer than 99 percent of anything else that has ever inhabited this planet. I was now witness to their preservation act—an act that defied the odds and transcended the centuries; an act that was as beautiful as a Tchaikovsky concerto, a field of mountain wildflowers, or a newborn baby.

Here were prehistoric creatures immersed in a quite modern environment, completely oblivious to the human being taking photographs and recording their sounds, intently carrying out their evolutionary imperative. Their persistence reminded me of the biomedical connections forged between horseshoe crabs and humans—connections that preserve and extend human life, but that also underscore our responsibility to respect and preserve these vulnerable creatures.

As I left the thriving orgy, I came upon one old horseshoe crab flipped upside down at the tail end of the beach. A male, he slowly moved his telson as he reached skyward with two or three legs. He had obviously been upturned by the surge of a departing wave during the last high tide. He was exhausted and stranded. I walked over, gently picked him up by the sides of his carapace, and placed him on his feet at the edge of the bay. He paused for a moment, seemingly to get his bearings, and then slowly, very slowly, he etched a double line of tracks into the waves.

He'd be back, as would I, next year…and next year…and…

How Horseshoe Crabs
Saved My Life

I N THE FALL OF 2011, AFTER COMPLETING THE MANUSCRIPT FOR this project and while it was being edited, I was scheduled for complete knee replacement surgery on my left leg. A combination of arthritis, thirty-five years of long-distance running, genetics, and two menisci (knee cartilage) that I tore severely while snow-blowing my driveway one day the previous winter made me an ideal candidate for a new knee.

Like our fictional friend Roger N. Parker back in Chapter 1, I was to have an implantable device inserted into my body. In preoperative conversations with my orthopedic surgeon—Dr. Michael Sicuranza of Orthopedic and Spine Specialists in York, Pennsylvania—I learned that I was to have a NexGen artificial knee, manufactured by 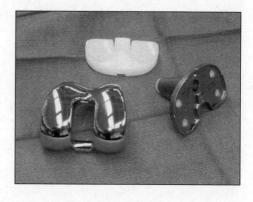 Zimmer of Warsaw, Indiana, inserted in place of my damaged knee. Just like Roger's heart valve, this implantable would have been tested for pyrogens by the manufacturer using LAL (*Limulus* amebocyte lysate). It's an odd coincidence that I underwent a successful operation that was dependent, to an extent, on horseshoe crabs so soon after writing about a hypothetical one. The irony was not lost on this author.

Dr. Sicuranza was kind enough to photograph the three major components of the artificial knee just prior to its insertion into my leg during the nearly two-hour operation. I want to take this opportunity to thank Dr. Sicuranza, the entire surgical team at OSS, and all my horseshoe crab friends for ensuring the success of this procedure.

Acknowledgments

THIS BOOK WAS INSPIRED IN LARGE MEASURE BY THE TALENTS, expertise, and dedication of several individuals. I am indebted to those who not only supported this project, but also unselfishly shared their visions, philosophy, research, and time.

My dear friend, Nancy Weikert, earns a gold medal for her unwavering camaraderie and encouragement over the years. She was both inspiration and reason for this book, and for that I am forever grateful.

That I was able to stand on the shoulders of giants in preparing this manuscript is one of the great joys of my literary career. I am particularly indebted to Carl N. Shuster, Jr., who unselfishly, through several interviews and informal discussions, provided me with incredible information, unmitigated determination, and delightful insights into the life and times of *Limulus polyphemus*. He is both motivation and inspiration! I am equally indebted to H. Jane Brockmann for her keen perspectives, wonderful stories, and dynamic research that opened my eyes to some of the enchanting mysteries surrounding this enigmatic creature. To Glenn Gauvry of the Ecological Research & Development Group (ERDG) goes wild and thunderous applause for his dedication to horseshoe crabs, his energy in promoting sound environmental thinking, and his vision for the future of the species. To Gary Kreamer goes my sincere appreciation (along with lots of high fives) for his deep commitment to positive educational principles, his unwavering promotion of Green Eggs & Sand, and his steadfast commitment to spreading the word about *Limulus*. And, although I never had the honor of meeting Robert Barlow, who passed away before this book was conceived, his influence, too, is liberally sprinkled throughout this book.

My visit to Florida would not have been complete without the assistance of two significant and influential individuals. Tiffany Black provided me with valuable facts and detailed information on horseshoe crab populations in the Gulf of Mexico. I especially want to acknowledge the contributions, insights, and perspectives of Anne Rudloe, whose exemplary commitment to horseshoe crabs ensures that their story will not go unnoticed. I am indebted to both of these individuals for their wisdom and energy.

To the good folks at Lonza—especially Maribeth Janke and Denise Wolf—go my undying gratitude. That they are contributing mightily to a better understanding of horseshoe crabs is a given; that they unselfishly shared their passion and respect for these creatures is a professional treasure.

I am particularly thankful for the incredible inspiration, unwavering dedication, and enthusiastic support of all the members of the Green Eggs & Sand project during our workshop at the Wetlands Institute in Stone Harbor, New Jersey, in May 2011. Teachers such as Walter Bauer, Tracee Panetti, and Janet Mead make the teaching and learning of science so incredibly exciting. Presenters including GE&S team members Karen Leskie (who also organized and hosted the workshop), Stacy Epperson, Jennifer Holmes, Cindy Etgen, and Mike Oates, as well as guest expert presenters Ron Berzofsky, Bill Pitts, Walter Chew, Heidi Hanlon, Jeffrey Brust, and Nancy Jackson continue to ensure the success of the GE&S workshop and its ultimate influence on the lives of children. All of the participants underscored the value of GE&S, its vitality in classroom settings, and its power in shaping the future of science education. They all merit a standing ovation.

Grateful thanks are extended to the Professional Development Committee at York College of Pennsylvania, which provided financial support and professional encouragement for much of the book's research. Special thanks go to the former chair of the Education Department at York College, Michael McGough, who approved generous travel funds for my various excursions both near and far.

This book would not have been possible without the editorial vigilance and consistent support of my editor, Daniel Kohan. We didn't always agree, but Dan's professionalism, dedication to the highest ideals of book publishing, and unwavering support of this project is to be celebrated. "Thanks" hardly seems appropriate for his personal contributions and professional investments in this project.

A hearty round of cheers (hip, hip, hooray) deservedly goes to my transcriber extraordinaire, Irene Altland. With her ever-present *joie de vivre*, Irene eagerly and patiently transcribed hours upon hours of interview tapes, producing comprehensive and detailed documents. She is as much a part of this book as any of the individuals whose names appear more frequently. Thank you, Irene.

I am especially appreciative for the enthusiastic and consistent support of my wife, Phyllis. She embraced this project from the very beginning and was especially excited about its development and design. Lost weekends, a (still) shamefully cluttered attic, and a dozen "honey do's" that never got done were some of the consequences of this literary effort. Yet, she was steadfast in her support and a passionate champion of the book's message. She is my love and my muse. Thanks, sweetheart!

But the ultimate gratitude, appreciation, and applause rightly goes to the legions of horseshoe crab fans, supporters, and promoters who unselfishly give of their time and talents to ensure the protection and survival of one of the world's most valuable creatures. I had the great fortune and honor to meet so many people (unfortunately unnamed) dedicated to preserving and admiring horseshoe crabs. It is their energy and commitment that truly warrant recognition and celebration. And, to those of you who may be equally inspired by this book to join the horseshoe crab community, you, too, are to be acknowledged and celebrated. The challenges are many, but the sustained efforts of this band of dedicated individuals deserves constant admiration for their work in ensuring the continued evolutionary success of one of nature's unique creatures.

Timeline

THE CHART BELOW PRESENTS A VERY SIMPLIFIED CHRONOLOGY of the history of the world and the horseshoe crab's place in it. I realize I may rouse the ire of my paleontological colleagues by simplifying their life's work this way, but I think this chart will provide you, dear reader, with a concise summary of the evolution of life as we know it. Doubtless there will be changes and adjustments to this information in future years as we learn more details about life in the past.

PRECAMBRIAN (4,600–542 million years ago)	
4.55 billion years ago	Formation of the earth
3,800 million years ago	Earth became capable of supporting life
2,400 million years ago	Oxygenation of Earth began
1,700 million years ago	Early multicellular plants and fungi appeared
580 million years ago	Earliest multicellular animals appeared

PREHISTORIC (542–65 million years ago)	
490 million years ago	Plants and invertebrates began to colonize the land
445 million years ago	Oldest horseshoe crab (*Lunataspis aurora*)
425 million years ago	Appearance of sea scorpions
370 million years ago	Vertebrates began appearing on the land
230 million years ago	Appearance of the first dinosaurs
150 million years ago	Birds evolved from a single dinosaur group
130 million years ago	Flowering plants appeared
65 million years ago	Extinction of dinosaurs; diversification of mammals

DISTANT PAST (65 million years ago–1000)	
40 million years ago	Shorebirds appear
6–7 million years ago	Common ancestor of humans and chimpanzees appeared
4 million years ago	Red knots evolve
200,000 years ago	Modern humans appeared
10,000 years ago	The period of recorded human history begins
10,000–5,000 years ago	The Delaware Bay forms

RECENT PAST (1000–now)	
1000–1500	Algonquin people use horseshoe crab shells for various implements
1558	First description of the "horsefoot crab" in scientific literature

1609	Henry Hudson makes the first recorded discovery of Delaware Bay by a European
1850s	Horseshoe crabs first collected in large numbers and used for fertilizer
Early 1900s	Fishing towns offer rewards for dead horseshoe crabs
1926	First studies of horseshoe crab eyes
1949	Carl Shuster begins his lifelong studies of horseshoe crabs
1950s–1960s	Most horseshoe crab fertilizer plants close
1953	Frederick Bang discovers a substance in the blood cells of horseshoe crabs that is extremely sensitive to endotoxins
1967	Dr. H. Keffer Hartline receives the Nobel Prize in medicine for his research on horseshoe crab vision
1977	LAL is approved as a test for endotoxins by the FDA
1995	The Ecological Research & Development Group (ERDG) is founded
1999	Atlantic States Marine Fisheries Commission (ASMFC) creates a management plan for horseshoe crabs
2000	First Green Eggs & Sand workshop is held
2000	Virginia fishermen adopt bait bags
2001	Carl N. Shuster, Jr., Horseshoe Crab Reserve is established at the mouth of the Delaware Bay
2002	Alarming declines in red knot populations noted

2002	The horseshoe crab is designated as Delaware's state marine animal
2003	Publication of *The American Horseshoe Crab* by Carl N. Shuster, Jr., Robert B. Barlow, and H. Jane Brockmann
2007	First International Symposium on the Science and Conservation of Horseshoe Crabs is held on Long Island, NY
2008	*Lunataspis aurora* fossil found
2011	Second International Symposium on the Science and Conservation of Horseshoe Crabs is held in Hong Kong

Bibliography

INTRODUCTION

Ecological Research & Development Group (http://horseshoecrab.org).

CHAPTER 1

Bang, Frederick B. (1953). "The toxic effect of a marine bacterium on Limulus and the formation of blood clots." Biol. Bull. 105: 447-448.

Cooper, I. F., J. Levin, and H. N. Wagner. (1971). "Quantitative comparison of in vitro (*Limulus*) and in vitro (rabbit) methods for detection of endotoxin." J. lab. Clin. Med. 78: 138-148.

Environmental Research & Development Group. (2003). Evolution. http://www.horseshoecrab.org/evo/paleo/paleo.html.

Evans, T. M., Schillinger, J. E., and Stuart, T. G. (1978). "Rapid determination of bacteriological water quality by using *Limulus* lysate." Appl. Environ. Microbiol. 35: 376-382.

Levin, Jack, and F. B. Bang. (1964). "The role of endotoxin in the extracellular coagulation of *Limulus* blood." Bull. Johns Hopkins Hosp., 115(3): 265-274.

Lonza. (2007). "Endotoxin & Microbial Detection." www.lonza.com/group/en/products_services/products/lal.html.

National Science Foundation. (May 19, 2011). "Replacing the Blue Bloods." Arlington, VA: Press Release 11-102.

Novitsky, Thomas J. "Biomedical Applications of Limulus Amebocyte Ly-sate." In *Biology and Conservation of Horseshoe Crabs.* Edited by John T. Tanacredi, Mark L. Botton, and David R. Smith. New York: Springer, 2009. Pp. 315-329.

Novitsky, Thomas J. (1982). "*Limulus* amebocyte lysate: life saving extract from the horseshoe crab." Aquasphere, J. New England Aquarium, 16: 26-31.

Sargent, William. *Crab Wars: A Tale of Horseshoe Crabs, Bioterrorism, and Human Health.* Hanover, NH: University Press of New England, 2002.

Science 2.0 (October 2009). "An Ancient Creature with a Modern Impact." http://www.science20.com/print/60496.

Swan, Benjie L. "A Unique Medial Product (LAL) from the Horseshoe Crab and Monitoring the Delaware Bay Horseshoe Crab Population." In *Limulus in the Limelight: A Species 350 Million Years in the Making and in Peril?* Edited by John T. Tanacredi. New York: Kluwer Academic/Plenum Publishers, 2001. Pp. 53-62.

U.S. Pharmacopoeia. (1995). Bacterial endotoxins test 23. NF 18: 1696.

The quotes from Thomas Novitsky are from: Thomas J. Novitsky. "How Does the Horseshoe Crab Protect the Public Health." (Little Creek, DE: Ecological Research & Development Group; http://horseshoecrab.org/med/med.html).

The information from the National Science Foundation is from: National Science Foundation. "Replacing the Blue Bloods." (Arlington, VA: National Science Foundation; http://www.nsf.gov/news/news_summ.jsp?cntn_id=119584&org=NSF&from=news, May 19, 2011).

The quote from *Crash: A Tale of Two Species* is from: PBS Nature. *Crash: A Tale of Two Species—The Benefits of Blue Blood.* (New York: PBS; http://www.pbs.org/wnet/nature/episodes/crash-a-tale-of-two-species/the-bene-fits-of-blue-blood/595/, 2011).

CHAPTER 2

Fredericks, Anthony D. *Walking with Dinosaurs: Rediscovering Colorado's Prehistoric Beasts.* Boulder, CO: Johnson Books, 2012.

———. *How Long Things Live: And How They Live as Long as They Do.* Mechanicsburg, PA: Stackpole Books, 2010.

Kihm, Richard, and James St. John (2007), *Walch's trilobite research—A translation of his 1771 trilobite chapter,* in Donald G. Mikulic, Ed Landing, and Joanne Kluessendorf, "Fabulous fossils—300 years of worldwide research on trilobites," *New York State Museum Bulletin* (University of the State of New York). 507: 115–140.

McPhee, John. *Basin and Range*. New York: Farrar, Straus and Giroux, 1982.

Rudkin, D. M., and G. A. Young. "Horseshoe Crabs—An Ancient Ancestry Revealed." *Biology and Conservation of Horseshoe Crabs*. Edited by John T. Tanacredi, Mark L. Botton, and David R. Smith. New York: Springer, 2009. Pp. 25-44.

Shuster, Carl N., Jr., "Two Perspectives: Horseshoe Crabs During 420 Million Years, Worldwide, and the past 150 Years in the Delaware Bay Area." In *Limulus in the Limelight: A Species 350 Million Years in the Making and in Peril?* Edited by John T. Tanacredi. New York: Kluwer Academic/ Plenum Publishers, 2001. Pp. 17-40.

Walker, J. D., and Geissman, J. W., compilers. (2009). *Geologic Time Scale*: Geological Society of America, doi: 10.1130/2009.CTS004R2C.

Walls, Elizabeth S., Jim Berkson, and Stephen A. Smith. (2002). "The Horseshoe Crab, *Limulus polyphemus*: 200 Million Years of Existence, 100 Years of Study." *Reviews in Fisheries Science*, 10(1):39-73.

The figures from the United Nations on life expectancy are from: United Nations. *World Population Prospects, The 2006 Revision*, Table A.17. Life Expectancy at Birth, Both Sexes (Combined), by Country for Selected Periods (New York: United Nations; http://www.un.org/esa/population/publications/ wpp2006/WPP2006_Highlights_rev.pdf, Pp. 80-84).

The quote from Dave Rudkin is from: Science Daily. "Oldest Horseshoe Crab Fossil Found, 445 Million Years Old." (www.sciencedaily.com/releases/ 2008/02/080207135801.htm, February 8, 2008).

The quote from Shuster and Anderson is from: Shuster, Carl N., Jr., and Lyall I. Anderson. "A History of Skeletal Structure: Clues to Relationships Among Species." In *The American Horseshoe Crab*. Edited by Carl N. Shuster, Jr., Robert B. Barlow, and H. Jane Brockmann. Cambridge, MA: Harvard University Press, 2003. P. 175.

The quote from Anderson and Shuster is from: Anderson, Lyall I., and Carl N. Shuster, Jr. "Throughout Geologic Time: Where Have They Lived?" In *The American Horseshoe Crab*. Edited by Carl N. Shuster, Jr., Robert B. Barlow, and H. Jane Brockmann. Cambridge, MA: Harvard University Press, 2003. Pp. 213-214.

CHAPTER 3

Anderson, Lyall I., and Carl N. Shuster, Jr. "Throughout Geologic Time: Where Have They Lived?" In *The American Horseshoe Crab*. Edited by

Carl N. Shuster, Jr., Robert B. Barlow, and H. Jane Brockmann. Cambridge, MA: Harvard University Press, 2003. Pp. 189-223.

Botton, Mark L., and J. W. Ropes. 1987. Populations of horseshoe crabs, *Limulus polyphemus*, on the northwestern Atlantic continental shelf. Fish. Bull. 85(4): 805-812.

Ecological Research & Development Group. 2003-2009. "The Delaware Bay: 11000 BC – Today." http://www.horseshoecrab.org/evo/ceno.html.

Encyclopedia Virginia. (April 5, 2011). "Samuel Argall (bap. 1580-1626)." (http://www.encyclopediavirginia.org/Argall_Samuel_bap_1580-1626).

National Geographic Maps. 1988-1999. Ocean maps. Washington, DC: National Geographic Society. On CD-ROM.

Physorg.com. (April 14, 2010). "The New *T. rex*: A Leech with an Affinity for Noses." (http://www.physorg.com/news190468932.html).

Science Daily. (April 8, 2011). "Simple Chemical Cocktail Shows First Promise for Limb Re-growth in Mammals." (http://www.sciencedaily.com/releases/2011/04/110406122207.htm).

Shuster, Carl N., Jr., 1997. Abundance of adult horseshoe crabs, *Limulus polyphemus*, in Delaware Bay, 1850-1990. In *Proceedings of the Horseshoe Crab Forum: Status of the Resource*. University of Delaware Sea Grant College Program (DEL-SG-05-97). Pp. 5-14.

Shuster, Carl N., Jr., and Mark L. Botton. 1985. A contribution to the population biology of horseshoe crabs, *Limulus polyphemus* (L.), in Delaware Bay. *Estuaries*. 8:363-372.

Spartacus. (no date). "Thomas De La Warr." (http://www.spartacus.schoolnet.co.uk/USAwarr.htm).

The quote from the "Contract with Henry Hudson" is from: Holland History. "The contract between Hendrick Hudson and the Dutch India Company." (http://www.hollandhistory.net/holland_overseas/the-contract-between-henrick-hudson-and-voc.html).

The quote from Captain Cornelius Hendricksen is from: Delaware Federal Writer's Project. 1938. "Delaware: A Guide to the First State." P. 6.

CHAPTER 4

Berkson, J., and Carl N. Shuster, Jr. 1999. "The horseshoe crab: the battle for a true multiple-use resource." *Fisheries*. 24:6-10.

Kreamer, Gary, and Stewart Michaels. "History of Horseshoe Crab Harvest on Delaware Bay." In *Biology and Conservation of Horseshoe Crabs*. Edited by John T. Tanacredi, Mark L. Botton, and David R. Smith. New

York: Springer, 2009. Pp. 299-313.

Liao Y, and Li X. "Poisoning from eating horseshoe crab and its prevention and treatment." http://www.ncbi.nlm.nih.gov/pubmed.

Milne, Lorus, and Margery Milne. *The Crab That Crawled Out of the Past.* New York: Atheneum, 1965.

Shuster, Carl N., Jr., and Mark L. Botton. 1985. "A contribution to the population biology of horseshoe crabs, *Limulus polyphemus*, in Delaware Bay." *Estuaries.* 8:363-370.

Shuster, Carl N., Jr. "King Crab Fertilizer: A Once Thriving Delaware Bay Industry." In *The American Horseshoe Crab.* Edited by Carl N. Shuster, Jr., Robert B. Barlow, and H. Jane Brockmann. Cambridge, MA: Harvard University Press, 2003. Pp. 341-357.

Shuster, Carl N., Jr. "Two Perspectives: Horseshoe Crabs During 420 Million Years, Worldwide, and the Past 150 Years in the Delaware Bay Area." In *Limulus in the Limelight: A Species 350 Million Years in the Making and in Peril?* Edited by John T. Tanacredi. New York: Kluwer Academic/Plenum Publishers, 2001. Pp. 17-40.

University of Delaware College of Marine and Earth Studies and the Sea Grant College Program. *Native Americans.* http://www.ceoe.udel.edu/horseshoecrab/humanuse/nativeamericans.html.

U.S. National Library of Medicine, National Institutes of Health. (March 2001). http://www.ncbi.nlm.nih.gov/pubmed/11321949.

The quotes from Thomas Harriot are from: Harriot, Thomas. *A Briefe and True Report of the New Found Land of Virginia* (Rosenwald Collection Reprint Series). New York: Dover Publications, 1972.

The ERDG quote is from: "Horseshoe Crab Management: Birds, Bait and Controversy." In *Horseshoe Crab/Shorebird Education Project*—a brochure produced by the Green Eggs & Sand Partnership, 2004.

CHAPTER 5

Grant, Dave. 2002. "Hitchin' a Ride." *Natural History.* June 2002: 66-69.

Hall, William. *Horseshoe Crab: A Creature That Crawled Out of the Past.* Newark, DE: University of Delaware Sea Grant Marine Advisory Service Bulletin, 2006.

Rudloe, A. 1983. "The effect of heavy bleeding on mortality of the horseshoe crab, *Limulus polyphemus*, in the natural environment." *J. Invertebr. Pathol.* 42:167-176.

Shuster, Carl N., Jr., and Lyall I. Anderson. "A History of Skeletal Structure:

Clues to Relationships Among Species." In *The American Horseshoe Crab*. Edited by Carl N. Shuster, Jr., Robert B. Barlow, and H. Jane Brockmann. Cambridge, MA: Harvard University Press, 2003. Pp. 154-188.

The quotes from *Attack of the Crab Monsters* are from: *Attack of the Crab Monsters* (a Roger Corman Production, Screenplay by Charles B. Griffith. An Allied Artists Picture, 1957).

The quote on "Taxonomy" is from: "Taxonomy." *Wikipedia* (accessed September 12, 2011).

The quote from Dave Grant is from: "Hitchin' a Ride," Natural History. June 2002. Pp. 66-69—an article adapted from his chapter in *Limulus in the Limelight: A Species 350 Million Years in the Making and in Peril?* Edited by John T. Tanacredi (Kluwer Academic/Plenum, 2001).

CHAPTER 6

Barlow, Robert B., J.M. Hitt, and F.A. Dodge, 2001. *Limulus* vision in the marine environment. *Biol. Bull.* 200:169-176.

Barlow, Robert B., L.C. Ireland, and L. Kass. 1982. Vision has a role in *Limulus* mating behavior. *Nature* 296:65-66.

Battelle, B-A. 2002. Circadian efferent input to *Limulus* eyes: anatomy, circuitry, and impact. *Microsc. Res. Tech.* 15:58(4):345-355.

Hartline, H.K., and F. Ratliff. 1958. Spatial summation of inhibitory influences in the eye of *Limulus*, and the mutual interaction of receptor units. *J. Gen. Physiol.* 41:1049.

Nobel Prize in Physiology or Medicine 1967. Nobelprize.org. Accessed September 29, 2011. http://www.nobelprize.org/nobel_prizes/medicine/laureates/1967.

Szaflarski, Diane. (undated) How We See: The First Steps of Human Vision. http://www.accessexcellence.org/AE/AEC/CC/vision background.php.

The quote on the typical eye exam is from: Wikipedia, "Eye Examination," accessed September 29, 2011, http://en.wikipedia.org/wiki/Eye_examination.

The quote by Aristotle is from: The Ex-Classics website, "Aristotle, The Famous Philosopher: On Eyes," accessed June 25, 2011, http://www.exclassics.com/arist/arist33.htm.

The quotes by H. Keffer Hartline are from: Hartline, H.K., H.G. Wagner, and F. Ratliff. 1956. Inhibition in the eye of *Limulus*. *J. Gen. Physiol.* 39:651-673.

The quotes by Robert Barlow are from: Barlow, Robert B., and Maureen

K. Powers. "Seeing at Night and Finding Mates: The Role of Vision." In *The American Horseshoe Crab*. Edited by Carl N. Shuster, Jr., Robert B. Barlow, and H. Jane Brockmann. Cambridge, MA: Harvard University Press, 2003. Pp. 83-102.

The quote on *The Crawling Eye* is from: *The Crawling Eye*. 1958 movie trailer, accessed June 25, 2011. http://www.youtube.com/watch?v=BDGwCMcLs_M.

CHAPTER 7

Brockmann, H. Jane. "Male Competition and Satellite Behavior." In *The American Horseshoe Crab*. Edited by Carl N. Shuster, Jr., Robert B. Barlow, and H. Jane Brockmann. Cambridge, MA: Harvard University Press, 2003. Pp. 50-82.

———. "Nesting Behavior: A Shoreline Phenomenon." In *The American Horseshoe Crab*. Edited by Carl N. Shuster, Jr., Robert B. Barlow, and H. Jane Brockmann. Cambridge, MA: Harvard University Press, 2003. Pp. 33-49.

Brockmann, H. Jane, and Matthew D. Smith. "Reproductive Competition and Sexual Selection in Horseshoe Crabs." In *Biology and Conservation of Horseshoe Crabs*. Edited by John T. Tanacredi, Mark L. Botton, and David R. Smith. New York: Springer, 2009. Pp. 199-221.

The quote by Mary Roach is from: Roach, Mary. *Bonk: The Curious Coupling of Science and Sex*. New York: W.W. Norton & Co., 2008. P. 15.

CHAPTER 8

American Eel Plan Development Team, 1997. American eel and horseshoe crab public information document. Atlantic States Marine Fisheries Commission.

Argo, Allison. (2008) *Crash: A Tale of Two Species* (PBS Nature/Argo Films). Chicago, IL: Questar Entertainment.

Botton, Mark L., and Brian A. Harrington. "Synchronies in Migration: Shorebirds, Horseshoe Crabs, and Delaware Bay." In *The American Horseshoe Crab*. Edited by Carl N. Shuster, Jr., Robert B. Barlow, and H. Jane Brockmann. Cambridge, MA: Harvard University Press, 2003. Pp. 5-32.

Crenson, Victoria. *Horseshoe Crabs and Shorebirds: The Story of a Food Web*. New York: Marshall Cavendish, 2003.

Crockett, Don. (August 1997). *Shorebird Crisis: The Horseshoe Crabs of*

Delaware Bay. http://www.virtualbirder.com/vbirder/realbirds/dbhsc/
index.html.

Delaware Estuary Program. (2002). *Horseshoe Crab and Shorebirds Fact
Sheet.* Dover, DE.

U.S. Fish and Wildlife Service. (August 2005). *Red Knot: calidris canutus
rufa.* http://www.fws.gov/northeast/redknot/facts.pdf.

Willis, Nancy C. *Delaware Bay Shorebirds* (brochure). Dover, DE: Delaware
Department of Natural Resources and Environmental Control, 1998.

The quote on the number of shorebirds on Delaware Bay is from: Wander,
W. and P. Dunne. 1981. Species and numbers of shorebirds on the Delaware
Bayshore of New Jersey, spring 1981. Occasional paper 140, New Jersey Audu-
bon Society. *Records of New Jersey Birds.* 7:59-64.

The quote by Gonzalo Castro is from: Castro, G., J.P. Myers, and A.R.
Place. 1989. Assimilation efficiency of Sanderlings (*Calidris alba*) feeding on
horseshoe crab (*Limulus polyphemus*) eggs. *Physiol. Zool.* 62:716-731.

The quote from Mark Botton on "augment their diet" is from: Botton,
Mark L., and Brian A. Harrington. "Synchronies in Migration: Shorebirds,
Horseshoe Crabs, and Delaware Bay." In *The American Horseshoe Crab.* Edited by Carl N. Shuster, Jr., Robert B. Barlow, and H. Jane Brockmann. Cambridge, MA: Harvard University Press, 2003. Pp. 5-32.

The quote on declining numbers of red knots is from: Stone, W. 1937. *Bird
Studies at Old Cape May.* Philadelphia: Delaware Bay Ornithological Club.

The quote on "Those creepy, crawling...." is from: Mucha, Peter.
May 25, 2011. "3 cited over harvesting of horseshoe crabs." *Philadelphia In-
quirer.* Accessed October 25, 2011. http://articles.philly.com/2011-05-25/
news/29582094_1_horseshoe-crabs-vietnamese-restaurant-harvesting.

CHAPTER 9

Botton, Mark L., Carl N. Shuster, Jr., and John A. Keinath. "Horseshoe Crabs
in a Food Web: Who Eats Whom?" In *The American Horseshoe Crab.*
Edited by Carl N. Shuster, Jr., Robert B. Barlow, and H. Jane Brockmann.
Cambridge, MA: Harvard University Press, 2003. Pp. 133-153.

Lovelend, Robert E. "The Life History of Horseshoe Crabs." In *Limulus in
the Limelight: A Species 350 Million Years in the Making and in Peril?* Edited by John T. Tanacredi. New York: Kluwer Academic/Plenum Publishers, 2001. Pp. 93-101.

Samis, Carrie. (May 2011). Horseshoe Crab Spawning Survey Starts This
Week. http://www.delmarvanow.com/fdcp/?unique=1306257537068.

Shuster, Carl N., Jr., and Koichi Sekiguchi. "Growing Up Takes About Ten Years and Eighteen Stages." In *The American Horseshoe Crab*. Edited by Carl N. Shuster, Jr., Robert B. Barlow, and H. Jane Brockmann. Cambridge, MA: Harvard University Press, 2003. Pp. 103-132.

World Health Organization. *World Health Statistics—2010*. Geneva, Switzerland. P. 12.

The quote by Carl Shuster is from: Shuster, Carl N., Jr., and Koichi Sekiguchi. "Growing Up Takes About Ten Years and Eighteen Stages." In *The American Horseshoe Crab*. Edited by Carl N. Shuster, Jr., Robert B. Barlow, and H. Jane Brockmann. Cambridge, MA: Harvard University Press, 2003. Pp. 103-132.

The quote from Samuel Lockwood is from: Lockwood, Samuel. 1870. The Horse Foot Crab. *Am. Nat.* 4:257-274.

CHAPTER 10

Bettendorf, Elizabeth. "A Place, A Purpose, A Panacea." *Florida State University Research in Review* (Summer 2009), Vol. XIX, No. 1; Pp. 30-39.

Cedar Key Chamber of Commerce. Cedar Key History and Culture. http://www.cedarkey.net/history.html.

Gerhart, Susan D. "A Review of the Biology and Management of Horseshoe Crabs, with Emphasis on Florida Populations." *Fish and Wildlife Research Institute Technical Report TR-12*, St. Petersburg, FL: Florida Fish and Wildlife Conservation Commission, 2007.

Panacea, Florida. http://en.wikipedia.org/wiki/Panacea,_Florida.

The opening lines from *Where the Boys Are* are from: *Where the Boys Are* (released December 28, 1960), distributed by Metro-Goldwyn-Mayer. Written by Glendon Swarthout (novel) and George Wells; directed by Henry Levin.

The definition of "red tide" is from: Centers for Disease Control and Prevention, "Harmful Algae Blooms (HABs)," accessed October 17, 2011, http://www.cdc.gov/hab/redtide/about.htm.

CHAPTER 11

Ecological Research & Development Group. (http://horseshoecrab.org).

Gauvry, Glenn. "Community Building: An Integrated Approach to Horseshoe Crab Conservation." In *Biology and Conservation of Horseshoe Crabs*. Edited by John T. Tanacredi, Mark L. Botton, and David R. Smith. New York: Springer, 2009. Pp. 605-612.

The source for the Margaret Mead quote has never been determined. Although it is the motto for many organizations and movements, researchers have not been able to locate when and where it was first cited. Current thinking is that it may have been something Dr. Mead included in a speech or spontaneously uttered during an interview. Nevertheless, it was the basis for much of her thinking and philosophy.

Quotes and statements about the Lone Ranger are from: Random House and are used with permission.

CHAPTER 12

Fredericks, Anthony D. *More Science Adventures with Children's Literature: Reading Comprehension and Inquiry-Based Science*. Santa Barbara, CA: Teacher Ideas Press, 2008.

Green Eggs & Sand Partnership. 2006. Dr. Carl Shuster/Horseshoe Crabs. Smyrna, DE: Green Eggs & Sand. On CD-ROM.

Shuster, Carl N., Jr., and Koichi Sekiguchi. "Growing Up Takes About Ten Years and Eighteen Stages" In *The American Horseshoe Crab*. Edited by Carl N. Shuster, Jr., Robert B. Barlow, and H. Jane Brockmann. Cambridge, MA: Harvard University Press, 2003. Pp. 103-132.

Shuster, Carl N., Jr. (1955). On morphometric and serological relationships within the Limulidae, with particular reference to *Limulus polyphemus* (L.). Ph.D. thesis, New York University (1958 Diss. Abstr. 18:371-372).

The quote by Bob Barlow is from: Green Eggs & Sand Partnership. 2006. Dr. Carl Shuster/Horseshoe Crabs. Smyrna, DE: Green Eggs & Sand. On CD-ROM.

CHAPTER 13

Green Eggs & Sand Partnership. 2004. "Horseshoe Crab/Shorebird Education Project." Smyrna, DE: Green Eggs & Sand. Poster.

O'Connell, Katy, Cindy Etgen, Gary Kreamer, and Michael Oates. "*Green Eggs and Sand*: A Collaborative Effort of Scientists, Teachers, Resource Managers, and Stakeholders in Educating About *Limulus polyphemus*." In *Biology and Conservation of Horseshoe Crabs*. Edited by John T. Tanacredi, Mark L. Botton, and David R. Smith. New York: Springer, 2009. Pp. 595-604.

CHAPTER 14

Atlantic States Marine Fisheries Commission. January 19, 2011. *Biomedical*

Companies Pledge Over $100,000 to Continue Horseshoe Crab Survey. Arlington, VA: ASMFC Press Release.

Shuster, Carl N. "Public Participation in Studies on Horseshoe Crab Populations." In *Biology and Conservation of Horseshoe Crabs.* Edited by John T. Tanacredi, Mark L. Botton, and David R. Smith. New York: Springer, 2009. Pp. 585-594.

POSTSCRIPT

Dunlap, Julie. *Extraordinary Horseshoe Crabs.* Minneapolis, MN: Carolrhoda, 1999.

PHOTOGRAPHY CREDITS

Photographs are by the author, except as follows:

- Page 13 by Jerry Hecht for National Institutes of Health (public domain)

- Page 33 by David M. Goehring (CC BY 2.0)

- Page 34 by Hannes Grobe (CC BY 3.0)

- Page 40 by Anthony Finley (public domain, copyright expired)

- Page 43 by Christina Kennedy (CC BY 2.0)

- Page 48 by Johannes Vingboons (public domain, copyright expired)

- Page 56 by John White (public domain, copyright expired)

- Page 69 by Stu Spivak (CC BY-SA 2.0)

- Page 73 courtesy Glenn Gauvry/ERDG

- Page 93 by Jeff Dahl (CC BY-SA 3.0)

- Page 109 by Chris Howard (CC BY-SA 3.0)

- Page 119, page 123, page 125, and page 129 by U.S. Fish and Wildlife Service (public domain)

- Page 126 by Dan Pancamo (CC BY-SA 2.0)

- Page 137 by Texx Smith (CC BY-SA 2.0)

- Page 143 by Horseshoecrab1 (CC BY 3.0)

- Page 150 by Ebyabe (CC BY-SA 3.0)

- Page 216 by Dan Centry (CC BY-SA 2.0)

Index

Al-Haytham, Ibn, 94-95

Al-Nafis, Ibn, 95

Alternative Gear and Supplemental Bait project, 178

Aquatic Resources Education Center (NJ), 200

Argall, Samuel, 47

Argo, Allison, 127

Aristotle, 93

Artificial body parts, 16, 19-21, 218-219

Associates of Cape Cod, 19

Atlantic States Marine Fisheries Commission (ASMFC), 21-22, 71, 150, 184, 189, 220

Atsena Otie Key, 153

Attack of the Crab Monsters, 76-79, 89-90

Bait bags, 72-73, 178

Bald Point State Park (FL), 163-164

Bang, Frederick, 15-16

Barlow, Robert, 100-102, 194, 196

Basin and Range, 27

Berzofsky, Ron, 208

Birds, 31, 59, 64, 71, 110, 117-132, 154, 164, 166, 186, 193, 206, 214, 219

Long-billed dowitchers, 119

Migration of, 70, 72, 119-123, 129-130, 193

Red knots, 119, 122-124, 126, 128-129, 202

Ruddy turnstones, 119, 122, 124-125

Sanderlings, 119, 122, 125-127

Semi-palmated sandpipers, 119, 122, 126-127

Swallows, 118-119

(The) Birds, 130-132

Black, Tiffany, 150-152

Bonk: The Curious Coupling of Science and Sex, 105-106

Botton, Mark, 122, 144

Bowers Beach, 199-200

Bradley, Abigail, 204

British Museum, 62

Broadkill Beach, 3-4, 174

Brockmann, H. Jane, 111-116, 195-196, 208, 211-212, 217-218

Brookdale Community College, 85

Byrd, Robert, 183

Cape Cod, 98, 107

Cape May (NJ), 30, 182, 190-191, 198-199, 207, 214

Carl N. Shuster, Jr., Horseshoe Crab Reserve, 182, 184

Castro, Gonzalo, 122

Catch shares, 211

Cedar Key (FL), 116, 149-153, 157

Cenozoic era, 28, 31

Census of Aquaculture (2005), 70

Center for Vision Research (NY), 100

Charles River Endosafe, 19

Cheltenham Art Center (PA), 177

Chew, Walter "Chewie", 210-211

Chin, Karen, 36-37

Circadian rhythms, 99-102

College of William and Mary, 184

Concept of lateral inhibition, 100

Corman, Roger, 76

(The) Crawling Eye, 103

Crichton, Michael, 30

CrabCam, 102

Crabs, true, 79-80

Crash: A Tale of Two Species, 22, 127-128

(The) Daily Pilot, 7

Dare, Virginia, 62

De Champlain, Samuel, 64

De La Warr, Thomas 41, 47

De Vries, David Pietersen, 50

De Walvis, 50

Delaware Bay, 3, 9, 53-55, 64, 82, 101, 107, 118, 120-122, 126, 128, 132, 134, 153, 182, 184, 188-189, 193, 199-202, 214, 220, 225

Formation of, 42-44, 51

History of, 41-55, 65-68, 70, 190-191, 211

Maps of, 40, 48-49,

Delaware Department of Fish and Wildlife, 199

Department of Natural Resources and Environmental Control (DE), 72

Descartes, René, 95

Dinosaurs, 30-31

Dutch East India Trading Company, 45-46

Eagle Pencil Company, 153

Ecological Research & Development Group (ERDG), 4, 72, 168-181, 219

Headquarters, 170

History of, 169-172

Horseshoe Crabs & the Arts Competition, 176-177

Horseshoe Crabs Conservation and the Arts In-School Program, 176

Just flip 'em! program, 175

Website, 177

Young Voices program, 176-177

Eels, 68-71, 128, 189, 202

Health benefits of eating, 69

Eicherly, Frank, 72, 178, 204-205

Elizabeth C, 190-191

Endotoxins, 15, 18-20, 23, 219

Environmental Protection Agency, 191

Epperson, Stacy, 208

Eyes, 91-103

Doctors, 91-93

Horseshoe crab, 9, 32, 83-84, 89, 96-103

Parts of the human, 94-97

Visual acuity, 92

Faber, J. Eberhard, 153

Faber Pencil Factory, 153

Fantastic Voyage, 135

Florida Fish and Wildlife Research Institute, 150

Florida Railroad, 153

Fordham University, 144

Fossils, 35-36

Coprolites, 36-37

Horseshoe crab, 31-33, 35, 37

Index, 36

Sea scorpion, 32-33, 35, 37

Trace, 37

Trilobite, 27, 33-35, 37

Galateia, 60

Gandy's Beach, 225-228

Gauvry, Glenn, 4-5, 169-180, 196, 219

Geissman, J. W., 28

Geologic Society of America, 28

Google, 106

Gorshin, Frank, 148

Gram-negative bacteria, 15, 18

Granit, Ragnar, 100

Grant, Dave, 85

Green Eggs & Sand, 9, 111, 191, 195-215

Gulf Specimen Marine Lab, 159-160, 162-163

Half-Moon, 46
Hamilton, George, 148
Hanlon, Heidi, 212
Harriot, Thomas, 62-63
Hart, Dolores, 147-148
Hartline, H. Keffer, 98-100, 102
Heart surgery, 12-13
Hendricksen, Cornelius, 47-50
Herrnkind, Bill, 158-159
Heyes, Peter, 50
Higbee's Luncheonette, 226-227
Hitchcock, Alfred, 130-132
Holmes, Jennifer, 208
Horseshoe crabs (*Limulus polyphemus*)
    Age, 85, 116, 137-138, 156, 187
    Anatomy, 4-6, 8-9, 32, 38, 75-90
        Anus, 83
        Arthrodial membrane, 17, 221
        Bleeding/blood, 15-23, 162, 178,
            220-223
            Clotting, 21
            Collecting, 21-22, 128
            Mortality rate as a result of, 22,
               220
        Book gills/lungs, 6, 32, 83-84, 135, 144
        Brain, 88, 97, 145
        Carapace/shell, 6, 19, 31, 64, 74, 84-85,
            88, 115-116, 138, 142-143, 154, 188,
            194-195, 212-213, 228
            Color of, 85, 116, 153, 162
        Chelae, 145
        Chelicera, 4, 83, 87
        Chitin, 19, 31, 87-89, 144, 195
        Eyes, 9, 84, 89, 96-103, 156
            Endoparietal, 97
            Experiments on, 99-100
            Lateral compound, 32, 83, 96-98,
               100, 176
            Median, 83, 97-98
            Model, 102
            Ommatidia, 96
            Photoreceptors, 97-99
            Rudimentary Lateral, 97-98
            Ventral, 97
        Genital pores, 89, 109

Gnathobases, 83, 144-145
Heart, 17, 84, 218
Immune system, 9
Legs, 87-88, 90, 144-145, 145
    Claspers, 4, 6, 88-89, 186-187, 213
    Pedipalps, 4, 87, 89, 108
    Pusher Legs, 6, 88, 109
    Walking, 83, 144
Median Ridge, 83
Mouth, 63-64, 83, 87-88, 145
Operculum, 84, 89, 109
Opisthosoma, 83, 85, 87, 144
Posterior opisthosomal projections
    (POP), 108
Prosoma/cephalothorax, 82-85, 136,
    213, 221
Spines, 83
Tarsus, 4, 6
Telson (Tail), 32, 61-63, 83, 86-87, 90,
    98, 135, 166
As bait, 70-72, 128-129, 178, 184, 189-190,
    202, 220
As fertilizer, 64-68, 189-190
Classification/taxonomy/names of, 15,
    60-63, 80-82, 190
Diet, 4, 54, 84, 87, 143-144, 192
Diseases and infections, 143-144
Educating people about, 22-23, 156, 172-
    176, 192, 195-215
Eggs, 9, 54-55, 63-64, 70, 72, 84, 88-89,
    98, 108, 117-132, 134, 145, 185, 193-194,
    204-205, 207, 214, 219
    Chorion, 134-135
    Fertilization of, 109-110, 135, 188
    Sites for laying, 112-113, 121
Evolution of, 8, 27-39, 156
Exoskeleton, 142
Fossils, 31-33, 35, 37, 186
    Synziphosurines, 37
    Xiphosurida, 37-38, 81
Growth and development of, 9
Habitat, 38, 53-55, 85, 110, 148-149, 193,
    206
Hitchhikers (epibionts), 85-86, 137-138,
    143-144, 153-154

Instar, 136

Larvae/young, 97-98, 110, 134-145, 201
  Development of, 134-135, 209

Life expectancy/span, 6, 137-138, 143, 188,
  213

Management plan, 71

Migration, 107, 120, 137, 149, 161

Molting, 135, 137-138, 140-142, 187-188,
  206-207, 215

Other species, 38
  Carcinoscorplus rotundicauda (Indo-
    nesian), 38, 81, 213
  Tachypleus gigas (Chinese), 38, 81, 81
  Tachypleus tridentatus (Japanese), 38

Population figures, 66-68, 71, 129-130,
  150-152, 178, 189-190, 193, 202, 212

Predators, 64, 72, 84, 110, 112, 117-132, 135,
  154, 161, 164, 166, 186, 193, 202, 206-
  207, 214, 219

Preservation efforts, 72-73, 172-175, 178-
  180, 184, 186, 202-203, 208

Protection (Federal) for, 152, 191

Range, 148-150

Size, 4, 115-116, 135-137, 153, 155, 163, 187

Spawning/mating/breeding, 4, 6, 8-9, 24,
  51, 53-55, 84, 87, 100-102, 104-115, 119-
  120, 128, 134, 149-150, 154, 156, 159, 162,
  168, 174, 184, 187, 189-190, 206-207,
  213-214, 227-228
  Amplexus, 108-109, 153, 163, 165, 217
  Behaviors, 111-115, 211-212
  Breeding season, 107
  Satellite males, 115-116, 163-164
  Scars, 108, 138, 186
  Sexual maturity, age of, 142
  Tagging, 22, 212
  Turning over, 87, 158, 166, 173-176, 228

Horseshoe Crab Fishery Management Plan
  (FMP), 71

Hudson, Henry, 45-47

Human
  Eyes, 94-97
  Life expectancy, 25-26, 139
  Skin, 138-140

Hutton, Jim, 148

Injectables, 14, 16, 19, 21, 218

Implantable devices, 16, 19-20

International Commission on Zoological
  Nomenclature (ICZN), 58-59

International Space Station, 219

Intracoastal Waterway, 51

Janke, Maribeth, 19-23

Jefferson, Thomas, 183-184

Johns Hopkins, 15

Jurrassic Park, 30

Kepler, Johannes, 95

Kimball's Beach (DE), 211

Kinsey Institute for Research in Sex, Gender, and Reproduction, 106

Kirkpatrick Research Lab, 150

Kitts Hummock, 174

Kreamer, Gary, 199-206

Levin, Jack, 15-16

Liao, Li X., 63

Lil Shark Beach (FL), 155-156

Limulus amebocyte lysate (LAL), 15-17, 23,
  178, 204, 215, 218-219
  LAL test, 16, 19-21, 209
  Manufacturers of, 19-22
  Regulation of, 21-22

Lincoln, Abraham, 183

Little Creek (DE), 169-180

Lockwood, Samuel, 142

(The) Lone Ranger, 167-168, 180-181
  Fan Club, 181

Lonza Pharmaceuticals, 19-20, 22, 220-223

Lott, Trent, 183

Lower Suwannee and Cedar Keys National
  Wildlife Refuges, 152

Manitoba Museum, 32

Maryland Department of Natural Resources, 208, 223

Mashes Sands State Beach (FL), 165-166

McPhee, John, 27

Mead, Janet, 207-208

Mead, Margaret, 168, 178

Merriam-Webster College Dictionary, 20

Mesozoic era, 28, 30-31, 42

Mid-Atlantic Sea Grant Programs, 63

Mimieux, Yvette, 148

Names
    Animal, 58-60, 132
    Creation of scientific, 58-61
    People, 57-58
National Marine Fisheries Service, 184
National Oceanic and Atmospheric Admin-
    istration, 63
National Science Foundation, 23, 111-112
Native Americans, 45-46, 50
    Fishing methods, 56, 61
    Use of horseshoe crabs, 61-62, 64
Nelson, Thurlow C., 185
Nestor, 26
New Jersey Audubon Society, 120
New Jersey Department of Fish and Wild-
    life, 208, 212
New Jersey Division of Travel and Tourism,
    197
New York Times, 36
New York University, 188
Nichols, Barbara, 148
Nobel Prize, 8, 100
Not of This Earth, 76
Novitsky, Thomas J., 15-16, 22
Nowlan, Godfrey, 32
Oates, Mike, 199-200
Odysseus, 60
Oil production and transportation, 44,
    170-171
Onrust, 47
Paleozoic era, 27, 29-30, 32-33, 37, 42
Panacea (FL), 116, 158-160
Panetti, Tracee, 206-207
Parker, Roger N., 8, 11-23
Penn, William, 50
Perkins Center for the Arts (NJ), 177
Pickering Beach (DE), 189-190, 174
Pitts, Bill, 208
Plate movements, 42-44
Polyphemus, 60
Precambrian era, 27, 29
Prentiss, Paula, 148
Prime Hook State Wildlife Management
    Area (DE), 3-4, 174
Pyrogens, 15, 23

Rabbit pyrogen test, 15, 21
Red tide, 160-161
Reed's Beach (NJ), 213-214, 215
Rehoboth Beach, 4
Roach, Mary, 105
Roosevelt, Theodore, 183
Royal Ontario Museum, 31
Rudkin, David, 31-32
Rudloe, Anne, 158-163
St. Jones Reserve (DE), 111, 208
Salah-ud-din bin Youssef Al-Kalal bi Hama,
    95
(The) Samurai, 177-178
San Juan Capistrano (CA), 118
Sea scorpions, 32-33, 35, 37, 194
Seahorse Key (FL), 111, 151-152
(Saint) Servatious, 26
Shadle, Albert R., 106
Shuster, Carl N, Jr., 9, 37-38, 67, 128-129, 136,
    184-196, 204, 212-213, 218-219
Siebert, Florence, 15
Slaughter Beach (DE), 176
Smithsonian Institution, 194
Snellen Chart, 92-93
Stiff: The Curious Lives of Human Cadavers,
    105-106
Sutures, 16, 19
Suwang, LP, 26
Tirasis of Thebes, 26
Tomasello, Ashley, 177-178
Trilobites, 27, 33-35, 37, 194, 213
Troutman, Jim, 184
U.S. Department of the Interior, 189
U.S. Food and Drug Administration (FDA),
    15-16, 20
University of Delaware, 63, 204
University of Florida, 208
University of New Hampshire, 20
University of Pennsylvania, 122
University of Wisconsin-Madison, 23
Vingboons, Johannes, 48-49
Virginia colony, 47
Virginia Institute of Marine Sciences Sea
    Grant program, 72, 178
Wako Chemicals, 208

Wald, George, 100

Walker, J. D., 28

Walking with Dinosaurs, 36

Washington, George, 183

West, Thomas, 47

Whelks/conch, 68, 70-72, 120, 189, 190

Where the Boys Are, 147-149, 166

White, John, 56, 61-62

Wildwood (NJ), 198

Williamstown Middle School (NJ), 207-208

Wolf, Denise, 220-221

Woods Hole (MA), 186

World Health Organization (WHO), 134

York College, 159

Young, Graham, 32

Young, Thomas, 95

Yulee, David, 153

Zhanjiang Ocean University, 63

"This logo identifies paper that meets the standards of the Forest Stewardship Council®. FSC® is widely regarded as the best practice in forest management, ensuring the highest protections for forests and indigenous peoples."

INITIATIVE

Ruka Press is committed to preserving ancient forests and natural resources. We elected to print this title on 100% post consumer recycled paper, processed chlorine free. As a result, for this printing, we have saved:

26 Trees (40' tall and 6-8" diameter)
10 Million BTUs of Total Energy
2,616 Pounds of Greenhouse Gases
11,794 Gallons of Wastewater
747 Pounds of Solid Waste

Ruka Press made this paper choice because our printer, Thomson-Shore, Inc., is a member of Green Press Initiative, a nonprofit program dedicated to supporting authors, publishers, and suppliers in their efforts to reduce their use of fiber obtained from endangered forests.

For more information, visit www.greenpressinitiative.org

Environmental impact estimates were made using the Environmental Defense Paper Calculator. For more information visit: www.papercalculator.org.